A Lady an explorer? a traveller in skirts?
The notion's just a trifle too seraphic:
Let them stay and mind the babies, or hem our ragged shirts;
But they mustn't, can't, and shan't be geographic ...

To The Royal Geographical Society
from *Punch*, London, June 1893.

For my sister,
Margaret Louise (Bluey),
one of the last passengers to sail
on the R.M.S. *Stratheden*, famous among
the '5 Straths' of the P&O Australian Fleet

and in remembrance of the wanderer's escorts
— the work horses, mules, camels, bullocks,
dogs and, on some journeys, cats —
whose transport and protection were
essential for travel within Australia and its
Territories for so many.

Venus in Transit

Australia's Women Travellers

1 7 8 8 – 1 9 3 0

Edited by

DOUGLAS R G SELLICK

Fremantle Arts Centre Press

Australia's finest small publisher

We contest in toto the general capabilities of women to contribute to geographical knowledge. Their sex and training render them equally unfitted for exploration, and the genus of professional globetrotters with which America has lately familiarised us is one of the horrors of the latter end of the 19th century.

George Nathaniel Curzon
in a letter to the Editor of *The Times*.

Contents

*Pack food rather than jewels when threatened
with shipwreck.*

Hints to Lady Travellers, c.1911.

Introduction

You will read here the marvellous true stories and the first impressions of varied journeys made out to and in Australia by adventurous and daring wanderers. Some were rather bothersome and unwilling, others grand or eccentric, all were independent, individualist and unconventional — and they were all women.

Travel was once thought to be a curious life for a lady! In 1847 the Council of the Royal Geographical Society in London recorded that 'it was not deemed expedient at present' to elect women to the Society. However by 1905 a medal was presented to a 'lady explorer and traveller' for her Himalayan work and for the fine example set by her 'feminine accomplishments'. In Europe and North America during the second half of the nineteenth century an increasing number of women were travelling abroad and returning home to write books, and were in constant demand to reveal their stories to a broad public by giving lectures. These lady travellers were journeying as far as the Indian Empire, Africa, the Pacific and even remote parts of Asia to the north. Australia was a major destination for many of them.

In this time, discussion raged bitterly about women travellers. George Nathaniel Curzon, lately home from travels in Persia, contributed an unpleasant letter to the Editor of *The Times* in which he wrote, 'We contest in toto the general capabilities of women to contribute to geographical knowledge. Their sex and training render them equally unfitted for exploration, and the genus of professional globetrotters with which America has lately familiarised us is one of the horrors of the latter end of the 19th century.'

The mechanics of transport were improving all the time while women were becoming freer in every way. Railway and ocean travel were pretty well established. Travelling hints dealing with these new modes of transport were published for the benefit of lady travellers, and were seriously noted. 'Do not bother to take a lady's maid with you by train! If you do, defy convention by keeping her with you in your first class carriage instead of in the correct 3rd class, where she can be of no use in an emergency.' 'Never eat a railway ham sandwich.' 'Pack food rather than jewels when threatened with shipwreck.'

The dreaded seasickness, not surprisingly I suppose, once occupied the mind of many a traveller before a journey abroad. One correspondent of a colonial newspaper offered her advice to women travellers in 1872:

> I have made three voyages to and from Australia, and previous to my coming to Australia I had travelled tolerably on coasting steamers, and have always, except on my last voyage to Australia, been exceedingly sick, usually the worst passenger on board. The usual remedies proposed by those well versed on the subject are, to drink plenty of beer, porter, or champagne, to eat ice, or have it placed on one's back,

also to eat heartily, and, when sick, to eat again, nothing daunted … All these remedies have I tried without any permanently good effect. My last but one voyage out to Australia I was sick from the Mediterranean to King George Sound … this voyage I went on board the mail steamer at Southampton in positive fear and trembling. I, with reason, expected to be very sick as usual, but contrary to my full belief, I was not once sick on the whole way to Australia. My remedy was this: I did not, like many sanguine passengers who felt so well and jolly with the sea-breeze and still water, go down to dinner, but sat quietly on deck till such time as I felt a little hungry, and then went down to my berth, had some toast lying down, though it was then rough and we were in the open sea, and slept well during the evening and through the night. I did not get up the next day, though I felt quite well, but by the steward's favour ate a good breakfast and dinner lying in my berth. I arose on the third morning, feeling perfectly well, and from that day and all through the voyage, I took my meals at table, ate heartily, having found as I then believed, and still am assured of, a perfect cure for seasickness. I may mention that fully one-third of the passengers were sick, and a number did not make their appearance at table till a day or two after me, and I can only attribute my unwonted immunity from this miserable complaint lying in my berth till such a time as my system had become accustomed to the rolling and pitching motion.

This may be so, but brandy and dry ginger ale must be the best cure.

The wardrobe for any journey was important and necessitated profound thought. What was to be packed for wear at sea and on shore? It has always been a problem! For a comfortable feminine outfit the following was suggested in 1909 by an experienced lady traveller:

On the voyage warm clothing is indispensable even in summer. Steamer chairs can be hired on board, and two travelling rugs or heavy shawls and two small cushions conduce to comfort on deck. Extra coats or wraps which can be thrown off for walking are desirable. An ocean voyage is a windy experience, and headgear must be chosen with that in mind.

For travel on land it is not wise to take much luggage. Foreign and Empire railways provide more generously than ours for hand luggage, and there are always plenty of reliable porters who for a few pence will help caring for it ... so two bags are to be preferred to a truck, and the canvas or linen 'hold-all' serves a good purpose.

Two walking gowns are the basis of everywoman's wardrobe. One should be somewhat warmer than the other, but both should be short skirt and light of weight. Shirt waists [blouse] of cotton, flannel, and silk are as useful as at home. Besides the walking gowns and the blouses a women needs at least one gown for evening wear. This should be chosen to bear packing well. A taffeta silk which comes out of a bag a mass of wrinkles is a trial to the owner. The toil of packing and re-packing can be reduced by a choice of materials that do not easily crumble.

The hat for travelling should be small and becoming, but without much rim at the rear to prevent leaning back in the railway carriage. The motor-car veil, gathered at the top and tied down over the hat, is a veritable boon to a woman at sea as well as on shore ... low shoes and gaiters are a convenient combination for footwear ... A light rain wrap must be carried; it is a sensible protection against rain, and can be used as a pillow, a blanket, or as a 'hold-all' according to the ingenuity of the traveller ... a bright knit jacket and one sensible thick skirt are excellent travelling companions.

Laundry work is generally done promptly abroad, but not always carefully, and fine skirts and blouses are likely to suffer where work is done by rubbing on stones in a brook. A linen laundry bag is a convenience, and a needle-book, with a good supply of threaded needles, is a precious appendage. A hot water bag is sure to be needed at times, and a tiny alcohol lamp and saucepan is a luxury if not a necessity ... a small folding parasol is useful to shield the eyes from the glare of the sea, and, sometimes elsewhere ...

When on an extended Empire journey, provisions are nowadays best and easiest purchased near the base of one's journey, but a few special things might be taken from home or the civilised region from which one departs. The selection is best left to the individual fancy. A small medicine chest with an ample supply of good quinine should certainly be obtained before one's departure and taken with one everywhere. If one wishes to reduce medicine to a few standard remedies, then select sugar-coated quinine tabloids of three grains each, chlorodyne (for dysentery and diarrhoea), Cockle's Pills, Eno's fruit salts and some form of peppermint for indigestion. The best general drink in the tropics is weak tea ... alcohol is very prejudicial to the health ... the least prejudicial form of and the least unwholesome distilled spirit is a gin cocktail, taken very occasionally 'if the flesh is very weak' ... the safest rule is no alcohol in any shape or form, for in the tropics even beer is bad for the liver ...

Lastly, heaps of books should be taken; not books heavily bound, but all that can be obtained in cheap editions and paper covers. Until you are travelling in the tropics you do not appreciate the joys of reading ...

The importance of proper tropical equipment — such as camp beds and mosquito nets; waterproof travellers' holdalls for carrying rugs, coats, cloaks and umbrellas; tin trunks of a convenient size for ship's cabins and for being carried on men's heads, or slung across the backs of mules, donkeys or camels; helmets, deck chairs, portable india rubber baths, air cushions, deck boots, stout watertight shoes, soiled linen bags, merino socks, and preserved provisions for travel — was emphasised in a letter from Rosita Forbes, the famous traveller, which was included in a periodical advertisement placed by a company special-ising in such serious matters. Her letter was dated 6 November 1920 and was sent from the Grand Continental Hotel, Rome. It reads:

Dear Sirs,
    I write to thank you very much indeed for all the

trouble you took over my camp outfit in London. I am very pleased indeed with all of it & am so grateful for the efficient & practical way you arranged the packing of all my goods. The huts will be most useful. In fact I think you have left nothing undone to secure the success of my outfit. Again very many thanks. I would certainly recommend you for all kinds of camp equipment down to the minimalist details, only I shall be in the Sahara for the next 6 months but I shall be delighted for you to use this letter & my name if it can be in any way useful to you.

Very different advice came from the authors of the *P&O Pocket Book* in 1924 who advised their intending passengers:

A few general hints to travellers may be of use. Ordinary tropical clothing is needed, with some pairs of common canvas shoes for beach walking. Riding cloths and saddles will be useful. A mackintosh is indispensable, as there is sometimes a good deal of rain. Ladies should wear a short skirt, in case of landings from boats in rough weather, or mountain climbs. Presents offered by natives should not, as a rule, be accepted without making a gift in return: to do so is considered 'unchieflike'. When staying in native houses it is necessary to carry one's own mosquito nets, rug, and pillow. Much luggage is not necessary; but it is a mistake to wear out old clothes in the islands, as the natives are very keen critics of white people's dress, and there is usually some official society in the different towns. The case of a number of politician tourists who landed on a highly civilised island in pyjamas has not yet been forgotten in the island world …

Wearing pyjamas would never have entered the mind of the fearless Miss Philippa Bridges, who appears later in this volume. Miss Bridges was a true Empire wanderer, purposeful and serious. She touchingly concluded her book:

This account of various journeys is necessarily both slight and incomplete, for I did not set out with the idea of writing about them, but of travelling for my own pleasure and education, glad to have an opportunity of gaining a little first-hand knowledge of this very important part of the Empire. Yet the writing of it has been a pleasure, for to some extent I have lived these journeys over again, and met again — if only in the realms of memory — men and women whose friendship I shall always prize. I owe them my thanks, not only for their kindness to me, but for what they taught me. Hands across the sea!

By the time Amy Johnson arrived in Australia with only a tiny suitcase and an equally tiny toilet bag in 1930, Australians had themselves begun to travel abroad in earnest, and in great comfort, not so much by aeroplane — this was to come — but by famous passenger ships furnished in the style of an English country house hotel.

Just as my task of editing was drawing to a close, I spotted a 1930s feature in *The Home*, once well known as 'the Australian journal of quality'. The article made a marvellous contrast to the unknown female convict in 1790, featured in

14

the first section of this book, who complained about her 'cloaths', and the difficulties faced by all the other travellers herein. It reads:

> The clangour of the ship's gong gives warning of the imminent departure. Soon the last streamer breaks, and the liner moves off down the harbour. The thoughts of the passengers inevitably veer from those they have left behind on the wharf to the new experiences that await them. For the women passengers much of their enjoyment will depend on how they have dealt with the question of clothes and luggage.
>
> In regard to the latter, conditions have changed greatly in the last few years. When the smart Australian woman sets off on her travels she is no longer satisfied merely to have her clothes correct and charming. Her luggage also must measure up to the same standard of perfection. Nowadays a chic voyageuse — whether hailing from Paris or Sydney — has trim new luggage as spruce in appearance as her charming self.
>
> One of the newest conceits is to have coloured luggage, and some of the new suit cases and hat boxes are striking studies in scarlet or bright blue. One advantage that is claimed for them is that they can be easily picked out from among an assorted heap of other people's impedimenta. Less conspicuous, and in better taste, are suit cases and hat boxes in shiny black, piped narrowly in red or blue, or plain navy blue and grey leather boxes.
>
> Last season we were introduced to the hat box of American cloth, with a soft lid. This light little

receptacle hangs from a strip at the wrist, and is ideal for carrying a special hat or two for a short trip. Now comes the suit case made on this principle, and very practical it is. They are definitely lighter than any other form of suit case we have seen. Probably they would never enter for the family heirloom stakes, but there has been too much inherited luggage in days gone by, so perhaps it is really an advantage that they should be somewhat ephemeral.

When it comes to heavy luggage, the wardrobe trunk is noticeably gaining ground. It is objected to by some humanitarians on the score of the excessive weight for porters, but there is no doubt that it solves the problem of packing as no other piece of luggage has ever done. It is a wardrobe and chest of drawers combined. When you arrive at your destination no unpacking is needed. You simply stand it up on end, open it out, and there you have a wardrobe on one side with frocks neatly strung on their coat hangers, and a chest of drawers on the other side, stacked with undies and oddments. In addition, there is a space for footwear, and last, but not least, a serviceable bag for soiled linen. For the visit lasting only one night, or for the train trip, a special bag has been evolved, known as the over-night bag. These have rather the air of a bloated handbag, swollen beyond all seemly proportions, but there is no doubt that they are delightfully easy to carry. They fasten with the popular Zipper lightning fastener, and are fitted inside with brushes, combs, mirror, and an array of bottles.

When one looks for clothes to pack into these trunks, one discovers that the designers have come wonderfully up to the demands of the voyageuse. Whole hosts of designs in sports frocks, quite uncrushable, have been created for travelling needs. The delightfully fleecy new Angora fabric is ideal for shipboard wear. You cannot crush it, and it is as light as a feather, while being quite comfortingly warm …

… Separate top coats of soft kasha, lined with crepe de Chine, and boldly embroidered in bright-coloured wools are perfect for shipboard wear. A fleecy lambs' wool coat … is most appealing. It would certainly soil easily in the vicissitudes of land travel, but would be ideal for 'the road without earth's road-dust' to quote John Masefield's picturesque phrase for the sea trail. Very spirited are bright-coloured cardigans in wool darned over net … All of these will withstand the rigours of unskilful packing, being entirely uncrushable.

For evening wear there is quite a big choice of fabrics that come up smiling after a sojourn in a trunk. Lace frocks are specially useful. Better still is a frock of the new crepe chiffon, with long lace sleeves … perfect for packing. The one fabric that must be eschewed is the treacherous taffeta, as it has a disconcerting habit of falling to pieces in the tropics.

In 1933 the travel writer Freya Stark wrote in her first book about what she called 'the art of travel'. An art, she considered, that could be practised by anybody on any journey anywhere. It's worth remembering. This is what she wrote:

To awaken quite alone in a strange town is one of the pleasantest sensations in the world. You are surrounded by adventure. You have no idea of what is in store for you, but you will, if you are wise and know the art of travel, let yourself go on the stream of the unknown and accept whatever comes in the spirit in which the gods may offer it. For this reason your customary thoughts, all except the rarest of your friends, even most of your luggage — everything, in fact, which belongs to your everyday life, is merely a hindrance. The tourist travels in his own atmosphere like a snail in his shell and stands, as it were, on his own perambulating doorstep to look at the continents of the world. But if you discard all this, and sally forth with a leisurely and blank mind, there is no knowing what may not happen to you.

In the extracts in this anthology I have in a very few places, for the sake of simplicity and euphony, modernised the spelling or explained quaint obsolete words or forms.

DOUGLAS R G SELLICK
Lower King, Western Australia
Spring 2002

Two Unknown Convicts

1788 and 1790

These two letters from female convicts, both recently arrived in Australia after slow and horrible voyages, were probably addressed to family members in the British Isles. Many female convicts were near starvation, desperately ill and too feeble to work or help themselves; most did not have adequate 'cloaths'.

Conditions gradually improved and freewill women settlers, explorers, travellers, wayfarers and wanderers came out to Australia under happier circumstances and recorded their first impressions of many parts of Australia.

Port Jackson, 14th November 1788.

J TAKE THE FIRST OPPORTUNITY that has been given us to acquaint you with our disconsolation situation in this solitary waste of creation. Our passage, you may have heard by the first ships, was tolerably favourable; but the inconviences since suffered for want of shelter, bedding, &c., are not to be imagined by any stranger. However, we have now two streets, if four rows of the most miserable huts you can possibly conceive of deserve that name. Windows they have none, as from the Governor's house, &c., now nearly finished, no glass could be spared; so that lattices of twigs are made by our people to supply their places ... As for the distresses of the women, they are past description, as they are deprived of tea and other things they were indulged in the voyage by the seamen, and as they are all totally unprovided with clothes, those who have young children are quite wretched. Besides this, though a number of marriages have taken place, several women who became pregnant on the voyage are since left by their partners, who have returned to England, are not likely even here to form any fresh connections.

Our kingaroo rats are like mutton, but much leaner; and there is a kind of chickweed so much in taste like our spinach that no difference can be discerned. Something like ground ivy is used for tea, but a scarcity of salt and sugar makes our best meals insipid. The separation of several of us to an uninhabited island was like a second transportation. In short everyone is so taken up with their own misfortunes that they have no pity to bestow upon others. All our letters are examined by an officer, but a friend takes this for me privately …

*****

Sydney Cove, Port Jackson, 24th July 1790.

WE ARRIVED HERE SAFE after a long voyage, in very good health … as we had everything that we could expect … and all our provisions were good. We landed here 223 women and twelve children; only three women died, and one child. Five or six were born on board the ship; they had great care taken of them, and baby linen and every necessary for them were ready made to be put on. The greatest part of the women were immediately sent to Norfolk Island, a place about 100 miles from here …

This place was in a very starving condition before we arrived, and on allowance of only 2 pounds of flour and 2 pounds of pork for each man for a week, and these were almost starved, and could not work but three hours in the day; they had no heart, and the ground won't grow anything, only in spots here and there. There is a place called Rose Hill, about twenty miles from this, where they say there are four cornfields, but it does not grow much wheat; we are now much in want of everything; we have hardly any cloaths; but since the *Scarborough*, *Neptune*, and *Surprise* arrived we have had a blanket and a rug given us, and we hope to have some cloaths, as the *Justinian*, a ship that came from London with provisions, will be bringing some cloth and linen and we are to make the cloaths.

Oh! if you had but seen the shocking sight of the poor creatures that came out in the three ships it would make your heart bleed; they were almost dead, very few could stand, and they were obliged to sling them as you would goods, and hoist them out of the ships, they were so feeble; and they died ten or twelve a day when they first landed; but some of them are getting better … They were not so long as we were in coming here, but they were confined, and bad victuals and stinking water.

The Governor was very angry, and scolded the captains a great deal and, I heard, intended to write to London about it, for I heard him say it was murdering them. It to be sure was a melancholy sight … I don't think I ever shall get away from this place to come again to see you without an order from England, for some of the men's times were out, and they went and spoke to the Governor … He told them he could not send them home without orders from London … I hope you will try to get an order for me, that I may once more see you all.

From *The Historical Records of New South Wales — The British Museum Papers 1783–1792*, Volume Two, Sydney, 1893.

Mary Ann Parker
1791–1792

Mary Ann Parker was the young wife of Commander John Parker RN of H.M.S. Gordon which had been commissioned to transport members of the New South Wales Corps to Australia. It was the custom of the day for senior officers of the Royal Navy to be accompanied by their wives on long voyages. Mary Parker's book of her travels is an extraordinary eighteenth century traveller's tale. She hoped that its novelty would earn enough royalties to keep her family comfortable after the early death of her husband in 1794. A review of her book in the Literary Anecdotes section of Monthly Review in 1795 commented,

> it is a rare circumstance to see a female in the list of circumnavigators; and when we consider that it is a disconsolate Widow who details the particulars, we are sorry for the immediate occasion … at the pressing request of an affectionate husband, [she] embarked with him on a voyage … of the occurrences which principally attracted her notice … both outward and homeward, she has given a plain, unvarnished, but not unentertaining recital.

WHEN THINGS WERE IN THIS STATE of forwardness, it was proposed to me to accompany Captain Parker in the intended expedition to New Holland. A fortnight was allowed me for my decision. An indulgent husband waited my answer at Portsmouth: I did not therefore take a minute's consideration; but, by return of post, forwarded one perfectly consonant to his request, and my most sanguine wishes that of going with him to the remotest parts of the globe although my considerate readers will naturally suppose that my feelings were somewhat wounded at the thoughts of being so long absent from two dear children and a mother, with whom I had travelled into France, Italy, and Spain; and from whom I had never been separated a fortnight at one time during the whole course of my life … [H.M.S. *Gordon* sailed from England in February 1791, and reached Australia six months later.]

AT SUNRISE WE SAW THE COAST of New Holland, extending from South West to North West, distant from the nearest part about nine or ten miles. During the night we were driven to the Northward, and passed Port Jackson, the port to which we were bound; however, on the ensuing day, the 21st September, we arrived safe in the above harbour. As soon as the ship anchored several officers came on board, and shortly after Governor King [Captain Philip Gidley King] of Norfolk Island accompanied by Captain Parker, went on shore, and waited on His Excellency Governor [Captain Arthur] Phillip, with the government dispatches: they were welcome visitors and I may safely say that the arrival of our ship diffused universal joy throughout the whole settlement.

We found lying here His Majesty's army tender, the *Supply*, with her lower masts both out of repair, they were so bad that she was obliged to have others made of the wood of the country, which was procured with great difficulty, several hundred trees being cut down without finding any sufficiently sound at the cove ... Also the *Mary-Anne*, a transport-ship that had been sent out alone, with only women-convicts and provisions on-board.

A dreadful mortality had taken place on-board of most of the transports which had been sent to this country; the poor miserable objects that were landed died in great numbers, so that they were soon reduced to at least one third of the number that quitted England ...

On the 30th Governor Phillip did us the honour to breakfast on board; so did also Mr. Collins, Judge Advocate; and Mr. Palmer, the Commissary. The conversation was very interesting; the one party anxiously making enquiries after their relatives in England, and the other attentively listening to the troubles and anxieties which had attended the improvements made in that distant colony. When the company returned on-shore, we amused ourselves with the pleasing novelties of Sidney Cove: from this Cove, although it is very rocky, a most pleasant verdure proceeds on each side: the little habitations on shore, together with the canoes around us, and the uncommon manners of the natives in them were more than sufficient amusements for that day; the next was occupied in receiving visits from several officers belonging to this settlement.

When we went on shore, we were all admiration at the natural beauties raised by the hand of Providence without expense or toil: I mean the various flowery shrubs, natives of this country, that grow apparently from rock itself. The gentle ascents, the winding valleys, and the abundance of flowering shrubs, render the face of the country very delightful. The shrub which most attracted my attention was one which bears a white flower, very much resembling our English Hawthorn; the smell of it is both sweet and fragrant, and perfumes the air around to a considerable distance. There is also plenty of grass, which grows with the greatest vigour and luxuriance, but which, however, as Captain Watkin Tench justly observes, is not of the finest quality, and is found to agree better with horses and cows than with sheep.

In Botany Bay there are not many land fowls: of the larger sort, only eagles were seen; of the smaller kind, though not numerous, there is a variety, from the size of a wren to that of a lark; all of which are remarkable for fine loud notes, and beautiful plumage, particularly those of the paroquet kind. Crows are also found here, exactly the same as those in England. But descriptions, infinitely beyond the abilities of her who now, solely for the benefit of her little flock, is advised to set forth this narrative, having been already published, it would be presumptive to attempt any thing farther.

Our amusements here, although neither numerous nor expensive, were to me perfectly novel and agreeable: the fatherly attention of the good Governor upon all occasions, with the friendly politeness of the officers rendered our séjour perfectly happy and comfortable.

After our arrival here, Governor King and his Lady resided on shore at Governor Phillip's, to whose house I generally repaired after breakfasting on-board: indeed it always proved a home for me, under this hospitable roof, I have often ate part of a Kangaroo, with as much glee as if I had been a partaker of some of the greatest delicacies of this metropolis, although latterly I was cloyed with them, and found them very disagreeable. The presents of eggs, milk, and vegetables, which I was often favoured with from the officers on shore, were always very acceptable; and the precaution which Captain Parker had taken, previous to our departure from the Cape of Good Hope, made me fully contented with my situation.

Our parties generally consisted of Mrs. King, Chaplain Johnson, and the Ladies who resided at the colony. We made several pleasant excursions up the Cove to the settlement called Parramatta. The numerous branches, creeks, and inlets, that are formed in the harbour of Port Jackson, and the wood that covers all their shores down to the very edge of the water, make the scenery beautiful: the North branch is particularly so, from the sloping of its shores, the interspersion of tufted woods, verdant lawns, and the small Islands, which are covered with trees, scattered up and down.

Upon our first arrival at Parramatta was surprised to find that so great a progress had been made in this new settlement, which contains above one thousand convicts, besides the military. There is a very good level road, of great breadth, that runs nearly a mile in a straight direction from the landing place to the Governor's house, which is a small convenient building, placed upon a gentle ascent, and surrounded by about a couple of acres of garden ground: this spot is called Rose-Hill. On both sides of the road are small thatched huts, at an equal distance from each other. After spending the day very agreeably at the Governor's, we repaired to the lodging which had been provided for us, where we had the comfort of a large wood fire, and found every thing perfectly quiet, although surrounded by more than one thousand convicts. We enjoyed our night's repose and in the morning, without the previous aid of toilet or mirror, we set out for the Governor's to breakfast, and returned with the same party on the ensuing day.

This little excursion afforded us an opportunity of noticing the beautiful plumage of the birds in general, and of the Emu in particular, two of which we discovered in the woods: their plumage is remarkably fine, and rendered particularly curious, as each hen has two feathers generally of a light brown; the wings are so small as hardly to deserve the name; and, though incapable of flying, they can run with such swiftness that a greyhound can with difficulty keep pace with them. The flesh tastes somewhat like beef. In this cove there are some cool recesses, where with Captain Parker and the officers I have been many times revived after the intense heat of the day, taking with us what was necessary to quench our thirst.

Here we have feasted upon Oisters just taken out of the sea; the attention of our sailors, and their care in opening and placing them round their hats, in lieu of plates, by no means diminishing the satisfaction we had in eating them. Indeed, the Oisters here are both good and plentiful: I have purchased a large three quarter bowl of them, for a pound and a half of tobacco, besides having them opened for me into the bargain.

The Inhabitants of New South Wales, both male and female, go without apparel. Their colour is of a dingy copper; their nose is broad and flat, their lips wide and thick, and their eyes circular. From a disagreeable practice they have of rubbing themselves with fish-oil, they smell so loathsome, that it is almost impossible to approach them without disgust.

The men in general appeared to be from five feet six to five feet nine inches high, are rather slender, but straight and well made: they have bushy beards, and the hair on their heads is stuck full with the teeth of fish, and bits of shells: they also ornament themselves with a fish-bone fastened in the gristle of the nose which makes them appear really frightful and are generally armed with a stick about a yard long, and a lance which they throw with considerable velocity.

The stature of the women is somewhat less than that of the men — their noses are broad, their mouths wide, and their lips thick. They are extremely negligent of their persons, and are filthy to a degree scarcely credible: their faces and bodies are besmeared with the fat of animals, and the salutary custom of washing seems entirely unknown to them.

Their huts or habitations are constructed in the most rude and barbarous manner: they consist of pieces of bark laid together somewhat in the form of an oven, with a small entrance at one end. Their sole residence, however, is not in these huts; on the contrary, they depend less on them for shelter than on the numerous excavations which are formed in the rocks by the washing of the sea; and it is no uncommon thing to see fifty or sixty of them comfortably lodged in one of these caves.

Notwithstanding the general appearance of the natives, I never felt the least fear when in their company, being always with a party more than sufficient for my protection. I have been seated in the woods with twelve or fourteen of them, men, women, and children. Had I objected, or shewn any disgust at their appearance, it would have given them some reason to suppose that I was not what they term their 'damely' or friend; and would have rendered my being in their company not only unpleasant, but unsafe.

Before I conclude my description of the natives, it is but justice to remark that, in comparison with the inhabitants of most of the South-Sea Islands, they appear very little given to thieving; and their confidence in the honesty of one another is so great, that they will leave their spears and other implements on the sea-shore, in full and perfect security of their remaining untouched.

From the treatment which I invariably experienced, I am inclined to think favourably of them; and fully believe that they would never injure our people, were they not first offended by them.

I cannot help observing that one of the men had a most engaging deportment; his countenance was pleasing, and his manners far beyond what I could possibly have expected. He was pleased to seat himself by me, changed names with Captain Parker, and took particular notice of the travelling knife and fork with which I was eating, and which I did myself the satisfaction to give him: he paid us a visit on-board the ensuing day, and shewed me that he had not lost my present, but made use of it, though somewhat awkwardly, whilst he demolished two or three pounds of the ship's pork.

The natives very frequently surrounded our vessel with their canoes. The women often held up their little ones, as if anxious to have them noticed by us. Sometimes, for the sake of amusement, I have thrown them ribbands and other trifles, which they would as frequently tye round their toes as any other part of their person.

Since my return to England, Bennelong, one of the natives brought hither by Governor Phillip, came to see me. To describe the pleasure that overspread this poor fellow's countenance when my little girl presented to him the picture of her dear father, is impossible; it was then that the tear of sensibility trickled down his cheeks; he immediately recognised those features which will never be obliterated from my memory, and spoke, with all the energy of Nature, of the pleasing excursion which they had made together up the country. The above is one amongst many instances which I could relate of the natural goodness of their hearts; and I flatter myself that the time is hastening when they will no longer be considered as mere savages; and wherefore should they?

In the course of this month (October), the *Britannia* transport anchored at this place, as did also the Admiral Barrington. The arrival of the latter afforded us the pleasure of seeing Mrs. Patterson again, whose company added much to the happiness of our little parties. The 25th was quite a busy day with us, it being the commemoration of His Majesty's accession to the throne: after amusing ourselves in the morning with looking at some ships which were busily employed in going out of the cove on a fishing expedition, and the full dress of our bark in compliment to the day, we repaired to the Governor's, whose unremitting attention to his guests rendered the day very agreeable, could we but have forgotten that it was the eve of our separation from Captain King and his Lady, whose affability had so much contributed to the pleasantry of our voyage thus far; and who, with Captain and Mrs. Patterson and several other military officers destined for Norfolk Island, set sail the next day, accompanied to the end of the cove by the Governor, Judge Advocate, Captain Parker, and many others who were anxious to be in their company as long as possible.

From the first of our arrival at Port Jackson, no time had been lost in preparing for our return to England. The embarkation of the marines, with their wives twenty-five in number, and their children forty-seven, the caulking of the vessel, the clergyman of the New Corps coming on-board to read divine service for the last time, in short, every thing began to remind me of our departure.

The ship, when ready for sea, was very differently stored to what it was when we left the Cape of Good Hope in July. In lieu of live stock and all kind of necessary provisions, our bark was now crowded with Kangaroos, Opposums, and every curiosity which that country produced. The quarter-deck was occupied with shrubs and plants, whilst the cabin was hung around with skins of animals. We had also procured a variety of birds. I was so fortunate as to bring to England a bronzed wing and two pair of Norfolk Island pigeons — they are now alive and well, and are, I believe, the only birds of the kind ever brought to this country.

The uniform attention which the Governor paid us during

our short stay at the colony will always be remembered with singular satisfaction: he may be justly called, like the Monarch of Great Britain, 'The Father of his People', and the Convict, who has forsaken the crimes that sent him to this country, looks up to him with reverence, and enjoys the reward of his industry in peace and thankfulness: indeed, the kindness which we experienced from all around was such, that to have left the colony without a considerable degree of regret at parting from them would have shewn much ingratitude.

On the 17th of December, after supping at the Governor's, we repaired on-board, where every one was busily engaged in lashing and securing such things as were intended to be conveyed to England: it was my occupation to look after the birds, and to place them in the safest and most convenient manner I possibly could.

18th. Anchor being weighed, we set sail at 7 o'clock p.m. ... I shall not here trouble my readers with the regular dates and little variations customary in these distant latitudes; but simply notice the weather, which was mostly fresh breezes, hazy, and squally — splitting of sails, passing rockweed, seaweed, and such like occurrences, met with by voyagers in general ...

From *A Voyage Round the World, in the 'Gorgon' Man of War: Captain John Parker. Performed & Written by His Widow; for the Advantage of a Numerous Family*, London, 1795.

Rosalie Hancorn Ambrose Hare

1827–1828

Rosalie Hancorn Ambrose was eighteen years old when in 1827 at Ipswich in England, she married Captain Robert Lind Hare, Master of the East Indian ship Caroline *of Calcutta and immediately accompanied him on a chartered voyage to Van Diemen's Land and Batavia. Rosalie Hare probably knew little of the world beyond the immediate surroundings of her home. She kept a voyage diary which formed the basis of her book published for the first time in 1927. The* Caroline, *a barque of 330 tons, carried sixty passengers, three hundred Saxony sheep, and cows and horses for the Van Diemen's Land Company Settlement on the north-east coast of Tasmania.*

JULY 17TH, 1827. WE BEGAN OUR VOYAGE [from Hull] towards Van Diemen's Land, having on board sixty passengers for the Company's settlement at Circular Head (Van Diemen's Land).

WEDNESDAY, AUGUST 8TH. A passenger, intoxicated and using mutinous language, the Captain ordered him to be put in irons. On attempting which he was rescued by four of the passengers, who took him below, when he declared there was a conspiracy in the ship and it should soon be seen. The Captain, Surgeon, Chief and Second Officers armed themselves, handcuffed [the passenger], and kept him a prisoner on the poop, during which time he threatened the lives of the Captain and Surgeon. At 9 in the evening he was liberated on his promise of future good behaviour.

THURSDAY, AUGUST 16TH. The Steward delivered up the keys of the store-room for wasting and adulterating the provisions of the passengers. Left the cabin and threatened revenge on the First Officer.

MONDAY, AUGUST 20TH. Mr. and Mrs. N. passengers, quarrelling with each other and declaring their intention to murder if possible. The husband was persuaded to continue on deck all night and his own clothes being torn, was supplied with others. At 9 in the morning the Surgeon was informed that Mrs. N— had inflicted a severe wound on his arm with a pen-knife, declaring that if he again came near her she would, as she before intended, 'cut his throat.' This she was prevented doing by the interference of one of the bailiffs. She was put in irons on the poop, where she continued threatening the lives of those who had confined her. There was now a cabin built for her on the quarter-deck. On entering it she declared she 'would not leave it the whole voyage', it being the most comfortable place she had been in, and she would reward the carpenter with her grog, should she again receive it, for making it so well. The next day, however, she began to break the door of her cabin in order to take vengeance. Breaking the venetian blind in pieces, she took two of the sticks to strike the Captain and Surgeon. Her child at her request was permitted to sleep with her, but she frightened him so much that he dare not continue in her cabin.

FRIDAY, AUGUST 31ST. Spoke [hailed] the ship *Othello* of Bristol, Captain Swainson of Calcutta, bound to Liverpool. Received from them a present of sugar and rice. Mrs. N— liberated on promise of better behaviour in future and sorrow for the past and reconcilement with her husband.

SUNDAY, SEPTEMBER 9TH. A brig passed about five miles to leeward with a French Ensign and Pendant flying at two o'clock in the afternoon in our wake, tack'd and stood after us. She fired her weather-bow gun. Hove our main-yard aback. When she came up, along our leeside, hailed us in

English, and ordered our boat with all the ship's papers on board immediately, and then fired a shot round us on our weather-bow. Mr. Drybrough, First Officer, went on board her with our papers. On going up the gangway he discovered the crew at their quarters, each armed with a cutlass, brace of pistols, and long Spanish knife. Two men with drawn cutlasses conducted him in silence to the companion and then ordered him below. On going into the cabin he was surrounded by ten or twelve men, each having a cutlass in one hand and a pistol in the other. The French colours were taken down and Spanish hoisted. We now began to feel anxious lest she should keep our officer — as is often the case. The Captain [the pirate] on coming out of his state-room questioned Mr. Drybrough through an interpreter as follows: 'Have you the ship's papers?'

'Yes'

'What was the reason you did not heave-to on first seeing us?'

'We took you to be a French man-of-war and supposed if you wanted to speak to us you would fire a gun.'

At this he appeared displeased ... he remarked that there was no part of the cargo of any use to them.

He ordered Mr. Drybrough to sign a paper, signifying that it was a declaration that he had not hurt us and telling him that he must sign the names of himself and his captain. When he had signed the paper he was ordered to go on board his own ship and return with one bolt of canvas and two sheep, the captain saying he would send us two better in return, remarking aside that we might think ourselves well off (which we certainly did).

He repeated to Mr. Drybrough: 'Remember we have not

injured you; we have not hurt you.' Mr. Drybrough, on taking the articles ordered to them, saw the marines discharge their small arms, which, with the long guns, had been pointed at us all the time. Our ship having forged on end they filled their main-yard and again placed themselves on our weather-bow in a menacing manner. We of course sent all that was demanded finding resistance would be perfectly useless, as she mounted 18 great guns, Spanish 12-pounders, and appeared to have 300 men. She was about 350 tons, flush-deck and billet-head. The men filled the deck boats, tops, and cross-trees.

There was no uniform or mark of distinction among them (the officers); the marines had on red caps made of cloth four square, similar to those of collegians. There were several Englishmen on board! Mr. Drybrough could not learn the ship's name or any particulars (although he asked) except that they were going on a cruise. Our officer noticed 16 or 18 trunks lashed with white line lying carelessly about the deck of the after cabins with arms of all kinds. They seemed to have plenty of provisions of all kinds on board, having five or six hands employed in baking. They sent us two sheep and a small quantity of wine which we had thrown overboard fearing all might not be correct. The crew had some wine and biscuit, which they ate and found good.

Her sails were much worn and rigging weather-beaten. There were drunken men lying all about her decks. On making sail she told us now we might go where we liked and enquired if we wanted anything.

Our passengers (with the exception of a few families), consisting of the lowest class of Yorkshire people, showed their true character. They who had daily denied the power of God now supposed there certainly was a God, while others declared that on the Captain alone depended their fate … The Surgeon, seeing so large a number of men on board the pirate, feared that they might send for him, but appeared determined to buy his life with his pistols or sell it as dear as possible …

No sooner did it appear that danger was over than vows were forgotten, quarrels renewed, and songs and mirth on board with many, finished up the eventful day. Only that very morning the Second Officer was giving us an account of a pirate that they had fallen in with during the last voyage, but much inferior to this.

TUESDAY, SEPTEMBER 18TH, 1827. One of the sailors quarrelling. The Captain, First and Second Officers, and the boatswain went below. The sailor, throwing his arms about, bidding defiance to everybody, was collared by the boatswain and put in irons. To the no small amusement of the Captain and Surgeon, the wife of one of the bailiffs stood by the side of them with a large bar of wood to defend them (as she said), and sure enough she would have been able to fight two men.

SEPTEMBER 19TH. Captain mustered the crew and warned them of the consequences of mutinous conduct. The prisoner, acknowledging himself sorry for his conduct and promising to behave better, was released and went to his duty.

SEPTEMBER 30TH. Divine Service on the quarter-deck.

MONDAY, OCTOBER 1ST. Spoke a French brig-of-war, bound to Rio Janeiro. On the sight of which considerable alarm was shown as it appeared exactly like our piratical friend — in company with another vessel which had sprung a leak. The man-of-war was towing her into Rio Janeiro. The First Officer went on board; Captain, very polite, sent his compliments to me with some very fine oranges. He had seen the Pirate but could not long give chase on account of the leaky vessel. Uncommon fine weather the last fortnight.

THURSDAY, NOVEMBER 8TH. Saw Table Mountain, Cape of Good Hope. The first land seen since leaving England.

SUNDAY, NOVEMBER 11TH. Ship brought to an anchor in Table Bay. Officers and steward left the ship, the officers only by mutual consent. Mr. Chamberlain joined the ship as mate. We were obliged to put into this port for water. I went on shore in the evening with my husband and the Surgeon … We slept on shore this night, and in the morning received a polite and friendly invitation to spend the time we might remain here at Mr. Heideman's — he being one of my dear husband's former ship owners — at their house in the country.

SUNDAY, NOVEMBER 25TH, 1827. We sailed from the Cape … towards Van Diemen's Land.

SATURDAY, DECEMBER 29TH. Strong gales with high sea the last fortnight. At 6 o'clock in the morning Mrs. B. delivered of a son, a fine child. This miserable, wicked woman would not take the trouble to make a few clothes for the infant, begging what she could, being too much engaged in smoking a short pipe in the cook-house from morning till night. Her husband and her three other children ran about half naked and covered with dirt. This woman had had eleven children, the others, the husband assured the Surgeon, had died of neglect. This inhuman mother was soon ordered about ... the Surgeon, after repeated orders, at last obliged her to go below to see to her infant. He discovered the child's flesh burnt in two places from her pipe ... The Surgeon supplied her with sago for the child, but she fed it with cold tea and biscuit.

SUNDAY, JANUARY 6TH, 1828. The Surgeon informed Mrs. B. her infant was ill. Mrs. B. begged that it might be baptised as 'she dared say it would die'. In the afternoon my husband baptised the neglected baby by the name of John. Weather too unsettled for Divine Service.

MONDAY JANUARY 7TH. One of the women on passing Mrs. B.'s bed awoke her telling her that her bairn was dead. She carelessly lifted it up and said: 'No, it has life in it yet.' At twelve her husband told her to feed it. She stuffed large pieces of soaked biscuits into its mouth without ever moving the little creature. The food was found in its throat and the women supposed it was then dead. Her husband expressed much sorrow ... John B. asked that the burial service might be read.

TUESDAY, JANUARY 8TH. My husband read the Burial Service ere the little unfortunate was committed to the deep. The father, dressed in his best clothes, was present and much affected. The service was read in the dining cabin as it rained very fast. I did not attend, being ill.

Saturday, January 19th. Saw the Pyramid, Van Diemen's Land. Passed Albatross Island, and the Hummock Island; brought to at one and a quarter of a mile from Circular Head. Much to my gratification, as I had been ill most of the passage from the Cape.

What was the disappointment of our passengers on their arrival! Their minds, like the minds of most settlers, had been painting fancy visions, and, instead of comfortable houses as they had been used to see in England, here there were tents, bark huts and huge mountains. Some of them were sent to a still less cultivated settlement, and all were displeased. Thus ended their voyage of hopes. Young men mechanics were stamping with passion, wishing themselves with their mothers, and all wishing themselves at home and the Directors of the Company, particularly Mr. Inglis in Heaven.

Sunday, January 20th. Mr. Curr, Agent to the Van Diemen's Land Company, came on board and invited us to dine at his house. This invitation we accepted, although doubtful if my strength would allow. With the assistance of my kind friends I managed it tolerably. This was indeed a new scene! The Head justly called Circular presented a rather desolate sight. Here were plenty of trees, but they were of Stringy Bark, so called from their bark continually falling off and hanging in strings. Leaves only at the top.

Mr. Curr's house, equal to a genteel English farmhouse,

stood on the top of a hill called Ladder Hill on account of a rude, narrow path with here and there a few steps dug out of the earth leading to the house.

Near the house is the garden which supplies the settlers with vegetables — a fine piece of ground neatly laid out and very flourishing, supplying vegetables every season. It has been but two years cultivated, and indeed that is but the age of the settlement. Round the house are cornfields and we had the satisfaction of seeing the first harvest gathered in. There are also beautiful plains not far distant called Western, Eastern and Lovely Plains, where most of the sheep are kept in good pasture. The large number of snakes in the grass prevented my going to see them.

This part of the settlement is very woody, and I was much pleased with the beautiful little parrots and cockatoos constantly flying about; the kangaroos skipping on their hind-legs are also very curious. The head of this animal is something like the head of a rabbit. The body very large in proportion, with a long tapering tail. The fore-legs not more than one-third the length of the hind-legs. They spring from place to place with great swiftness upon their hind-legs and tail. The natives are very expert at catching them and train their dogs for that purpose, so that they may never be at a loss for food. They are very fine stewed into what is here called a steamer. I had an opportunity of frequently tasting them. Mrs. Curr's son had a small kangaroo, tamed in some measure, about the house. Our sailors had also many on-board. The taste of this animal's flesh resembles that of venison, and I should imagine it is a species of southern venison.

The height of Circular Head appears about four hundred

feet. I ascended it in company with the Surgeon without much difficulty. We found sheep grazing on its summit and kangaroo leaping about in all directions. Here I picked up the upper jaw of a kangaroo, intending to take it to England, for I suppose I shall find but few who have seen this curious animal, peculiar to Van Diemen's Land, and New Holland. The descent from the Bluff we found very unpleasant and rather dangerous.

Some of the passengers being destined for another settlement, and my dear husband finding it necessary to have the ship entered at the next town [he] was obliged to proceed there ere he could land the stock. Anxious as I was to see a little more of this interesting colony, my own health rendered it desirable (after having received a kind invitation from our friends) that I should remain with Mrs. Curr at this uncommonly healthy settlement, while Mr. Curr and my husband proceeded to Launceston.

The ship being there delayed three weeks, I had an opportunity of entirely establishing my health and the satisfaction of seeing a few native women who visited the settlement with a few sealers and a Government Surveyor. Surely of all uncivilised creatures these are the worst! They commonly wear no dress of any kind, but Mr. Curr will not allow any of them to be brought into the settlement without decent clothing. It is surprising with what agility these women climb trees to catch the opossum and with what swiftness they hunt kangaroo. They also dive for crawfish, plunging without fear from very high rocks. Many of them had large scars upon them where they had pitched upon rocks under water.

The woman whom the Surveyor had given the name of

Mary to, paid us a visit at Highfield House. She had learned a little English and appeared more intelligent than most of her race. She was astonished at all she saw, particularly at the chairs, tables and beds, never before having seen any other dwelling-house than a hut of the bark of trees made over a hole dug in the earth with a fire at the entrance. She insisted, much against my inclination and Mrs. Curr's also, upon kissing us and the children. The next day three other native women, or young girls about fifteen, paid us a visit. These poor creatures had joined the crew of a sealing boat while they were looking for seals along the coast and were brought by them to Circular Head. How was my very soul shocked when two of these girls took off their kangaroo-skin coats and showed the inhuman cuts these European monsters had given them when they had not been able to find them food. Mrs. Curr's feelings were instantly aroused for the youngest of these poor girls, and she thought it might be possible to teach her to take care of the children. But on consideration it appeared dangerous — as they have been frequently tried as servants, but universally proved traitorous …

I had one sweet little boy (belonging to a fisherman, his mother a native) on board the *Caroline* some days, and a more sensible child I never saw in England. He was five years old, very tall and stout, and had black curly hair; his complexion was copper-coloured. He spoke English very well. His dress was, generally a shirt, pair of trousers buttoned at the knees and little kangaroo skin coat which we never could prevail on him to take off when he slept, nor would he sleep on a bed, preferring a mat on the bare deck. He had begged to come off with my husband to the ship and cried very much when obliged to leave us. His father, a cross old man, had not much affection for him, but would not part with him or this little stranger would most likely have seen England. We wished very much to have him.

The natives near Circular Head (the Northern coast) are much better looking than those of Hobart Town (Southern coast). The former are stout, well-made, their faces nearly round, with good eyes: noses not very flat and mouths of pretty tolerable width (such as I never saw in England). Their hair woolly, their lineaments in general are more pleasant than those of African Negroes. The men wear their beards long and smear them and their hair with red ointment. The latter are exceedingly ugly, with long spears, but remaining at the settlement I had no opportunity of seeing them.

The natives are terrible robbers and do all the mischief they can to the settlers. They had, a short time previous to our arrival, speared three hundred sheep belonging to the company. They do not eat mutton and do it but from mischief. Burning the huts of the shepherds and stealing their dogs are also the works of these incendiaries when they find them on the plains and wastes …

The climate is very healthy; two of our women were reduced to skeletons almost and appeared in consumption, but no sooner had they got on shore than they improved very rapidly and were, when I left, in particularly good health. Here, by the assistance of my good friends, I perfectly recovered, and my dear and anxious husband on his return from Launceston could scarcely believe me the same pale, thin creature he had left.

The morning before we left the Surveyor wished to bring

his native women on board to see the *Caroline*. They, on being told of it, asked if the vessel was going to Macquarie Harbour or England. The convicts who are too bad for any other place or beyond all hope of amendment are sent for life to Macquarie Harbour. Therefore the natives were a little afraid.

What was the surprise of the Surveyor in the morning to find (after having been with him for some time and treated by him with the greatest kindness) the native ladies had eloped with the sealers' ladies and taken all the dogs, a thing of great importance in an uncultivated country, as the men depended entirely upon their dogs for food for months together.

So we are to judge that these women, for the sake of the dogs, had been with them the whole way along the coast and had been with them long enough to learn enough English to be understood. But this was not all, for they stopp'd at the hut of a shepherd and robbed it of everything moveable. These people generally live among the bushes in considerable numbers and are called bushmen. They thrust their long spears from the roof of the huts and generally make too sure an aim — murdering their unfortunate victims. But we are not to suppose the Europeans in their turn take no revenge. We have to lament that our own countrymen consider the massacre of these people an honour. While we remained at Circular Head there were several accounts of considerable numbers of natives having been shot by them (the Company's men), they wishing to extirpate them entirely, if possible.

The Master of the Company's cutter *Fanny*, assisted by four shepherds and his crew, surprised a party and killed twelve. The rest escaped but afterwards followed them. They reached the vessel just in time to save their lives.

The natives are extremely superstitious and dare not travel by night. They are afraid of thunder and terribly alarmed at the sound of guns. They travel all together for many weeks, sleep together promiscuously, except when disturbed by their frequent enmities and assassinations. The women on the birth of an infant leave the party for one day only, then rejoin them and travel without fatigue for many miles. No religion whatever is known, although they have a faint idea of a future existence and believe their people return to the clouds whence they originally fell ...

One tribe, numerous and muscular, have the singular prerogative of extracting a tooth from the young men of other families — a token of subordination or government. It is, however, not improbable that these practices may be mere initiations ... the children are seldom disfigured and their sight is very acute. The language is reported to be grateful to the ear, expressive and sonorous, having no analogy with any other known language; but the dialects of the various regions seem entirely different.

Little can be said by me on the affairs of the Company. The sheep, whose wool alone renders them objects of care, flourish well. The harvest, of course very small, answered the expectations of those concerned, the wheat being of a very fine quality. It must be remembered that the Settlement, three years ago, was entirely uncultivated and covered with fern. I could not but feel pleasure in seeing the little companions of my voyage so happily employed gleaning this year at the opposite side of the world to that which they had gleaned in last.

Thursday March 6th. After enjoying all the sweets of friendship and comforts of shore, and a mutual promise of correspondence, we sailed for the unhealthy but fine island of Java, East Indies; with our hearts filled with thankfulness for the friends everywhere raised up to us. Had we reached Van Diemen's Land two months before, we should not have found a friend there.

From *A Journal of a Voyage From England to Van Diemen's Land & Batavia in the ship* Caroline *of Calcutta, AD 1827–8*, by Rosalie Hancorn Ambrose Hare, London, 1927.

Katherine Kirkland

1839

Katherine Kirkland made two very difficult inland journeys in the short but unhappy time she spent in the Colony of Victoria. The first was immediately after her arrival when she, her husband Kenneth, daughter Agnes and a few servants travelled inland from Corio Bay by spring cart, with a heavy bullock dray loaded with household belongings, poultry, rabbits and cats followed by horses, sheep, goats and dogs intending to farm at Trawalla (approximately forty kilometers west of present-day Ballarat). The journey took twelve days. She was probably the first white woman to go 'so far up the country'. Not long after this, Mrs. Kirkland was required to undertake a second hazardous journey, this time to Melbourne for the birth of her second child. Shortly after her return to Scotland in about 1842, **Chambers Miscellany,** *a popular periodical, printed her story based on her letters to her mother.*

WHEN ALL OUR LUGGAGE and animals were landed, we began to pack our own, and Messrs. Donald and Hamilton's dray. This took us a long time. The Messrs. Baillie were also with us with their drays, so we made a strong party. When all was ready to start, I got into a spring-cart which Mr. Thomson borrowed from Mr. Fisher for me; but indeed my share of it was small. It was already so well filled that I could scarcely find a seat. Our shepherd's wife, who was no light weight, took up more than her share of the seat; she carried Agnes (the infant) on her knee. I took possession of the other seat. At my feet were four little dogs of Mr. Baillie's, also three cats, some cocks and hens, and a pair of rabbits; at our back were three pigs, and some geese and ducks. We were a noisy party; for at times our road was very rough, and some of the animals were rather inclined to be quarrelsome. The spring-cart went first, then came the five drays, and all the gentlemen walking along-side, with the dogs running beside them. Most of the gentlemen had either pistols at their sides or a gun in their hands. Little Nanny followed behind, accompanied by old Billie, who had a wonderful long beard …

We got to Mrs. Fisher's about seven o'clock, she received us very cordially. We found tea awaiting us and I there tasted damper for the first time. I liked it very much; it is like bread but closer and heavier. I said to Mrs. Fisher that she must think we had taken a great liberty in coming in such force upon her; but she did not at all seem to think so. She said she was quite accustomed to have many gentlemen visitors, but she never had had a lady before … A bed was made up for me, little Agnes and her maid, on the parlour floor, and all the gentlemen were sent to the wool-shed, to sleep as they best could: fifteen slept in it that night. A few of them had blankets or rugs, but most of them had nothing.

We remained here a week. Next day we saw some of the natives; they were very ugly and dirty. Some of them wore skins sewed together, and thrown over their shoulders; a few of them had some old clothes given by the settlers; and some were naked. They kept peeping in at the windows to see us, and were always hanging about the huts. Mrs. Fisher called them civilised natives, and said they were always about the place … my servant Mary was very afraid of the natives … she would take comfort from no one, and was quite sure she would be killed by the wild natives when she got up the country.

We had fixed to begin our journey up the country, and the gentlemen had gone to Geelong to load the drays. I waited for them in Mr. Fisher's hut, when in a moment it got quite dark, and the wind roared tremendously. It was the most awful sight I had ever witnessed; we were afraid to move … the storm passed, but many trees were unrooted …

It was now too late for us to begin our journey, so we remained another night at Mr. Fisher's and started early in the morning. On this occasion we had much difficulty in getting the horses to start; they were ill broken in, and many times they stopped on the road, so that we had often to take some of the bullocks out of the other drays to pull them on again. We travelled the first day thirty miles, quartering for the night at Mr. Sutherland's hut which he kindly gave up for our accommodation. Next day we had to rest the bullocks, so we walked over to Mr. Russell's station, about three miles distant, and remained there a night.

In the evening we went to see a meeting of the natives, or a corobery, as they call it. About a hundred natives were assembled. They had about twenty large fires lighted, around which were seated the women and children. The men painted themselves, according to their own fancy, with red and white earth. They had bones, and bits of stones, and emu's feathers, tied on their hair, and branches of trees tied on their ankles, which made a rushing noise when they danced. Their appearance was very wild, and when they danced, their gestures and attitudes were equally so. One old man stood before the dancers, and kept repeating some words very fast in a kind of time, whilst he beat two sticks together. The women never dance; their employment is to keep the fires burning bright; and some of them were beating sticks and declaiming in concert with the old man. The natives, when done with their corobery, were very anxious that we white people would show them how we coroberied; so we persuaded Mr. Yuille to dance for them, which he did, and also recited a piece of poetry, using a great many gestures. The natives watched him most attentively and seemed highly pleased. After giving the natives some white money, and bidding them good night, we returned to Mr. Russell's hut.

Next morning our bullocks were lost — a very common occurrence, it being impossible to tie them, as in that case they would not feed; and unless one has a very good bullock driver who will watch them, it generally takes several hours to find them in the morning. Numbers of natives came this forenoon to see us. They examined my dress very attentively, and asked the name of everything, which they tried to repeat after me. They were much amused with my little Agnes, and she was much pleased with them. I wondered what her grandmamma would have thought, could she have seen her in the midst of a group of savages and the life of the party. Whenever Agnes spoke, they all laughed aloud, and tried to imitate her voice; and the pickaninny leubra's dress was well examined. I put a little night-cap on a native baby, with which its mother was much pleased, and many little black heads were thrust out for one also.

I now began to be a little disgusted and astonished at the dirty and uncomfortable way in which the settlers lived. They seemed quite at the mercy of their hut-keepers, eating what was placed before them out of dirty tin plates, and using a knife and fork if one could be found. Sometimes the hut-keepers would cook the mutton in no way but as chops; some of them would only boil it, and some roast it, just as they liked; and although the masters were constantly complaining of the sameness, still it never seemed to enter their heads to make their servants change the manner of cooking: but the truth was, they were afraid to speak, in case the hut-keeper would be offended and run away. The principal drink of the settlers is tea, which they take at every meal, and indeed all day. In many huts the tea-pot is always at the fire; and if a stranger came in, the first thing he does is to help himself to a panikin of tea. We had neither milk nor butter at any station we were at; nothing but mutton, tea and damper, three times a day. Every meal was alike from one week to another, and from year's end to year's end. I was so sick of it, I could scarcely eat anything.

Next day, we had our bullocks ready in good time, as we had a long journey before us; at least we hoped to get on a good way. The heat this day was very intense, and we had no shade. I could scarcely bear it; and before evening we had drunk all the water we had brought with us. I thought I should have died of thirst, and we were all suffering alike. Poor little Agnes cried much; at last we got her to sleep and forget her wants. My husband was driving one of the drays, and was so thirsty, that when we came to a muddy hole of water on the path, which the dray had passed through, he lay on the ground and drank heartily. One of our party, who knew something of the roads, told us we were near water-holes, which raised our spirits. At last we came to them, and both people and animals took many a long drink, although the water was bad, and quite bitter from reeds which grew in it. We filled our cask, and continued our journey a few miles farther, to a place where we were to sleep in the bush ...

We had soon lighted a fire at the foot of a tree, and put on a huge pot of water to boil, two or three handfuls of tea were put into it, and some sugar. One of the men made some thick cakes of flour and water, and fried them in grease. We had also some chops cooked, which we all enjoyed, as we had not stopped to eat anything on the road. The tea was not poured out; every one dipped his panikin into the pot, and helped himself. Mary, Agnes and I had a bed made with some blankets under the dray, and all the others slept round the fire, taking by turn the duty of watching the bullocks before going to rest. The bullock driver made a large damper, which he fired in the ashes for our provision next day.

We got up at daybreak, had breakfast, and we went on again, and travelled through a forest on fire for forty miles. I was often afraid the burning trees would fall upon us; and we had sometimes to make a new path for ourselves, from the old tracks being blocked up by fallen timber. The fires in the bush are often the work of the natives, to frighten away white men; and sometimes of the shepherds, to make the grass sprout afresh …

We rested for two hours and cooked some dinner, chiefly that our bullocks might feed and rest during the heat of the day. Mr. Yuille and I made some fritters of flour and water. I thought them the best things I ever ate. The Scotch clergyman from Melbourne passed us on the road. He rebuked our bullock driver for swearing at his bullocks; but the man told him that no one ever yet drove bullocks without swearing; it was the only way to make them go.

This night we slept at Mr. Anderson's hut. He was from home, but had an old woman as hut-keeper, who made us up as comfortable as she could; but it was a cold night, and the wind whistled very keenly through a door made of rushes. This was one of the most neatly kept huts I saw, and the owner of it one of the few gentlemen who kept himself always neat and clean in the bush …

I was glad when my husband came to take us to our station, which was about thirty miles farther up the country. Part of the country we passed through was the most beautiful I ever saw, while other portions were very cold and bleak. We stopped at one or two huts, and had mutton, tea, and damper, at each of them. We passed an immense salt lake, which is gradually drying up …

When we passed the salt lake, the country began to improve. I thought we should never come to our own station, the bullocks travel so very slowly. At last Mr. Thomson told me to look forward as far as I could see: we were now at the end of a large plain or marsh. I looked, and saw our pretty little hut peeping through a cluster of trees. I cannot say how it was, but my heart beat with delight the first time I saw that place … I was the first white woman who had ever been so far up the country …

I now hoped that my travels were ended for some time … [but] in the month of September I had to proceed to Melbourne as I was expected to be confined, and we were too far up to ask a medical man to come. I was much grieved at leaving my little girl; but Mary promised faithfully to take great care of her. The weather was very unsettled and rainy, and the roads very bad. I was in a dray, covered by a tarpaulin, which made it very comfortable; it was like a covered wagon, and when we could not get to a station at which to sleep, I slept in the dray. My husband was with me, and read to me very often; but we had often to come out of the dray, to allow it to be pulled out of a hole. I have seen the bullocks pull it through a marsh when they were sinking to the knees every moment: we were often in dread of the pole breaking.

We received much kindness at every station we were at … We remained at Mr. Reid's hut two days, as both I and the bullocks required rest … At this time his hut was full of company; but one room was prepared for us, and about twelve gentlemen slept in the other.

I there met our friend Mr. William Hamilton. He gave us

a sad account of the state of the rivers. He said he was sure we could not cross them — it was difficult for him to cross them three days before, and it had rained ever since. Mr. Reid sent off a man on horseback to see the river: he did not bring back a favourable account, but I was determined to try it. Mr. Reid and several gentlemen went with us to help us over our difficulty. We crossed one river without much difficulty, though the water was so deep that both bullocks and horses had to swim; but when we came to the next river, the 'Marable', it was so deep that we were at a loss how to get over. It was thought decidedly dangerous for me to remain in the dray while it was crossing. Many plans were talked of — at last it was fixed to fell a tree and lay it across, that I might walk over. But in looking about for one of a proper size and position, one was found lying across, which, from appearance, seemed to have been there for years: it was covered with green moss and stood about twenty feet above the water; notches were cut in it for me to climb up and give me a firm footing, and I walked over, holding Mr. Reid's hand. On landing, I received three cheers. Many thanks to Mr. Reid and others for their kindness to me on that journey. My husband was too nervous to help me cross he thought his foot might slip. The gentlemen then went to see the dray across, while little Robert Scott and I lighted a fire at the root of a large tree, which we had in a cheerful blaze before the gentlemen came. We then had tea in the usual bush fashion, in a large kettle: it did not rain, and we had a very merry tea-party. I retired to the dray soon after tea. The gentlemen continued chatting round the fire for some time, and then laid themselves down to sleep, with their saddles at their heads, and their feet to the fire.

We breakfasted at daybreak, and started again after taking leave of the gentlemen, except Mr. Anderson, who was going to Melbourne: he rode on before us to the settlement, to tell Mrs. Scott (who expected us at her house) that we were coming. Mrs. Scott was a particular friend of my husband at home, she came out to meet us, and I really felt delighted to see her. I had not seen a lady for eight months. Mrs. Scott was exceedingly kind to me, and would not allow me to go to lodgings, as I had intended. Next day being Sunday, I went to church — least the room where the congregation met, as no church was yet built in Melbourne. The ladies in Melbourne seemed to consider me a kind of curiosity, from living so far up the country, and all seemed to have a great dread of leading such a life, and were surprised when I said I liked it ... but I really felt at a loss upon what subjects to converse with ladies as I had been so long accustomed only to gentlemen's society, and in the bush, had heard little spoken of but sheep or cattle, horses, or of building huts ... my little boy was born four days after I came to Melbourne ...

From *Chambers' Miscellany*, London, 1845.

Elizabeth Ramsey-Laye

1853

Elizabeth Ramsey-Laye became a novelist and essayist after travelling out to Australia with her husband, a colonial official at the Diggings. As was the custom for many early travellers, they decided on an extended stay, choosing a visit to Melbourne before returning home to England. Life in Melbourne was comfortable for them; fashions, she thought, were both elegant and decorous. Social life was well organised, as in the best of London and Edinburgh. With enthusiasm she enjoyed the social life of the city: '… dinners, balls, and picnics follow each other in rapid succession, scarcely giving breathing time to the votaries of pleasure.'

THE HOUSE WE SOUGHT was quite close to the Richmond Punt, and almost opposite the Cremorne Gardens. It was built of brick, and the rooms were all on the ground floor with a wide verandah running round three sides. The stables were good, whilst a paddock, a very large fruit garden and a vineyard made it a desirable residence. The rent at first seemed very high, being four hundred and fifty pounds a year, but on consideration we took it for a term of five years, as we were anxious to get settled as soon as possible, and then commenced the arduous, puzzling and yet delightful toil of furnishing.

In Collins Street we purchased almost everything we required as good as we could have procured in England. The newest inventions and the most fashionable patterns are sent out here immediately after their appearance in London or Paris. These things, however, are no means cheap; our furniture was the most expensive, a sofa cost 15 pounds, and the chairs in proportion; but we found the tradespeople most civil and obliging ...

Our attention was next turned to the garden. As the produce was far too great for our consumption, we hired a gardener and made arrangements with him after supplying us with fruit and vegetables, he was to dispose of the remainder. The sum thus obtained went some way towards the rent of the house. Then I bought poultry, and, as eggs were six shillings a dozen, I used to send a few dozen every week to my grocer, for which he gave me credit in his bill. I soon became very expert in rearing chickens and always had the produce of the farm-yard to fall back on in the hot weather. We also kept three goats, as milk was a shilling a quart. Every morning the butcher used to send for orders and bring the meat, as in the hot weather we were obliged to eat it the very day it was killed.

The greatest plague in Melbourne is the flies; they are more disgusting if possible than those at the diggings, for they alight on your plate at dinner and leave such disgusting traces that all idea of dining is at an end. We found a storeroom very much wanted, so we agreed with our landlord that we should build one on our own plan, if he paid something towards the expense. This he willingly promised to do; we therefore erected a large square brick room immediately over a tank in the yard, thereby ensuring coolness. The roof was of slate, very shelving [sloping] and projecting; an opening was made through the roof and ceiling, so that a current of air might pass freely through the apartment; the windows were protected by fine canvas wire to prevent the flies coming in. We had shelves and cupboards made, also a trap-door in the floor so that the tank might be cleaned when required without inconvenience. The tank held fourteen or fifteen thousand gallons of water and, as our roof was slate, the water was perfectly good for every purpose and we never had to buy any, which was of some consequence to us, as it was sold for four shillings a load or barrel. The storeroom we found succeeded admirably; it was always deliciously cool and fresh.

The mosquitoes were so very annoying in summer that, besides mosquito curtains for our beds, we nailed 'lino', a kind of net, to the window frames so that we were not obliged to close windows at night, which was a great luxury.

Our establishment consisted of two maid-servants, a housemaid, a cook, and the coachman, who also waited at table. The women-servants, as is the custom in this country, did the washing between them, so we had a washing machine and also a patent mangle; thus, though their wages were high, we had no washing to pay for. The coachman and cook were a married couple; they received eighty pounds a year; both were most excellent English servants, perfectly trained in their several departments. The housemaid, who also acted as parlourmaid, was Irish; she got up the fine things beautifully; her wages were thirty-five pounds.

I would very strongly recommend Irish servants to anyone settling in the colonies as I found, from my own experience and observation, that if properly managed and well treated they become different beings when away from Ireland, attaching themselves strongly to the family and making light of many a little inconvenience which would scare an English servant.

We kept two riding horses and a dog cart, which prevented our having to hire a carriage when we went out, which was the greatest expense of visiting. Two pounds ten shillings is frequently the charge for conveyance to and from a party. We also had a boat, which was a source of much enjoyment during the hot months. When it was not convenient for us to use our own horses to go into town, we used to hire a boat and row down the river. The charge for each person was only a shilling. I need hardly say that the boat was a far more agreeable mode of conveyance than the other alternative, the omnibus, the fare was sixpence ...

From Elizabeth Ramsey-Laye, *Social Life and Manners in Australia: Being the Notes of Eight Years' Experience by a Resident*, London, 1861.

Alice Mary Frere
1865

Alice Mary Frere, afterwards Lady Alice Clerk, wife of General Sir Godfrey Clerk, Groom-in-Waiting to Edward VII, spent her early years in India where her father Sir (Henry) Bartle Frere was an administrator in the Indian Civil Service and later Governor of Bombay. On being recalled to London Sir Bartle decided to make the journey home via Australia, the Far East and the United States for the benefit of his youngest daughter Alice. He and Alice travelled with their Goanese factotum Lucien, who had been one of their table servants in Bombay. Alice might not have been a typical traveller but her impressions of her journey contrast interestingly with those of other travellers of the period.

'*A* 'SPOSE WHUM YE GUT hom y' intend t' write a buke?' was the half-questioning remark made to me in Peking by a young man fresh from the wilds of Scotland, who was hoping, in the course of years, to grow into a diplomatist! ...

My letters had been carefully preserved, but they were in the form of diaries. As such, judging by my own feelings in reading the published diaries of others, they would be tedious and uninteresting to all except immediate friends. Not to mention the 'slip-shod' style which is, I fear, only too commonly employed in letter-writing, and which it is almost impossible to avoid, when the letters are written under the circumstance, amid scenes, and in the position, in which travellers in out of the way places often find themselves. At the same time, I wished to leave the substance of these letters, as much as possible, in the original form, so as to fulfil the original intent, viz., to convey to the minds of the reader the impression left upon that of the writer, by things seen, heard, and felt, in the course of short visits paid to comparatively unknown parts of the world. This is all I wish to say in the way of explanation ... I shall console myself with the thought of having done my best, and that, as a philosophical old woman in our village used constantly to affirm, 'We can't do no more than we can — can us?'

IT WAS WITH SAD and melancholy feelings that we parted from the many relations and friends who had come to take leave of us, when quitting Bombay, on the 15th April, 1865.

Four days steaming down the coast with a calm sea, brought us to Point de Galle [Ceylon] … we were warned that our steamer would leave in the evening, the English mail having arrived. About sunset we left harbour, and commenced our voyage to Melbourne; and a very long weary voyage it proved. Not all the civility of the captain and officers could render the *Northam* anything but most uncomfortable. Neither could the confidence, which every one ought to have felt in the captain, prevent a certain amount of uneasiness being experienced by those who found themselves on board an old steamer, the engines of which had proved out of order before she had left harbour twenty-four hours. This uneasiness was not lessened when, later in the voyage, the weather was such that the following entries were made in the ship's log —'Terrific gale' — 'Heavy squalls' — 'Mountainous sea'. So bad, indeed, was it that the captain deemed it advisable, on approaching the coast of Australia, to lay to for twelve hours. I hope it may never again be my lot to undergo the same misery in such a sea, and when occupying one of the foremost cabins. Two very small stern-cabins, in which the rattle of the rudder-chain rendered sleep almost impossible, being all that we could hope should be given us to ourselves, and more than the first it seemed likely we should obtain.

For the long run as from Galle to King George's Sound, 3330 miles, without touching or sighting land, we were obliged to carry 100 tons of coal on deck. This made everything horridly dirty, and also caused the vessel to be so low in the water, that we were unable, even once, to have the ports open, notwithstanding the great heat of the first week. Our progress was very slow. The discharge pipe of the engine, which had burst almost before we were well out of sight of Galle, was patched up, but burst again two days later. This hardly increased our mental comfort, when informed that we had run into the tail of a cyclone.

The only break we had in the voyage was at King George's Sound (Albany is the name of the little village or town as it wishes to be considered), which we reached in sixteen days. It is a dreary, dismal-looking place, but it was such a relief to get out of our prison, if only for a short time, that we were inclined to look upon it, and its inhabitants, with lenient eyes. The neat cottage bonnets and the rosy faces of certain small children we met, trotting along the road on their way to school, were refreshing to those who had for some time seen nothing but the sallow, wan faces, and dirty finery, of the few children of English parentage who in India occupy a somewhat similar position in the social scale. There were gangs of evil-looking convicts at work on a road; and in front of the hotel, near the landing place, many natives were lounging about, hoping to earn an easy shilling or sixpence by throwing the boomerang or jumping about, in what, for the benefit of the passengers, they call a 'corroboree', i.e. the native dance, to which, we were told by those who knew, it bore as much resemblance as it did to a deux-temps valse!! A wretched-looking set of beings they were, clad in kangaroo skins piled one over the other, with the heads and legs dangling in a ghastly sort of fringe. Their faces were smeared with oil and red ochre, and their hair matted and knitted. I never saw a more painfully degraded appearance than these miserable creatures presented.

We climbed to the top of a very steep hill, behind the village, to gain as extensive a view as possible of this our first halting-place on Australian ground. But the prospect was not cheerful. For the first time we beheld, in the distance, the apparently interminable forest of dull dead green, or rather greenish grey, gum trees, with which, before long, we were to become so familiar. We found, however, that amongst the shrubs and 'scrub', through which, in preference to the beaten path, we clambered to the top of the hill, there were many curious plants entirely new to us; and on returning to the village, we were shown a very perfect 'hortus siccus', containing some very strange, some very lovely, flowers. They had been collected by a little old man [James Drummond, a colonial botanist] who, I believe, had spent the greater portion of his life, and, being a good naturalist, had chiefly occupied himself, in making collections of dried plants, skins of animals, and other curiosities, which he sent to all parts of the world. He was well known to all naturalists and curators of museums in Australia, and by them acknowledged as the person to discover or entrap any rare plant or animal …

We had required this refreshing run on shore to help us to contend against the miseries of the ensuing week. The temperature had become cold and raw, and the weather was very bad. One afternoon I was sitting at the head of the companion-ladder while all the rest of the passengers, who were well enough to be up at all, were at dinner; soon a loud report was heard, followed by a flapping sound; and then the hurry-scurry among the sailors announced the pleasing intelligence that a sail had been blown away. A little while after, I saw some sailors carrying a man forward, evidently much hurt. This was one of the three steersmen; he had been lifted completely over the wheel, after which four men at a time were considered necessary at the helm.

Presently the captain came up, and recommended my going below, as he had made his mind up to lay-to for the night, and thought that while the steamer was being put about, the chances were in favour of our shipping a good many seas, which proved to be the case. The waves continued to break over the deck all through the night, dashing down into the cabin in a way that, even in remembrance, is very unpleasant. Right glad, therefore, were we when we arrived at Port Phillip Heads; and yet gladder when, after a long steam up the Yarra-yarra River, in a dirty little steamer, with a thick drizzle constantly falling, and everything wet and muddy, we at last found ourselves in a comfortable, but very small room, in the Port Phillip Club Hotel, Melbourne.

I do not know whether, after visiting America, the manner of servants, shopkeepers, and persons generally in that rank of life in Australia, would strike strangers as being so extremely free-and-easy, brusque, and independent, as it appeared to us, who had just left a country where a deferential, not to say obsequious, bearing prevails among the same classes. The patronising air of the waiter at our hotel and his tone, which seemed to imply, 'Where can you have lived not to know that?' when we asked for information upon any subject, was most amusing. No less so was the condescension of a young woman, who, on my inquiring for a workwoman, had been recommended by the headchambermaid as a 'young lady' who would do all I required. Nobody, I imagine, could be found less like 'a young lady' than this impudent, wild, Irish girl, who, with her deft fingers, seemed to have discovered in Melbourne 'El Dorado'. Having but a few warm clothes with us, I set to work the day after our arrival to procure some, and suggested to this young woman that she should go to one of the large shops near and bring me some warm cloaks, and woollen patterns to look at. This suggestion she met by a proposal, that I should put on my bonnet, and under her guidance go myself to the shop, as Mr. What-ever-his-name-was would be sure to produce the best of his goods for any one introduced by her! ...

There were several theatres. We went now and then to hear particular pieces, or when the Governor [the Freres were now staying at Government House] was asked to be present, and were quite surprised at finding the houses so large, and the acting so good.

One soon discovers here the fallacy of the notion that the nature of the Anglo-Saxon race is to 'take their pleasure sadly', and that they are incapable of enjoying simple, out-of-door holiday-making, unless it includes riot and debauchery. I believe this to be entirely owing to the climate of damp, dull, foggy old England, and not to the nature of the people. Here, under the influence of a bright, clear sky and in the crisp, dry air, the 'people' are quite as ready as any foreigners to find enjoyment in spending a day with wives and children and friends, in the open air by the sea-shore, or in the fields and meadows. The strictness with which they hold to their Saturday's holiday and

Wednesday's half-holiday, is a proof of this. On these days the shops are deserted, shut-up, or left to the charge of an errand boy, or maid-of-all-work. Their owners, meanwhile, flock out to some place of gathering, taking their provisions with them and apparently enjoy their quiet, periodical holiday quite as much as children themselves.

The Queen's Birthday Ball, given by the Governor, was at the Exhibition building ... everybody who has inscribed his name in the visiting-book at Government House is invited to these balls ... before dancing commenced, everyone passed in front of [the Vice-Regal party] making their bows and curtseys, or what did duty for the same. Sometimes a whole family would pass like a class of school children, holding each other's hand, tumbling over each other's heels, giggling, and turning their heads away from the throne where Her Majesty was represented. Even the nods they gave in passing were directed to the other end of the room.

It is difficult to describe the peculiarity of some of the dresses. The style apparently intended to represent 'elegance and simplicity' consisting in many cases of a thick, dark-coloured decolletee linsey-woolsey, made in the most antique fashion, hardly touching the ground, and trimmed with light coloured satin ribbon. Those who appeared, on the other hand, to have determined upon spending an extravagant sum in honour of the occasion, adopted another fashion; that of putting on several distinct dresses, one over the other. I took particular note of one of these costumes, worn by a small woman, who had managed to heap upon herself the contents of an ordinary miller's show-room. While standing still her dress appeared to be white net, worked with coloured silk, over a handsome blue silk trimmed with lace; but when she began dancing she held these up, after the manner of a person crossing a muddy street, and displaying a white lace dress, and under that, another complete dress of pink moire-antique, with deep lace flounces!! The coiffures were no less marvellous than the dresses. Flowers were worn ad lib, many of which looked as if they had been bought at the grocer's as they exactly resembled the little wreaths sold there for putting round candles ...

Soon after this we paid a visit to Ballarat, the great mining town of Victoria ... we went first to the Band-of-Hope Gold Mine ... we were taken into the manager's room to be equipped for a descent into the mine, and reappeared completely disguised. We were put into enormous boots, long Macintosh coats, with huge collars sticking up all round, our handkerchiefs were tied over our ears, and regular 'sou'-westers' put over them. The result being, that only the end of our noses were left visible! By very close packing, the manager of the mine, another man, and I, contrived to squeeze into one of the little waggons, which had just brought up a load of mud, and were trundled on to the 'drop' at the mouth of the shaft. As soon as we arrived at the level of the river, and all the way below that, we were in a regular shower-bath, which, on arriving at the bottom, we found turned into a mud-bath. The manager, an immensely tall, powerful Scotchman, took charge of me, lifting me in and out of the waggons as if I had been a baby. Apparently he forgot that I was not; for, what with his height and mine, the top of my head suffered considerably from the wooden beams which supported the gallery.

On returning to the surface, the light revealed us to each

other in a most unrecognisable condition of mud and wet. But there was a good fire in the manager's room, wine and biscuits were on the table, and we were quite dry and comfortable in half-an-hour, by which time the day's gold was brought in to be cleaned and weighed.

... we were told that many of those working in the mine were shareholders, and very rich men. From our own experience we learnt how much truth there was in the almost incredible stories one used to hear of miners and miner's wives in the first days of gold digging. Very few of these men have the slightest idea of the value of money, or of how to spend it. They live on in their little wooden houses, treat their friends to 'nobblers' (i.e. glasses of spirits) on every possible occasion, and when they go down to the nearest town, they buy the most expensive dresses for their wives that they can find. Very few of them have any higher idea of the pleasure, or the advantages, or even of the comforts to be attained by the possession of wealth. Many of those who can count their money by thousands, live on in the same little shanties which they erected on first coming to the diggings ...

Two days after our return we set off for Sandhurst [Bendigo], another gold field about four hours by rail from Melbourne ... Sandhurst is a regular 'digger-city', and a very 'rowdy' place. There was but one hotel, to which we had been told, it would be possible for us to go. When we arrived there the master insisted upon knowing our names before he would admit us. I don't suppose he was much the wiser when he heard them, but he then condescended to take us in. We found the only rooms disengaged were three, en suite, with the sitting room at the further end, the inconvenience of which is obvious. There being no other we took them, and could have put up with the inconvenience had there been any civility, or attempt at cleanliness, on the part of the people of the house.

On leaving Sandhurst we went by rail to Echuca, about two hours distant. This is the terminus of the railroad. The country through which we passed was essentially Australian in character ... the solitude and silence, the perfect absence of savage animal life of any kind, must be enough to drive a man mad. Many of the shepherds, we are told, after enduring it for many months, will come to their masters with tears in their eyes, begging to be put to work at anything, for any wages, rather than undergo such banishment from their fellow beings. This intense silence, together with the extreme clearness of the air, may also account for the 'coo-ee' or bush call, being heard at a distance of three miles.

We left Melbourne on the 10th July for Sydney, in the *City of Melbourne*, one of the small and not over-clean steamers which run regularly between various ports. We had a very uncomfortable passage, and bad weather, which threw us back eighteen hours. We were unable to get cabins to ourselves, and it is certainly an infliction to be compelled to share the very limited accommodation with persons as are generally met with on board these steamers ...

We left Sydney for Brisbane on the 7th of August [the Freres spent some time visiting friends in the Blue Mountains and then hurried to Queensland] ... we were more fortunate in our fellow-passengers than when coming from Melbourne. There was only one lady besides myself, and she was a quiet body enough. But she was

77

accompanied, unhappily, by a brother, who was never sober during the whole voyage for more than a quarter of an hour at a time. He was the terror of my life, by constantly coming to the door of the Ladies' Cabin, with some excuse of wanting to speak to his sister, making a terrific noise on finding it fastened, and trying to persuade the stewardess that it would be much better to leave it wide open, as then we should have plenty of fresh air!! What weather it was: pouring rain, seas constantly washing over the vessel, which was very heavily freighted, and everything swimming about in the cabin! There was nothing to do but lie in the narrow berth, and speculate upon the chances of having hair and eyelashes at least, devoured, if one ventured to sleep, by a multitude of cockroaches; for the panels all round were lined with innumerable pairs of feelers belonging to these horrid creatures!!

The town of Brisbane is striking new, and the whole place presents a curious mixture of savageness and rapid progress. The pit-falls and quagmires in the streets are painfully numerous; but some of the country roads are good, and for riding particularly pleasant … the houses in this part of Australia are complete bungalows with large and numerous windows opening on to wide verandahs, the latter well sheltered from the sun. With this style of architecture, it needed not the multitude and viciousness of the mosquitoes to show us that we had arrived within the tropics.

After staying ten days at Brisbane we left for a short visit to the Darling Downs … we had hired a small drag [a private coach], very light and roomy, and a pair of good horses to take us and our baggage; and, on making trial of them previous to our departure, were well satisfied with both. But when the day on which we were to leave arrived, we found that neither the driver, nor the carriages, nor the horses, were the same as those we had engaged. The driver was a surly fellow, who seemed to think he was conferring a great favour by taking us at all. The carriage was a heavy, open fly, with little room for baggage. The horses, too, were heavy cart-horse-looking animals, not promising at all well for long days' journeys over bad roads. The voluble Irish stable-keeper, from whom we had hired them, declared that it was not his fault that we did not have the others; and, after a fashion of promise-breakers, assured us that what he had sent was in every way superior to what we wished to have, etc. etc, to which, though we could by no means agree, we were obliged to submit; and packing our selves in, and Lucien and the portmanteaux on the box, as well as we could, we proceeded to Ipswich. We were nearly five hours accomplishing this twenty miles, which, considering that it is a very good road, did not raise our opinion of our Irish friend nor of the horses that fallen to our lot …

It was late before we arrived at Gatton, but the latter part of the way we had been amused by watching several sets of drovers and carriers making up their camps for the night. The moon was bright, and very picturesque the people looked by her light and that of the camp-fires, making up their beds or cooking their suppers, with the unharnessed oxen or horses grouped around. They seemed so comfortable that we quite longed to join them, instead of jogging along in our slow vehicle. We were destined to spend the night in a very 'lath-and-plaster' inn, in which sleep became impossible from the opossums running about the roof all night long.

The next day we left Gatton early, expecting to arrive in Toowoomba, twenty-five miles off, by about 2 p.m. Our wretched horses, however, found the carriage heavier to drag through the bush and up steep hills than even over the bad roads at Brisbane, though the plausible stable-keeper assured us that they were used to the work. When we arrived at the Main Range, a mountain pass of four or five miles with steep incline the whole way, our case seemed hopeless. At the top of the first steep place we came to a stand-still. And there we stood; the worst of the horses looking the very impersonation of obstinacy as he hugged the pole, with eyes half shut, his head in the air, and his ears laid back. We now discovered that the horses were the property of the driver; subsequently, he did not choose to give the flogging, which was the proper way to treat such an animal, but left us, and went off to see if he could meet a dray coming down the hill, from which we might borrow a pair of leaders.

The heat of the sun was intense as we waited here till our coachman returned, announcing the approach of an empty dray, drawn by a team of eighteen bullocks, from which two were to be detached to help us on our way. The team was guided by a man and a woman. The speech of the former seemed intelligible to none save himself and the bullocks; but the latter was incessantly shouting, talking, and swearing. She addressed each one of the team by its own particular name, so that by the time we arrived at the top I had become well acquainted with all of them ... when the worst was over, the coachman was of the opinion that the horses could manage the rest of the way by themselves. They went fairly so long as the road was level; but at the first rise our old friend [the horse] stopped short, and began gibbing [baulking], and no exertions on the parts of Lucien and the coachman would induce him to move forward. So we had to wait till the dray reappeared, and beg renewed assistance from the old woman, who seemed to think that we deserved our fate.

Sunset was approaching when we arrived at Toowoomba, but we were assured that from thence the road was good, and that there would be no difficulty in reaching our destination, ten miles off, before midnight; and our being late would not signify, as there was a good moon. So the horses were baited [refreshed], we had some tea, and set off again for Westbrook [station]. We soon lost our way, but fortunately met a man, more civil than sober, who after wandering about a field in a vague kind of way for some time, found a particular gate. From this point he took his bearings, and put us into a bushtrack, which ultimately brought us to our destination. We had been eleven hours doing thirty-five miles. We spent a couple of days here very pleasantly, learning the mysteries of a squatter's life. The houses are comfortable — perfect bungalows with low, sloping roofs, extending over the wide verandahs, on to which the rooms open. The head station is in fact the 'home-farm' and is surrounded by out-buildings. One of these is devoted to the accommodation of any person, squatters, managers, head-men, or in short any travellers, who, without being known to the proprietor of the station, claim hospitality and shelter for themselves and their beasts, simply and solely on the plea of being wanderers.

It requires but a short experience of bush-travelling to appreciate fully the weariness and misery which must be suffered by those who have to undergo much of it, and alone. I could imagine a solitary man, being driven well-nigh out of his mind by the horrors of going on day after day without seeing 'a kindly human face' or hearing a 'human voice', perhaps without the song of a bird to break the intensity of the silence, and the oppression of the solitude ... [after an extensive tour of many stations, continually having trouble with carriage and horses, the Freres decided to return to Brisbane, then Sydney, en route for New Zealand, and later Tasmania] ...

On the 27th of November we took our leave of our kind friends here, with much regret, and set off in the steamer which takes the mails to meet the P&O boat for Galle. There were no other passengers, and we had a good enough though rough passage, arriving at King George's Sound late in the evening of the 1st of December. We landed the next morning, and went to the dingy little inn, with its very grumpy landlord, hoping to get rid of the whirr of the steamer by spending a night and day on shore.

The P&O steamer *Bombay*, which was to take us to Galle, arrived the same afternoon, and we were summoned to be on board next day at noon; punctually at which time we steamed away ... we bade farewell to the New World, where we had passed many months so pleasantly, and had been treated on all occasions by the inhabitants with so much cordiality, kindness and hospitality ... we now turned out thoughts to Ceylon.

From Alice M Frere (Mrs. Godfrey Clerk), *The Antipodes and Round the World; or Travels in Australia, New Zealand, Ceylon, Japan, and California*, Second Edition, London, 1870.

Harriet Douglas

1870

Harriet Douglas was the eldest daughter of William Bloomfield Douglas (1822–1906) a Royal Naval officer and a South Australian public servant when he was appointed Government Resident of the Northern Territory of South Australia. His family and servants sailed to Palmerston, later called Darwin. Harriet, an accomplished writer, recorded her experiences during the inter-colonial voyage via Brisbane in the schooner Gulnare. *She married Dominick Daly in 1871 and for many years wrote a column from London for the* Sydney Morning Herald.

SHORTLY AFTER THE RETURN of Mr. [George] Goyder's surveying expedition to Adelaide in April, 1870, my father was appointed Government Resident of the Northern Territory. For a time he was undecided whether he would not leave his family in Adelaide, but the idea of a separation from those nearest and dearest to him was so distasteful that it was arranged we should accompany him to Port Darwin.

The Government had some time previously bought a fast sailing Canadian-built schooner, the *Gulnare*, about two hundred tons burthen, for the use of the Northern Territory, and in this little vessel we left Adelaide for our future home. Our furniture and the numerous packages for which no room could be found on board the *Gulnare*, were dispatched by the *Bengal*, a barque that followed us to Port Darwin.

Ours was a large party to arrange for in so small a ship. Counting the maid we took with us, we mustered ten, all told, and the captain of the *Gulnare* carried his wife and a baby with him. There were two mates and a proper complement of seamen. The only other passenger was a police trooper, whose quarters were forward, on his way to join the mounted force stationed in Port Darwin.

It took several days to get used to our very limited accommodation besides the inevitable suffering from sea-sickness that ensued. From this malady I was always and still am fortunately exempt. Therefore I was able to minister to the wants of less privileged mortals in this respect than myself. My mother was the principal sufferer of the party; she never entirely got over her tendency to 'mal-de-mer', during the long voyage this one eventually proved to be ...

Our maid, Annie, deserves some special mention here; for being the only servant we took with us, she was a very important appendage to our party. A good-looking, clean, active, Australian born girl, with great capabilities both for hard work and flirtation; surely no very uncommon combination! Of her first named accomplishment, we had had actual experience, but in such close quarters, watching the latter developing itself afforded us a considerable amount of amusement. Annie's affaires de coeur were so numerous, and followed each other with such startling rapidity, that nothing short of a conquest of the entire ship's company seemed likely to happen.

My usual mode of occupying myself, was as follows. Those of our party who were well enough went on deck before breakfast. The invalids with some assistance made a somewhat unsatisfactory toilette afterwards, and then wearily and with a dejected air they betook themselves to the warmest and most sheltered position to be found on deck, lying down on an improvised couch, composed of tarpaulins, rags and shawls; and here they remained for the rest of the day. I then did a little 'house maiding' downstairs, for we carried no stewardess; and for some time, at least, Annie proved herself a very indifferent sailor. This portion of my duties over, I gladly snatched an hour or two's quiet, reading and working till the dinner-bell rang, generally about one o'clock. I afterwards looked at the chart, talked surreptitiously to the man at the wheel, and slept if possible till teatime. Not a very amusing voyage to write about. Our first halting-place was Warrnambool, one of the Victorian outports, where we were becalmed for some hours. Advantage was taken of our enforced stoppage to lower a boat, and send letters ashore, reporting our progress thus far on our journey. This slight detention proved a most provi-dential circumstance, the extent of which we did not fully realise until afterwards.

Soon a breeze sprang up, and we sailed rapidly along, with every stitch of canvas set the schooner was able to carry. The *Gulnare* was a fast sailer, built for a slaver originally, but fast as she was, she did not prove fleet enough to compete with the cruisers on the coast of America. A few days after leaving Warrnambool we ran into the radius of a hurricane; the low state of the barometer had warned us that some unusual atmospheric disturbance was at hand. Soon it seemed to us that we were in the thick of the storm, and as may be imagined we were very uncomfortable in our overcrowded quarters. The vessel pitched and rolled incessantly, and the wind howled as if it came through a funnel. The rigging thrilled as the wind beat against it, and added to this there were sounds of hurrying footsteps overhead all night, mingled with the giving of orders, and the angry swirl of the troubled sea against which we were trying to hold our own.

As my father remarked to me when I stole on dock to view the state of affairs, the sea was a 'cross one', and very difficult to steer against. However, we were weathering the storm as well as we possibly could expect in such a small vessel, carrying only just sufficient canvas to keep her head to wind. The mainsail was 'scandalised' — a nautical mode of describing a sail reefed at both ends; that, and a very small jib, were the only sails we could safely use. Frequently and against orders I made my way on deck, tired of being battened down in the saloon, and wearying for a breath of air, fierce though the elements undoubtedly were.

Breakfast was an impossibility, as the sea was washing clean over the galley, and the sailors, who had been on deck all night, were unable to obtain the cup of coffee usually served at four o'clock every morning. Our morning meal consisted of sherry, cheese, and biscuits, not a very appetising repast, but the only one to be obtained under the circumstances.

Sometimes, when an unusually heavy sea struck our little vessel, she stood still for a moment or two as if fairly stunned from the shock, while tons of water came sweeping along the decks, carrying every movable thing with it, and finding its way into every imaginable corner below. At times we felt anxious, and wondered whether the vessel would continue to weather the storm as bravely as she had done for the last twelve hours.

The steward, who invariably took the brightest view of everything, never lost his spirits. He tried to cheer us up by bringing frequent bulletins of the weather, and of the progress we were making. Hearing, however, of the loss of a boat from the davits, and the damage done to our most cherished possession — a beautiful Alderney cow — we were not much reassured by his reports, favourable as he intended them to be, nor did it point to a very improved state of things on deck.

The worst danger, however, had yet to be faced. The

trooper, who was perhaps the only unoccupied man on board, while leaning against the taffrail [stern rail], smoking his pipe, and looking about him, suddenly exclaimed, 'Surely that is land!' pointing to something to leeward of us that resembled a thick bank of cloud low down on the horizon. He immediately rushed aft to where my father was standing, and called his attention to what he had seen. At first it was considered impossible that we were anywhere in the vicinity of land. But a closer examination proved we were no great distance from a rock-bound island — not more than three to four miles to leeward of us. Being so far out of our reckoning was a very serious matter, but it was easily accounted for, from the fact that the sun had been obscured for two days, consequently no sights could be taken, and at night all the attempts to get lunar observations were frustrated by the overclouded state of the sky … we were fully forty miles out of our course. In our case, in spite of all our precautions, the current wafted us perilously near a dead lee shore, for the land we had so unwillingly sighted proved to be one of a melancholy cluster of scantily-clad islets, some distance from the Queensland coast, known as the Solitary Islands.

There was, of course, no time to lose in altering our course when once our critical position was ascertained. We were too near land to put the ship about and sail on the opposite tack; the only remedy was to 'wear ship', always a hazardous thing to do, and especially dangerous in such rough weather and at such close quarters. The schooner had to be turned round bodily, more sail made, and then to 'claw' off the land as best she could.

I heard the captain's clear-sounding voice giving his

orders amidst the din and bustle overhead. 'All ready!' he shouted in stentorian tones; and as he turned the wheel hard over we heard the cry of 'Wear slip!' With a tremendous lurch, that seemed as if the masts would be wrenched out of her, and with a shudder which thrilled the little vessel from stem to stern, she quickly obeyed her helm; and for the next twelve hours this plucky little schooner fought her way against apparently overwhelming odds. The weather moderated towards nightfall, and by midnight the wind entirely ceased, when we were left rolling helplessly from side to side in the swell that remained as a legacy of the gale.

Had it not been for those few hours detention at Warrnambool, we might have shared the fate of many others who were lost in the storm that night; for instead of perceiving our danger in daylight, we should probably have run straight on to the Solitary Islands in the middle of the night. The storm lasted exactly thirty-six hours, and during the whole time my father never once left the deck.

The following morning was a very different one from the day before. The air was deliciously cool and fresh, the sun shone out brightly, and the waves resumed their wonted dark blue colour; the swell had gone down, and a more happy state of things prevailed. But the clearer atmosphere only revealed more vividly the battered condition the ship was in.

We had lost two of our boats, and of those that remained only one was fit for use. The deck was in a dismantled, disorderly, and untidy state. I myself had witnessed a huge iron tank that we carried on deck, burst from its lashings, and make a rapid swoop to leeward the day before; if the men had not at once thrown it overboard, its weight would have carried away a portion of the bulwarks. As it was, these were 'started' and 'stove' in several places. A careful survey was then made of our damages, the result of which determined my father to run straight for Brisbane, for in the condition we found ourselves, it was impossible to go any further on our journey to Port Darwin …

We anchored in Moreton Bay for some hours till a steam tug came down for us, and towed us later on up the long winding Brisbane River. It was dark when we reached our anchorage, and everybody was thankful for a quiet night's rest after the knocking about we had experienced …

Of course the arrival of a Government vessel from a neighbouring colony could not pass without some special recognition from the harbour officials. We were lying near Her Majesty's ship *Pearl* — a surveying schooner, commanded by Captain [Edward P.] Bedwell [Royal Navy]. When eight bells were struck she hoisted her ensign and pennant; we of course followed suit with ours. This at once proclaimed that our vessel was no ordinary merchantman, but a colonial Government ship bent on a special mission. Then followed some visits from harbour authorities, and the health officer being satisfied with our papers, our only decent boat was lowered. In spite of our battered appearance we managed to muster a crew, turned out in true man-o'-war style. The captain donned his uniform and took the yoke lines, and my father went off to leave cards on board the *Pearl*, and thence ashore to pay a state visit at Government House — a ceremony never omitted by any one visiting a colony on official business.

Telegrams were sent to Adelaide explaining the circumstances that rendered our visit to Brisbane a necessity; and our friends were relieved by hearing of our safety — for a report had reached South Australia that we had shared the fate of so many others who were lost during that disastrous gale.

To our great delight we found we had arrived in Brisbane just in time for the Queen's Birthday Ball, a festivity never omitted in the Australian colonies. In addition to this it was the race week, and the town was full of squatters, down from the bush, bringing not only their families but their horses with them. Planters left their estates in the care of their Kanaka labourers for a time. One and all seemed bent on gaieties and amusement, in all of which, with kindly Australian hospitality, we were asked to join.

But, oh! our distress about frocks for these coming gaieties. Had we not forsworn, amidst bitter tears, and with vain regrets, balls and dances forever? Moreover, all our superfluous toilettes and every article of finery we possessed were at this moment lying in the hold of the *Bengal* — then on her way to Port Darwin.

We had only brought with us the actual necessaries for the voyage. We did not even possess 'two coats apiece' — our ordinary costume being waterproof monkey jackets, sailor hats with puggarees twined round them, and some simple white muslin or fresh cotton dresses. However, it was soon decided to make good the deficiency from which we were suffering. Materials were purchased, and the saloon having been transformed into a workroom, the necessary evening dresses were speedily forthcoming.

The next three weeks were spent in one continuous round of amusement. Part of the time N. and I paid a visit on shore to some newly-made but very kind friends, who, with proverbial Australian hospitality, did everything in their power to amuse us. We went to dinner-parties, picnics, dances, and boating-parties, thoroughly making the most of our time, and I gratefully remember these three weeks spent in Brisbane as amongst the happiest recollections of my life ...

All this time carpenters, shipwrights, and boat builders were hurrying on with the *Gulnare*'s repairs, and when their labours were over the little vessel looked her pretty self once more — smart as any yacht one would wish to see. The three weeks had passed away like a dream and we sincerely regretted the awakening was so near at hand.

With many adieux to our new friends, photographs having been given and exchanged, and promises on all sides of letters, we were once more under weigh [pull up the anchor and sail away]. Dipping our ensign to the *Pearl*, a compliment she speedily returned, we bid farewell to Brisbane, carrying with us nothing but happy memories of a charming and unexpected visit ...

We were, as I have said before, merely a family party, and depended solely upon our own efforts for any amusement on board. Sometimes the days passed monotonously enough. But when we drew farther north, the lovely scenery we sailed through, and the interesting character of the navigation, supplied any want of amusement and excitement we had hitherto felt ... There is no doubt that it is a difficult piece of navigation, and I never yet passed through without seeing wrecks here and there, and sometimes vessels lying hard and fast on the rocks. A great deal of this is due to a want of care on the part of the navigator. The Admiralty have made most careful surveys all over this much-dreaded passage, and the charts they have published are very perfect specimens of the hydrographic art, every danger is pointed out, and the soundings are given with unerring correctness. Thus danger is guarded against as far as possible, if sufficient care is taken to follow the directions ...

The distance between the coast and the island [Hinchinbrook] is very narrow indeed, and though we anchored very close in shore that night, none of the men were permitted to land. Natives in this part of the country bear an evil reputation. It is more than suspected that they are cannibals. Some years afterwards a vessel was wrecked near Hinchingbrook Island, the blacks swarmed off to the wreck and killed every survivor they could find; and during a gold mining rush, the body of an unfortunate Chinaman was found half-roasted on a wurley fire. Cannibalism does not openly figure amongst Aboriginal misdeeds, but in the northern part of Queensland it is no uncommon vice.

Though we must have been very near the black fellows at times, they only once showed themselves. One Sunday evening, sailing close in shore, under a heavy press of canvas, going fully nine knots an hour, we saw a party of natives rush down a steep defile in the cliffs overhead; all day they must have been watching us, for from one point to another fires were lit, and the smoke, as it curled away into the light, dry air, announced the approach of a vessel. The men brought bundles of spears, and ran along the beach, levelling them at our vessel. Some of them tried to launch their canoes, hoping, I suppose, to overtake us. They hooted and yelled as we left them behind, feeling savage, no doubt, that our pace was too good for them to overtake us.

Many tales are told of deeds wrought amongst the native tribes on this part of the coast by the black policemen, who are brought from one of the southern colonies to serve in the force. They are excellent marksmen. When a raid has to be made on a neighbouring tribe to punish some cruel deed of murder or theft, the native troopers divest themselves of their uniforms, retaining only their caps as a distinctive badge in case of accident. They creep silently, in true Aboriginal fashion, into the bush, carrying a rifle and revolver, stalking their prey with all the skill of a practised bushman. The inspecting officer, generally a European, asks no questions on their return. The men hold up one, two, or three fingers, as the case may be, showing the number of lives taken. The older and more experienced hands cut notches on the stocks of their rifles to remember the number of lives that have fallen into their hands …

As yet I have not mentioned our way of spending Sunday, and as a day of rest was a very welcome one to most of our ship's company, I will describe it. The first and prevailing feature pervading a Sunday morning was a general air of cleanliness. The decks were holystoned and washed earlier than usual, the brass work had an extra polish, and everything looked its brightest. The children, of course, all turned out in clean clothes … Willy, my other brother, a handsome, sturdy, bronzed boy of eight, was captured, washed, dressed, and, amongst many struggles, inducted into his boots and socks, articles of clothing he disliked, and which he only endured as a concession to the conventionalities of the Sabbath. Then followed a clean Eton collar fastened on his best suit, and his Sunday toilette was over. The little girls appeared, looking fresh and cool in pretty pink cottons, and we two elder ones seized the opportunity of making a more elaborate toilette than usual. Breakfast once over, the order was given to 'rig the church'. The Union Jack was spread over the end of the skylight. The places were found in Bible and Prayer-book. Camp-stools were arranged in pew-like order, and, the men having been duly inspected, filed aft, and, when everyone had taken their places, the morning service began. My father read the prayers and the lessons, and never omitted, wherever he was, the regulations observed in the navy on Sundays. The service usually progressed very solemnly, and the congregation was a model of reverence and good behaviour, though I must say there were [some] distractions for which we were hardly responsible …

We were now approaching the end of our voyage, which had been far longer than we anticipated, for we left Adelaide in April, and June was now very nearly over. However, the three weeks' detention in Brisbane fully accounted for our long passage. Bidding the inner route of the Barrier Reef goodbye, and having left its beauties behind us, we sailed into Somerset before we rounded Cape York, the most northern point of Australia. Here we anchored and remained for two days, the crew employed in cutting firewood and filling our tanks with fresh water. It is a pretty little spot, clothed like the rest of North Queensland with tropical vegetation down to the water's edge.

The Resident [Magistrate], Captain [Henry] Chester, came off [rowed out] to see us, and to him we were indebted for a pleasant little visit — an agreeable break to the monotony of our long voyage.

There were several pearling vessels at anchor, some just

arrived from a long cruise in the Straits, and others getting ready to go to sea again, all manned by South Sea Islanders — Kanaka boys, as they are usually called — fine looking, brown-skinned young fellows, with well-cut features, rather wistful, soft, dark eyes, and dressed in English-made clothes. There had been an epidemic of fever amongst them, and I saw the thinnest and most wasted-looking child at Somerset I ever saw in my life — a slender girl of ten years old. She was too weak to stand, and was carried by some of the 'boys' on a pillow; I was quite struck by their gentle manner, and by the tenderness with which they nursed the sick child.

The Kanakas are very often badly treated by the owners of the pearling schooners. These are frequently a low order of white men, of no distinctive nationality, the greatest bullies afloat. They thrash and ill-treat their brown-skinned sailors, defraud them of their pay, and their hands are not quite guiltless of murder; though this sweeping assertion does not hold good as a general rule. When the schooners belong to some properly-organised Company, and are commanded by respectable men, the very opposite conditions prevail.

Leaving Somerset, we sailed through the narrow strait between Australia and New Guinea, and then we ran into open sea. We anchored for some hours off Boob Island — the ocean post-office, as it used to be called. This is a small island lying right in the track of vessels from Java, India, and China on their way to Australia, a well-known resort of shipwrecked crews. There is a cave in the centre of the island, where ships in passing used to land stores and provisions for the benefit of any shipwrecked crews who might chance to find their way to this little oasis in the waste of waters. We had stores to land here on behalf of our own Government; the name of our vessel and the date of our calling was duly entered in a book kept there for the purpose. I am sorry I did not land, for I believe there were some curiously written inscriptions to be seen in this isolated 'visitors' book'. Our visit was an uneventful one. No shipwrecked sailors were waiting to be saved. We simply left our casks of beef and biscuit and proceeded on our way. Our course lay right across the Gulf of Carpentaria. Here the sea was rough, but the wind and weather favoured us. As we had done hitherto, we lived almost entirely on deck, the little saloon being too hot to allow us to remain long below … Here we were seen by some natives, who paddled off in canoes to meet us. Long before they came alongside, their gesticulations and signs showed us that their intention was to warn us of a danger they thought we were unaware of. This proved to be a reef near the Vernon Islands, on whose coral bosom several ships met their fate.

The blackfellows clung on to a rope we threw to them, and hauling their narrow bark canoes alongside, cleverly scrambled on deck. We at once entered into conversation with our savage visitors, though somewhat under difficulties, for our knowledge of their language was nil, and their acquaintance with ours extremely limited — such expressions as 'my word', 'very good', 'tum tum', when they saw a supply of food being made ready for them to take ashore. 'You gib me baccy', and 'big one ship come on', were intermixed with a voluble flow of the Woolna dialect. However, their hands and gestures were far more intelligible than their tongues, and our unclad visitors left us in a very amiable frame of mind, giving us in exchange for a supply of tea, sugar, tobacco, and flour some curious shells that were used to bale the water out of their canoes …

We anchored off the Vernon Islands for the night, strangely enough, sighting the *Bengal*, who, with worse luck than our own, was hard and fast ashore. She had been in this unenviable position since the last ebb tide. She was not however in any danger, having fortunately grounded on a soft sandy patch near one of the islands. Amongst the passengers were some intimate friends of our own, one of them a celebrated explorer, John McKinlay. Immediately we dropped anchor the *Bengal* lowered a boat, and our friends paid us a visit. From them we learnt all the latest Adelaide news, for they had sailed fully a month after we did, and were surprised to find we had not arrived in Port Darwin before them. They were a party of land selectors, on their way to select land in the Northern Territory for the capitalists and on whose behalf the survey was made. It was a curious meeting, away on the wild northern coast so far from our old home, and with the future one as yet an indistinct shadow in the distance …

We got under weigh very early, an obliging flood tide lifted the *Bengal* off her unwelcome resting-place, and the two ships sailed almost side by side into the harbour of Port Darwin …

We sailed along, passing smooth white beaches, on to which waterfalls from the overhanging cliffs shed glittering streams of crystal, dancing and shimmering in the sunlight. The air was warm and light, and a fair wind wafted us each moment nearer our future home. Beautiful it certainly was; but oh! so lonely and desolate, not a sign of human habitation could we yet discern; no living creature, not even a solitary blackfellow walked these lovely beaches. It was all just as nature had made it, just as it had remained from the beginning of time, untouched and untrodden by the foot of man; a region known only to the degraded tribes of savages, who had hitherto been the sole occupiers of this magnificent piece of country.

The scene of our exile — for such we deemed it then — though surpassingly beautiful in itself, was, from this very loneliness, hardly inviting to N. and myself, for we were at that time far too strongly attached to the pomps and vanities of this wicked world to appreciate being banished from all we had hitherto enjoyed so keenly.

At last we came in sight of the little settlement; it was situated in a gully on a broad tract of level ground between two steeply rising hills, having the sea on both sides. The 'camp', to use the name so familiar to every one, and which to this day it has retained, consisted of a number of log and iron houses on either side of the gully. On Fort Hill to our right — a steep hill with a flat summit, one of the most prominent landmarks of the harbour — was a flagstaff, on which the Union Jack was flying. It was delightful to find the familiar flag in this far-away corner of the British Empire. Close to the flagstaff was a lonely grave, the last resting-place of a young surveyor who was treacherously murdered at Fred's Pass by the natives, during the surveying expedition a year before. The opposite hill was covered with green shrubs, and at this moment it literally swarmed with black men and women. These unclothed spectators were the 'oldest inhabitants' of this part of the world — members of the Larrakiah tribe. The heads of the clan were amongst this eager and excited crowd. But as far as we could discern, there was nothing to distinguish them from the lesser lights of that barbarous horde of natives.

My young brothers and sisters looked very awestruck at this first glimpse of barbaric life, and I fear many of the theories they had formed about going into the wilds alone, and experiencing some Robinson Crusoe-like adventures, were suddenly knocked on the head, to use a forcible colonial expression, one, however, which rather pointed to their probable fate if they had attempted anything of the kind.

A closer view of the camp did not tend to raise our spirits to any very exalted elevation — a handful of log huts, with crowds of natives looking over our heads; and this tiny settlement literally the only one in the vast tract of Northern Australia. Looking straight through the gully, away over the roofs of the buildings, one beheld a long stretch of water, bounded like the other parts of the harbour by a mass of densely wooded and uninhabited country, which extended as far as the eye could reach. We realised, too, that no hope of regular communication with the outer world could be looked for, as the settlement had not become sufficiently important to induce a line of steamers to call there ...

The arrival of these two ships in one day was a great event in the history of the Northern Territory. Nothing had been done since the survey was finished, and progress was at a standstill. We brought letters to those in camp from friends and relatives far away. And the *Bengal* whose mails were of a later date than ours, brought the welcome news that an agreement had been concluded between the British Australian Telegraph Company and the Adelaide

Government to bring Australia into telegraphic communication with, not only the mother country, but the whole world. And Port Darwin was to be the connecting link, for the submarine cable was to be landed here when the overland line was completed ...

In the meantime boats were coming off to us, and we received a most hearty welcome from old friends who had preceded us to the settlement, and from those of the officers to whom we were introduced. Some months having elapsed since any news had reached them, our visitors were eager for news, and every scrap of intelligence we could give was listened to with great interest. Every item of Adelaide gossip was gone through: who was married, dead, or engaged. Politics were freely discussed, especially those questions which affected the territory itself; and the projected telegraph line afforded a subject of conversation which lasted during the whole of my stay in Port Darwin. After the Resident had landed and the official reception was over we went on shore.

I think the judgement we had formed from the deck of our schooner was rather a harsh one. On a closer inspection we found a pretty, well-kept, and neatly laid-out camp. The married people lived on the left hand side below the Larrakiahs' camp, in log huts, with neatly thatched roofs; at the farther end on the same side was the stable, a long shed made of logs, roofed with sheets of bark, and well filled with horses, we were glad to see. Close to the stable were the police barracks, bearing a military air of neatness, quite in character with the morale of the force. Several tall troopers were standing outside, still wearing their pretty blue uniform, for they had just come off duty, and were smoking their pipes and reading their letters and papers. The quarters assigned to our use were two huts, not large enough to accommodate such a party, but they were pleasantly situated close to the sea, and were, moreover, the best the place afforded. Until our furniture was landed and unpacked, we lived on board the *Gulnare*, and when the time came to leave the little vessel we were truly sorry, for we had become very fond of her during our three months voyage.

While we were getting settled, the land selectors were busily engaged in preparing for their expedition into the interior, and until they were ready to start, lived in a camp on the hill overlooking our own.

The first thing we turned our attention to after landing was to arrange our small quarters in the most comfortable manner and to make them as homelike as possible. The huts were very rough, and it was only by dint of management that we fitted into them at all. The sleeping apartments were in a large log hut divided by partitions. The spaces between the poles were plugged with 'paper-bark' — a species of gum tree whose bark is nearly white, and peels off in loose flakes; our roof was of bark also; indeed this material was called into requisition very freely throughout the settlement. The ironbark trees are 'rung' at a certain height top and bottom, and the bark detached in one sheet; it is then wetted, and laid out flat on the ground, huge stones being placed to keep it from rolling up again. This was laid on the framework of the roof when it was ready for use, and then saplings were laid across and lashed down so as to prevent it blowing off in a sudden squall. The floor of our hut was made of mud, pressed flat, and mixed with gravel, sand and limestone, well rolled till a smooth surface was obtained.

Glass windows were unknown — our windows were frames filled with unbleached calico, and they swung on a pivot, propped open by a stick which was fitted for the purpose. The floor was a great trial of patience, for every clean dress we put on became soiled round the edges immediately. We had only one sitting-room, which was joined to the sleeping apartments by a covered way. This was a galvanised iron hut, about twenty feet long, lined with deal and possessing the luxury of a wooden floor; its windows were sheets of iron propped open in the usual way; there was a door at each end, and we habitually sat in a draught for the sake of air. The iron roof was shaded by bark, but it was a very hot room at any time.

We arranged our furniture here to the best advantage, but owing to the incongruous medley, the room reminded me of nothing so forcibly as a broker's shop — chests of drawers, sideboards, chiffoniers, tables of every description and shape elbowed each other, seeming as lost as we were at the strange and novel associations in which they found themselves.

After a time we got things into some degree of order, and became so used to living in this cramped space that it seemed wonderful we ever wished for anything larger. We made a verandah, which added greatly to our comfort, by means of saplings fixed in the ground, and covered with a canvas awning. Here we spent the greater part of our time; a table and all the most comfortable chairs were put here; it quite answered the purpose of an extra sitting-room, and was by far the most favoured resort of our small quarters. Here in the evening the gentlemen smoked pipes or cigars, yarns were spun, and discussions on every topic of interest took place in spite of occasional onslaughts from sandflies and mosquitoes ... the next day was an uneventful one and with it my account of the voyage terminates.

From Mrs. Dominic D. Daly [Harriet Douglas], *Digging, Squatting, and Pioneering Life in the Northern Territory of South Australia*, London, 1887. Courtesy Peter Bridge Collection.

Rosamond and Florence Hill

1873

Florence Hill was travelling companion to her elder sister Rosamond, both seasoned travellers at home and on the Continent. They made an Australian trip to see relatives of their father who had died the year before. They made their long voyage to Australia longer still by travelling via Paris, Cannes, Florence, Venice, Ancona, Brindisi, Alexandria, Suez, Aden and Galle, and so to Albany on King George Sound before disembarking at Glenelg in South Australia. It was not an unusual itinerary for some and their description of going out to Australia is unusually good. The sisters were keen observers.

AN EXPEDITION TO AUSTRALIA is a very different undertaking in the present day from what it was comparatively only a few years ago, before the Peninsular and Oriental Steam Navigation Company had extended their traffic farther than the shores of India, and when no means existed for the regular conveyance of the mails to our antipodean colonies, letters being dispatched thither at irregular intervals in sailing ships. In those days the transit to the nearest point in Australia required at least from three to four months, sometimes a much longer period, for its accomplishment. Large and expensive outfits were indispensable for the voyage, including cabin furniture and some amount of food. At the present day, should the traveller choose the mail steamer for his mode of conveyance, he will reach his destination in less than half the time formerly consumed, and at no greater expense. Every requisite is provided by the Company, including comforts undreamed of by the pioneers of Australian travel ...

Nevertheless this expedition, when undertaken by ladies travelling alone, is still considered extraordinary; especially when the programme, as ours did, at first included Japan, and a possible return through America. We learned this from the manner in which the news of our intended journey was received by many of our acquaintances, who, if they did not set us down as absolutely crazy, yet thought we must at least be eccentric. Happily, their opinion was modified when it was distinctly understood that we were going to visit relatives for many years settled in South Australia. Our French friends in Paris were naturally even more amazed than any at home had been on learning the intention of two ladies, unmarried and unattended, to make a tour of the world, and their national courtesy was sorely tried to excuse a proceeding so opposed to their sense of propriety … our expedition, therefore, was no longer audacious or eccentric; it had become heroic.

Yet, apart from the deep interest excited by the different countries we passed on our route, the voyage itself, which has always appeared to our friends the most difficult part of our enterprise, prove to be almost prosaic. We encountered no gales of any severity, have to record no alarming adventures, and returning to England, after sixteen months' absence, convinced by experience that to persons of average health and strength the difficulties of such a journey exist only in the imagination. It may, we feel sure, be accomplished with ease and comfort by ladies unprovided with servants or escort. We constantly met with kindness and attention; everybody was ready to afford us assistance and information; and we regard the inhabitants of our Australian colonies as among the most good-natured and helpful people it has been our good fortune to meet.

We travelled advisedly without servants. Though strongly recommended by many of our friends to take at least a maid, the anticipation of the inconvenience and discomfort she would have had to encounter in so extended an expedition, added to the urgent counsel we had received from travellers accustomed to long voyages, not to embarrass ourselves with a female servant on ship-board, decided us to dispense with such an attendant. We never regretted our decision. The stewardesses were kind and efficient substitutes, and experience convinced us that the responsibility of having a maid to care for under the circumstances of our journey would have far outweighed to us the convenience of her service.

With regard to dress, we would remark that an extensive outfit is quite unnecessary. Shops are now so good in the principal capitals of Australia that any article wanted may be purchased at a cost not much exceeding that at home. As the fashions are sent out by the mail, those most devoted to the toilet need not be more than a couple of months behind Paris in adopting the new modes ...

We went on board the good ship *Pera* at Venice, and soon won the approval of our captain, and the envy of many a suffering fellow-passenger, by our regular attendance at breakfast, tiffin, dinner, and tea ... we observed the gentlemen on board (unless they were seriously ill), when suffering from sea-sickness, were considered by all true 'salts' as weak-minded individuals — fair objects for good natured jokes, not however untinctured with reproach; whereas if they were happily free from that wretched infliction — well, they were only fulfilling their commonest and most obvious duty. But when ladies were sea-sick, they at once became objects of the deepest compassion; and if they escaped this too common malady, they were treated as heroines, considered patterns of excellence, and commanded universal respect. We travelled to Australia and back again on this pinnacle of esteem.

Let us here pause a moment to express our gratitude for the courtesy we received from the officers and servants of the P&O Company, and the comforts we enjoyed in their well founded vessels. Complaints were sometimes heard of shortcomings; but on the whole surprise was not that some luxuries were wanting, but that so many could be provided. Vegetables and fruit, taken onboard at one port and kept fresh in the ice-room, never failed to last, in the best-managed ships, till we reached the next. Our bill of fare included daily a variety of flesh and fowl, and the delicate pastry and other sweet dishes would have done honour to a London confectioner.

Had we the opportunity of whispering in the ear of so august a personage as the chief steward, we would suggest that tea and coffee never can be good if dealt with wholesale, and that the raw material, however excellent, requires, like many other things, individual treatment to develop its most precious qualities. A little army of tea and coffee pots, each to be used as a factory, and not merely as a channel for conveying the liquid from huge cauldrons to the consumer's cup, would, we are sure, win lasting gratitude from passengers the most robust — how much more, then, from the miserable being who, after days and nights of prostrating sickness, revives sufficiently to long for tea or coffee, and receives a black and sometimes even nauseous draught, bearing little resemblance in taste and smell to the beverage of his yearning. How grateful we recall, among many acts of kindness, the morning tea sent to us from his own pot by one of the higher authorities on board, with whom it was our good fortune to travel.

There are, of course, discomforts far more serious and

irremediable than bad tea and coffee to be put up with in ship life. Indeed one of our captains, in his consideration for 'the sex', laid it down as an axiom that 'no woman ought ever to go to sea', and that each and all who violated this rule should be in a position to 'justify' the action. They should, at any rate, be able and resolved to bear the annoyances it entails with patience, and, if possible, with cheerfulness ...

We joined the *Malwa* at Suez ... reached Aden in a fine sunset on the fifth day after Suez ... it was too late to land and we steamed away by five o'clock next morning ... Galle Harbour, which we reached in nine and a-half days from Aden, has, in one respect, an unenviable character. Ships rarely go in or out by night: rocks on which well-known vessels have split, sad remains of some notorious wreck, are sedulously pointed out by lovers of the sensational to awe-struck passengers. We suppose we must have had an especially courageous captain from Galle to Australia, as he weighed anchor at 1 a.m. ... the channel we pursued was marked with buoys, while on each buoy was perched a Cingalese bearing a lighted torch, so probably we ran no real risk. It was, however, with a certain feeling of relief that we saw from our port, our pilot take his departure, and we knew we were once more fairly out at sea.

At Galle we transferred ourselves from the *Malwa* to the *Sumatra*, then one of the prettiest boats in the P&O Company's fleet, built, we are told, regardless of expense; and so well managed that everything seemed to go on oiled wheels. Here we saw the picturesque Sunday muster, usual on board these vessels, but which had not taken place during our voyage on the *Malwa*. The crew included

Lascars, Chinamen, Malays, Nubians, and a few of our own countrymen who perform the superior service on board …

Few travellers on the ocean, however good sailors they may be, fail to weary of their voyage long before its termination. Life on board ship 'drags its slow length along', except for the happy few whose heads are as clear there as on land, and whose capacity for work remains the same where privacy is unattainable, as in their own studies. Gambling is a common resort from ennui among the gentlemen, whether with games of chance, or in betting upon every conceivable uncertainty. The number of knots that will be made from noon to noon; the hours, minutes occupied in a run from port to port; the foot the pilot will first put on deck, etc., etc., are all subjects on which to hazard money, and so beguile the time. Souls above gambling still find light reading, chess, or needlework severe occupation; and smoking by the gentlemen and sleeping by both sexes are largely indulged in, to while away the lingering hours. Experience bought on our outward voyage made us resolve to try upon our return the effect of regular exercise, and we rarely fell short of two hours walking daily … If you are idle, you are lost!!

Theatricals are a frequent refuge from the monotony of sea-life; they require, however, one or two energetic people to set them going, and in none of our voyages did any passengers so distinguish themselves … dancing found little favour, except that a children's ball given by the captain proved a great success, though when first announced a rolling sea and the thermometer at 88 degrees made us anticipate it with dismay; for we were all expected to take part in entertaining the little ones …

Of living creatures outside our ship we saw comparatively few. Occasionally the pretty flying fish skimmed along the surface of the water, looking like flocks of little fawn-coloured birds. On the Australian coast hundreds of sea-gulls would sometimes collect above our vessel, circling round us and approaching near enough for us to appreciate the exquisite colouring of their dove-like plumage and coral-tinted beaks and feet … a few days after leaving Galle we became aware of a very uncomfortable amount of motion. The trade-wind was hard to catch, nor did it promote our ease when caught [through the porthole]. Our experience each way brought us to the conclusion that when it blew with us we rolled, and when it blew against us we pitched. Often were our ports closed, causing, while we were in the tropics, great discomfort. A heavy sea, which was admitted by the authorities to be 'half a gale' while it was blowing, and a very respectable whole one when well over, seriously aggravated our sufferings. Public opinion, however, was on the side of cheerfulness, and fortunately very few onboard were made really ill. The Australian waters are proverbial for their roughness …

There had been rough weather for several days, which by delaying our progress and postponing the termination of our voyage, had somewhat depressed our spirits. But now was 'the winter of our discontent made glorious summer!' One morning we came on deck to find the wind fallen, the sun brilliant, the sky cloudless, and the air balmy. This, we were assured by a fellow-passenger, was 'real Australian weather', and he promised us that by-and-by we should have 'months of it'. A delicious odour pervaded the air, such as greets one on a summer's day when thyme is in blossom, and fir-trees are not far off. Wafted to us 180 miles across the sea, it was recognised as the smell of a bush-fire. This, then, was our first Australian experience!!

But real Australian weather proved now, as often afterwards, very evanescent. The wind freshened that night, the ports were again closed, and we were rocked to sleep or kept awake as the case may be, by the tossing waves. Sailors say it is almost always rough near Cape Leeuwin, which we rounded the next day. When land was proclaimed to be in sight, everyone, whether colonist returning home or stranger who had crossed the world to see it, was eager to catch the first glimpse of the Australian coast; but as yet sailors alone could perceive it, though we strained our eyes to the utmost. 'Where is the land?' 'There,' replied the quartermaster, pointing to the horizon; 'don't you see it?' as if it were a signboard three yards square, about ten feet distant from our eyes!! … nor until some hours afterwards was the coast visible to landsmen. A barren, inhospitable shore it looked at first; but as we approached we could distinguish some patches of vegetation on the long line of sandy hills.

The sea remained high until we had reached King George's Sound. This was doubly depressing after our short taste of 'real Australian', and it cast a gloom over the spirits of the passengers. Under the circumstances it was cheering to observe that the roughness could afford pleasure to some living creatures. Several albatrosses of the small species common in this part of the world were flying backwards and forwards, now touching with the tips of their wings one wave and then wheeling off to another, circling with graceful motion in the air, evidently thoroughly enjoying both wind and weather.

It was with a sense of exultation that, steaming up the narrow entrance to the inner harbour [Princess Royal Harbour] of King George's Sound, we felt we had happily accomplished so large a portion of our voyage. In consequence of the delay in our arrival, we expected to find the branch mail-boat, which was to convey us to Adelaide, with steam up, ready for starting. Indeed, the captains of these vessels were represented as being so impatient to carry off their mails, that cargo and even passengers might easily be left behind. The reason for this extraordinary haste, we were told, was the natural desire of the South Australians to obtain their English news as quickly as possible, and — softly be it whispered — before the Victorians got theirs … this cause of rivalry between the two colonies is now at an end, as under a new contract the P&O steamers on their way to and from Melbourne, call off Glenelg to deliver and take in the outward and homeward mails. But this alteration had not taken place when we reached Australia.

The thoughtful captain of the *Sumatra*, in order to expedite matters as much as possible, had ordered all our luggage to be placed at one gangway, while the sacks of letters, sixty-three in number, lay at the other, and we stood on deck prepared for instant transit to the Adelaide steamer in the captain's gig, which he had kindly placed at our disposal. But this preparation proved needless — the South Australian steamer had not arrived.

Before five o'clock on the morning of April 2nd, and consequently long before it was light, our bed-room steward knocked at our cabin door, telling us the Adelaide boat had arrived during the night, and would start at six precisely. There was no time to be lost, and we dressed as quickly as possible. Several of our fellow passengers, having heard we were departing, appeared in various forms of dishabille to wish us farewell. On going on deck we found the captain's gig lowered and manned in readiness for us, and himself waiting to bid us good-bye before he 'turned in', to make up while he could for much sleep lost during our late rough weather. Under his chief officer's courteous escort, six Chinamen rowed our one-fellow passenger for Adelaide and ourselves in a very few minutes to the *Rangatira*, but on reaching her deck we saw plainly she was not on the point of starting. She had not even finished discharging her cargo for the Sound, and had yet to take in all we had brought her for Adelaide.

The sun, just risen, was lighting up the harbour from point to point, this radiance stealing over the water, now smooth as glass ... the morning aspect of the Sound was very pleasing ... while the little township of Albany, close to the water's edge, with its English looking church and one or two pretty country houses on a slight eminence, has a neat and well-to-do air.

Hour after hour passed and there was no sign of starting, and two or three had elapsed before any appeared even of breakfast. We watched with hungry eyes the preparations that at length became visible; and whether it was our long fast, or the freshness of the provisions which made that first Australian meal so delicious we have never been able to decide ... the provisions might indeed have seemed anything but fresh, for all except the milk had been brought from Adelaide. The bread, though five days old, was excellent, and continued excellent for the five remaining days of our voyage ... we had supposed these provisions would be taken onboard at Albany for the return voyage, but we were informed that the inhabitants, far from raising such articles of export, actually themselves import ordinary farm-produce from the other colonies ... the inhabitants of Albany are admitted not to be industrious, and the same reputation attaches in greater or less degree, though with doubtless many honourable exceptions, to the West Australians generally ... we had already heard of the suspicion with which most other colonies regard new arrivals from West Australia, lest they should prove to be escaped prisoners or ex-convicts. Police officers were on board the *Rangatira* during the whole time she lay at the Sound, to prevent any such objectionable persons coming on board and getting themselves conveyed as stowaways to Adelaide.

We started for Adelaide at last ... at 3 a.m. on the 7th of April, the stoppage of our engines and some bustle on board indicated that we had reached Glenelg ...

From Rosamond and Florence Hill, *What We Saw in Australia*,
London, 1875.

Constance Gordon-Cumming

1875

Constance Frederica Gordon-Cumming, the sixth daughter of Sir William Gordon-Cumming, Bt, was a professional empire traveller and a writer, one of a family of noted explorers. She wrote a number of instructional world travel books which were popular with the general public and ranked her among the upper echelons of travel authors at the time. In 1875 she accompanied her Colonial Service husband to Sydney where she remained while he went on to Fiji to prepare his new staff position at Government House and their home. Constance kept her sisters in Scotland fully informed by letter of all the Vice-Regal happenings and the journeys she made in New South Wales. Constance later lived abroad for many years. Chinese culture interested her and while a resident of China in 1898 she invented and published A Numeral Type for China — By the Use of which Illiterate Chinese, Both Blind and Sighted Can Very Quickly Be Taught to Read and Write Fluently *for use in missionary schools.*

Sydney
New South Wales.
June 2, 1875.

𝒟EAR NELL,

My last letter home was posted at Rockhampton, two days before we reached Brisbane. The latter lies twenty miles up a river, so a little steamer comes down to meet the big one and carry letters and passengers to and fro ... I should scarcely think Brisbane was a congenial atmosphere. It seemed to us a singularly uninteresting place, its botanical gardens being almost the only resource. Of course, in a semi-tropical climate like that of Queensland, there is always the attraction of very varied foliage; but we thought even this was somewhat stunted.

We had lovely weather on our two days' voyage from Brisbane, and also the day we arrived here. Unfortunately we just missed seeing the festivities for the Queen's birthday, when every ship in the beautiful harbour was dressed, and there was an immense volunteer review. There are no military here, and the volunteers only meet on this one day. Sir Hercules [the Governor] and Lady Robinson is, however, to have a great ball to-night, when she promises to show us any number of Australian beauties.

The accommodation of Government House is so very limited, and the family party so large, that it was as much as she could do to find room for Sir Arthur [Governor of Fiji] and Lady Gordon and the children. All the gentlemen have found quarters at an hotel; and Commodore [James Goodenough R.N. Australian Station Royal Navy] and Mrs. Goodenough, a most hospitable and kind couple, have managed to take me in. Lady Robinson kindly says that, though not living under her roof, I am nevertheless her guest. So I dine there most nights.

How you would revel in the exquisite loveliness of the camellias! The dinner-table is most often decorated with delicate pink camellias and maidenhair fern; and the loveliest white ones are abundant as snowdrops in an English spring. Beautiful as these are, I am not enamoured of what we have hitherto seen of Australia as contrasted with Ceylon and India. To begin with, I have contrived to catch a severe cold, not improved by all these starlight walks to and from Government House, which is just too near to be worth driving to; and the climate is apparently as changeable as in England. We have had four consecutive days of incessant rain and cold, raw air, so on every side you hear people coughing and sneezing; and we are glad to cower over fires — for which, by the way, the coal comes from Newcastle.

It is so absurd to hear the old familiar names out here. A man tells you he has just come from Morpeth, Oxford, or Hyde Park, Norwood or Sydenham, Waterloo, Waverley or Paddington, Birkenhead or Liverpool, Brighton or Cremorne, Clifton, St Leonard's, Darlington, Anglesea, &c. It is quite a relief to hear so wholly novel a name as Woolloomooloo!

But truly all the attractions which have hitherto delighted me in foreign lands are here conspicuous by their absence. Apparently no native population. Certainly no rich colour; no statuesque tropical undress; no graceful cocoa-palms. Everything is British, even to the ploughman riding his horses home at night, and the four-horse omnibuses, and the hansom cab, which drives you about the town at 4s. an hour, and the genuine unadulterated cockney accents of men born and bred in the colony. Of course it is interesting to see this Greater Britain mushroom, but it is difficult to believe that we are 14,000 miles from London!! and I hope, before long to get glimpses of bush-life. We went to the opera last night. The most remarkable thing about it was the drop-scene, which was simply a huge advertisement sheet, with puffs of all sorts, from the newest sewing machine to the most efficacious pills! Imagine the effect of this descending between each act of [Donizetti's] Anna Bolena! I regretted much that I had not rather accompanied Commodore and Mrs. Goodenough, who spent the evening with a large party of blue-jackets. It is quite touching to see their cordial kindness to all the men, and extreme interest in all that concerns them; and yet the Commodore has the name of being stern. I can only say I never saw a face which more thoroughly revealed the genial nature within.

June 10th.

WE HAVE HAD SEVERAL PLEASANT expeditions in the neighbourhood. Last Monday, Sir Hercules having ordered a special train to take us to see the Blue Mountains, we started early and went as far as the wonderful zig-zags by which the rail is carried across the mountains. I had the privilege of sitting on the engine [two chairs were placed on a small platform just above the cow-catcher], so I obtained an admirable view.

The following day [our Colonial staff] started for Fiji in H.M.S. *Barracouta*, so our first detachment is fairly under weigh. Sir Arthur is waiting for telegrams from England, and is to follow in H.M.S. *Pearl* with Commodore Goodenough. It has been decided that we are to remain at Pfahlert's Hotel till he sends us orders to follow, which we hope may come soon.

Meanwhile we find some attractions here. To-day we drove out to the South Heads, and had a most lovely walk along the cliffs. At the entrance to the harbour we came to a pretty little church perched among the rocks, and listened to the choir practising 'The strain upraise', while we sat basking in the sunshine, the whole air fragrant with the honeyed blossoms of the red and white epacris, which grows in profusion, and is suggestive of many coloured heaths. Though the everlasting gum tree is apparently the only indigenous growth, there is lovely foliage of all sorts in the gardens of innumerable villas, which lie dotted all over the countless headlands, and along the shores of the many creeks which branch off from this immense and most lovely harbour ... One of the favourite 'ploys' here [when on a picnic] is to start armed with a small hammer, a bottle of vinegar or some lemons, and slices of bread and butter, and find a feast of oysters on the rocks!

Two days ago, the weather being warm and sunny Lady Robinson took us in her steam-launch fourteen miles up one of the creeks. It was like a beautiful Scotch lake; and we caught glimpses of many lesser creeks branching off to right and left, all tempting us to explore. Now I must dispatch my letter. So good-bye.

Your loving sister.

Pfahlert's Hotel, Sydney,
Sunday, June 20.

I TOLD YOU IN MY LAST that the first detachment of our party started for Fiji in the *Barracouta*. Now so many have followed that we feel quite forsaken. This day last week Sir Arthur and Lady Gordon went to a farewell lunch on board H.M.S. *Pearl* with Commodore and Mrs. Goodenough and on Monday the *Barracouta* sailed. We sat in the beautiful botanic gardens to watch her pass down the harbour, carrying away so many of our friends ... The people here are not encouraging as to our prospects. Many of them have lost a great deal of money which they had invested in Fijian plantations; and those who have had friends or relations there, in some cases ladies and children, give us most lamentable accounts of the hardships they had to undergo from want of the commonest necessaries of life, and dangerous voyages in open canoes. From all we hear, I think there can be no doubt a planter's life in the Isles must be a most unenviable lot; but of course, as far as we individually are concerned, the way will be made smooth.

I am preparing for emergencies by attending the infirmary several days a week, to pick up a few ideas about simple nursing. It is under the care of Miss Osborne, a cousin of Florence Nightingale. Evidently her whole heart is in her work, and everything is done thoroughly; and kindness and order reign supreme. I have been very much interested in some of the patients, especially in one poor sailor who hails from the parish of Dyke in Morayshire.

Nothing strikes me more here than the exceeding loyalty of the inhabitants. Every one speaks of England as 'home', though neither they nor their parents or grandparents ever saw the old country; and certainly our Queen has no more devoted subjects. To-day being her Majesty's Accession, the churches were crowded; and at St. Andrew's Cathedral this afternoon we had the Coronation Anthem, and then God save the Queen.

I find here that it does not do to use the word native, as we are wont to do, with reference to the brown races. Here it is applied exclusively to white men born in the country, the hideous blacks being invariably described as Aborigines. Hideous indeed they are, far beyond any race I have yet met with; and of so low a type that it is impossible, in their case, to regret that strange law of nature which seems to ordain the dying out of dark-skinned races before the advance of civilisation, and which is nowhere so self-evident as in Australia, where they have simply faded away, notwith-standing the strict observance of their own most elaborate marriage laws, which set forth the various degrees of rela-tionship between different tribes, and the rotations in which alone they are permitted to marry. Perhaps, however, if all tales be true concerning the ruthless policy of extermination practised by too many of the settlers on the frontier, and the manner in which tribes have been shot down wholesale for daring to trespass on the lands taken from them without any sort of right, the extinction of the Australian black may be found to be less a law of nature than an illustration of the might that makes right. But certainly the few specimens we have come across have been unspeakably wretched, living in gipsy camps far more miserable than those of any British tinker, altogether dirty and debased.

Pfahlert's Hotel,
July 15.

DEAR EISA,

I have been all the morning waiting for the mail, sure of a letter from you, but I again have drawn a blank in that tantalising lottery. You can scarcely realise what a matter of interest the mails become in a place like this — the perpetual comings and goings of the steamers, the signalling of their approach from the Heads, then watching them come up the harbour, right past Government House to their respective creeks. Such a lovely harbour as it is, and every headland dotted with picturesque villas! We have had both time and weather to enjoy it, the latter having been faultless ever since the rainy week which greeted our arrival, when it did pour with a vengeance.

The days slip away pleasantly, many kind friends plan delightful excursions for us, by land and water; and I learn what carriage springs are capable of enduring when I see the daintiest little pony-phaetons driven, apparently at random, through the bush, across fields, or over the roughest cart tracks. When we come to a paling, we deliberately take it down, and, of course, put it up again. Sometimes we come to dells where the loveliest maidenhair fern grows wild, and we fill our carriage with it and pink epacris. As to the sweet wild geranium which abounds, it is thought quite extraordinary that we should care to gather it!! Yesterday we went by rail to Parramatta, and drove to the great orange gardens, and noticed one group of trees from 40 to 50 feet high, the stems being nearly a foot in diameter, and the lowest branch three feet above my head.

From a Tiny Cottage at the Weatherboard in the
Blue Mountains, New South Wales.
Begun, August 19, 1875.

Dear Eisa,

You see I have contrived to escape from the region of fine clothes and prolonged meals! Oh dear, what a trial it is to be invited to luncheon at some lovely place, where you go expecting a pleasant day out of doors, and find an immense party assembled for a stiff dinner of many courses, which takes nearly the whole afternoon! The donors of the feast console themselves by a quiet evening stroll and late tea; but the poor guest has to return to undergo a second long dinner as usual. Nevertheless I have had many delightful days in the neighbourhood of Sydney.

You have no notion what a size the harbour is, and how immense is the amount of shipping always coming and going! Great ships, and steamboats, and yachts, and tiny steam launches — sometimes I have counted eighteen or twenty steamers in sight at once … I have also spent some pleasant days with the Morts, whose lovely house,

Greenoakes, is built as a dream of Alton Towers — all gables outside, and good old carved oak inside ... you perceive my handwriting is shaky. I am in the train, returning to Sydney, whirling past orange orchards, and endless dull bush, all of gum trees. But everywhere there is an undergrowth of lovely bush flowers ... the glory of the bush is the feathery mimosa, which takes the place of our broom, and is covered with sheets of fragrant gold.

Duntroon, near the Murrumbidgee Hills,
Sept 2.

Dear Eisa,

Here I am really in the Australian bush, though I find it hard to reconcile the term with living in a fine large house, with every appliance of the most advanced civilisation. I can assure you we were glad to find such comfort at the end of a long and very cold journey ... this is the property of the sole descendants of the old Campbells of Duntroon ... we came about two hundred miles, half by rail and half by posting, to this place to see a true station. There are about 30,000 sheep, 500 horses, and 1000 head of cattle on the station; a most comfortable house, and everything most luxurious; lots of horses for riding or driving; I am getting over my belief that all Australians horses are buck-jumpers. Yesterday we had a great picnic to a waterfall eighteen miles off. I drove there, sketched, and rode back over fine grassy country. It was characteristic; for, as we went along, we picked up recruits till we numbered in all seventeen riders — the brake with four horses, a dogcart, a buggie, and a cart.

As to roads, no one here thinks of them. Without the slightest hesitation about springs, the brake and four will turn off into the bush, drive in and out among the trees, grazing the old stumps which stick up in every direction, and the felled or half-burnt timbers with which the ground is everywhere strewn, dodging morasses, and choosing the easiest bits of creeks, where you think you must overturn, through fords, etc. etc., for miles after miles.

A good deal of the country here is open, rolling downs, which afford very pleasant riding — miles without a fence. We have just been to a ploughing match, at which the chief noteworthy fact was seeing all the farm lasses riding. Every lass has her own pony; and a good many households' servants arrive at their new situation on their own horse, just turn it out in their master's paddock, and catch and saddle it when ever they want to ride to town ...

Sir Arthur writes to Lady Gordon that the house in Fiji is very tolerable, and that he has begun to build the new rooms, so we hope to find our Fiji home ready when we arrive. Good-bye.

From C.F. Gordon-Cumming, *At Home in Fiji, Volume 1,*
London, 1881.

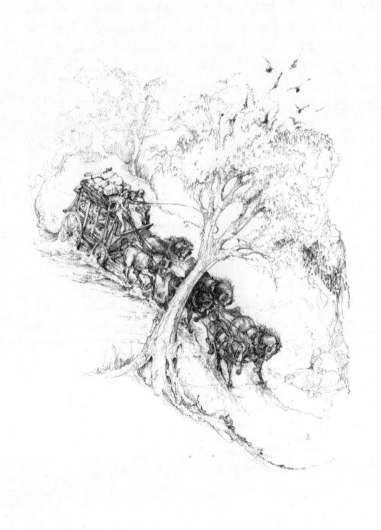

Emily Soldene

1877

Emily Soldene was an English opera singer and novelist, a successful singer of comic opera with a fine mezzo-soprano voice and a chic style of acting. She made many Empire tours returning often to Australia, which retained an especially happy place in her memory. On her first visit she made what was then a heroic overland journey from Sydney to Melbourne by Cobb & Co Royal Mail coach — while most of the Touring Company wisely went by inter-colonial steamer.

WE LANDED IN SYDNEY, September, 1877 ... We put up at the Oxford Hotel, the proprietor then being Mr. Curran, who gave 5000 pounds to the Home Rule fund, and is now M.P. for Sligo. We had rooms opening on to a balcony, and looking straight over to St. James's Church [King Street], the oldest one in Sydney. I used to watch Sir Hercules and Lady Robinson going to the morning service. Sir Hercules always stood on one side to let 'me lady' pass; you see, the door was narrow, and her ladyship was not. There was a nice-looking aide too — a Captain St. John ...

We found the city very hot, and our first Sunday was passed at Botany Bay. We dined or lunched at the hotel, and lounged about the grounds in the afternoon. Botany Bay had never previously associated itself in my mind with anything floral, but with other things distinctly disagreeable. When I saw the ground covered with heaths of the most rare description; heaths, white, pink, yellow, purple, red, large waxy blooms, that in Covent Garden cost from 1s. to 2s. 6d. per spray, and big flowers as big as pint pots and quite as useful, and hedges of geraniums, and trees of fuchsias, then I began to understand that Botany Bay meant flowers not convicts. That was a day to be remembered, for as we drove home, the sun went down suddenly; there was, to our surprise, no twilight, no moon, all dark, four horses pretty fresh, a driver new to the country. We were nearly lost. But we got home to the hotel all right.

We opened at the Royal and a royal time we had. We began with 'Genevieve de Brabant', but during our stay played the repertoire. I personally made a furore with 'Silver Threads Among the Gold', 'I Love Him So', and 'Marriage Bells'. The Theatre Royal was not too lovely, and the walls of the pit were greasy from much leaning against. Coming from an American theatre this was the more noticeable. The theatre was crowded every night, but the receipts seemed small after the States, where, in the class of house we played in, the lowest price was fifty cents. Coming to Australia, we found that people thought as much of a shilling as the Americans thought of a dollar …

The season finished up with my benefit. Patronised by the Governor and Lady Robinson, and the entourage, the suite and the elite, and all the city. It was really delightful, and Mr. Sam Lazaar, the local manager, made a speech, and presented me with a jewel casket made of an emu's egg and mounted in Australian silver. It was beautiful, and I appreciated it very much. We left Sydney with a good deal of regret and some apprehension, for people said, 'What went in Sydney was a dead frost in Melbourne' — and we had been so successful in New South Wales that we felt we should be an utter failure in Victoria.

Most of the company went to Melbourne by steamer, and got stuck in the mud outside that charming city, but four of us went overland. Such a journey, on a 'Cobbs' coach, drawn by six young horses, who galloped up mountains and flew down them, driven by coachmen more or less under the influence of the weather. One told us he had been out on a 'burst to a wedding, not slept for three nights,' but should be all right when he had had a 'nobbler'. We looked forward with much pleasurable anticipation to the 'nobbler', but were horrified when we saw it — 'half a tumbler of whisky'. Our driver tossed it off. He had not overstated its merits. It pulled him together splendidly, not that it made any difference in his driving, which was dare-devil and perfect, as was that of all the other boys. Fancy a track of soft sand, cut into deep ruts, piled high up in banks, winding in and out of huge trees, sharp corners, unexpected fallen trunks, monster upturned roots, every kind of obstacle, six horses always galloping, the coach banging, creaking, swaying from side to side!! Then suddenly down we go, down over a mountain as steep as the side of a house, down into and through a rushing, roaring, tumbling, bumping, yellow river!! Splash, dash. Then with a 'Houp!' 'Hi!' and a big lurch, out again and up the opposite side, galloping always galloping, breathless; the driver shouting, cracking his whip, and the horses shaking the water from their sides, tossing their heads, and jingling their harness; then out on to the level, soft and springy, covered with mossy turf and beautiful trees like an English park; away over more sand, and leaving the mossy turf, and plunging through sharp, cutting, stiff, rusty looking, tall grass, growing in huge tufts, far apart. At last we come to a hut, full gallop, and the driver, without any preparation, pulls the horses up on their haunches … It was all lovely except for the jolting, and my hands were blistered with holding on. I liked to sit on the box, though it made one sick, not with fright exactly, but with excitement and the anticipation of some possible calamity.

My first flock of flying cockatoos disappointed me dreadfully. They looked exactly like a flock of pigeons. The driver told me that when one was wounded or hurt, and could not go on, the others dispatched him, pecked his eyes out and tore him to pieces. I fancy I have seen something like that in more civilised regions. We went through groves, forests of gum trees, where there was no shade, but a delicious perfume. At night we heard the laughing jackasses, making an awful noise, but they laughed so well, that we joined in. That's another circumstance I've noticed in more civilised regions. At Gundagai there is an immensely long bridge, and we galloped over it in fine style. The approach to Gundagai, like every other mining town I have ever seen, was distinguished by a marvellous display of rubbish of all sorts, old boots, tin cans of every description, meat cans, milk cans, oil cans, fish cans, fruit cans, old stays, old bonnets, old bats, old stockings, heaps of more cans, strewn for miles. It takes all the romance out of the scene. Gundagai was surrounded by large, middling, and small heaps of pale red sand; the place was full of 'Holes in the ground', empty holes in the ground, as if herds of gigantic fox-terriers had been hunting out their best rabbits. This is the sign of deserted gold-diggings. Can anything be more lonely or more miserable? Nothing. I have seen them in gullies in America, in gullies and plains in Australia, in the heart of the mountains of California, in secret places of the Sierras, in little desert places in Nevada. But they are all alike — miserable, lonely, deserted, except by the wily, patient Chinaman, who goes over again the much gone over ground, 'making a Celestial's fortune out of the white devil's leavings', and disputing with the thin-legged, big-bellied, bearded goats, the abandoned tin cans. Still, at Gundagai there was a nice hotel. We had boiled fowls for dinner, and I left behind something I prized very much, a 5-cent palm leaf fan I had carried all the way from Cincinnati.

We opened at the Opera House, Melbourne, in 'Genevieve de Brabant', and falsified our anticipations by making a big success. We lived at St Kilda, at Mrs. Gardiner's ... The St Kilda residence was a pleasant one — a long low house of one story, built on piles, with a broad passage running down the centre, and ten or twelve rooms opening off on each side. St Kilda is close to and looking over the sea, so close to the sea, in fact, that a man-o'-war practising miles away had sent a big shot through the local pianoforte shop just before we arrived. It was a delightful place, but we seemed to have a good many hot winds there. They always gave me a horrible headache.

At Melbourne we added two operas to our repertoire — 'La Perichole', with the expurgated last act, and 'Girofle-Girofla'. During the rehearsals of 'La Perichole', when Mr. Campbell and I made our first entrance, the carpenter's dog, a fox-terrier, always accompanied us, and, wagging his tail, sat down with much gravity in the centre of the stage, with his back to the footlights, and, at one particular part of my opening song, lifted up his voice and gave a gruesome and most dismal howl. This went on for several mornings, the dog always howling at the same place, always paying the same tribute to my vocalisation. It was very funny and I thought we might utilise it. So for the performance we had a 'Toby' frill made for my appreciator. We went on as the street singers, spread our carpet, tuned our mandolins, and commenced to sing. Directly I began, doggy took up his cue beautifully, howling long and loudly. It was great — terrific applause and encore. Everybody said, 'How clever', 'Who trained the dog?'

Mr. and Mrs. Saurin Lyster [the impresario] made us socially very welcome. We went out to their delightful place at 'Fern Tree Gully', drove in a four-in-hand down a 'corduroy' road constructed at an angle of 45 degrees, had a lovely dinner and a lovely day, crept down the gully and saw the huge fern trees, rode bush ponies over stumps, through and over and under the trees, emulating and nearly sharing the fate of Absalom; saw heaps of cows milked mechanically, and the fine horses sent out to sleep in the paddock instead of in stables. Then in the evening we played halfpenny nap. I lost eleven shillings. Of course; what can one expect, playing cards on a Sunday? We drove home to St Kilda by the light of the moon, and very nearly had an awful spill. But a miss is as good as a mile, they say … We had a good time in Melbourne …

From Emily Soldene, *My Theatrical and Musical Recollections*, London, 1897.

SUNBEAM

Goodbye & Thanks

Lady Anna Brassey

1887

Anna Brassey, who always called herself Annie, was the
wife of the first Earl (Thomas) Brassey (1836–1918),
later the Governor of Victoria. Lady Brassey was a
writer and a wealthy professional empire traveller
whose journeys were in grand style, taking husband,
children, pets and servants in all departments aboard
her fully crewed private yacht. The 531 ton Sunbeam
could be converted from a steam yacht into a sailing
ship as weather and circumstances dictated, making it
one of the most luxurious ocean going yachts of the
time. Lady Brassey spent much time in travel and
wrote, for the benefit of her friends, accounts of many of
her voyages. Her popular books were compiled from her
weekly journal, which she forwarded to her family at
home. She was responsible for the establishment of
several St John Ambulance Association centres in
Australia.

MONDAY, MAY 9TH. At 11 a.m. we lowered the mainsail and raised the funnel. At noon we had run 190 miles and were half a mile to the northward of Eclipse Island. At one o'clock we passed inside Vancouver's Ledge. The coast seemed fine and bold ...

About two o'clock we rounded Bald Head, soon after which the harbour master of King George Sound and a pilot came on board, and were the first to welcome us to Western Australia. Over the lowland on one side we could see a P&O steamer, with the Blue Peter flying. Accordingly we sealed up all our mails and hurried them off, having previously hoisted the signal to ask if they could be received. By four o'clock we were at anchor in King George Sound, which reminded us much of Pictou in Nova Scotia.

Albany is a clean-looking little town, scarcely more than a village, built on the shore of the bay, and containing some 2000 inhabitants. We were soon in the gig, on the way to the P&O steamer *Shannon* to see our old friend Captain Murray. After looking round the familiar decks, and having tea on board, we exchanged good wishes for a fair voyage, and rowed ashore, landing on a long wooden pier.

Carriages are not to be hired in Albany, but we found an obliging carter, who had come to fetch hay from the wharf, and who consented to carry me, instead of a bundle of hay, up to the house of Mr. Loftie, the Government Resident. We have decided to remain a week — in order to give me a chance of recruiting [Lady Brassey was a patron of St John Ambulance]; besides which the *Sunbeam* needs a little painting and touching-up to make her look smart again after all the hard work and buffetings she has gone through.

Most of the party stayed on shore to dinner, for the kitchen range on board the *Sunbeam* has got rather damaged by the knocking about of the last few days. I went back however, in my primitive conveyance as far as the end of the pier, and then returned straight on board, feeling very tired with even so short an expedition. In the course of the afternoon a large sackful of letters and newspapers from England was delivered on board, much to our delight.

TUESDAY, MAY 10TH. A busy morning with letters and telegrams. Dogs are not allowed to land in any part of Australia until they have performed six months quarantine, but I was able to take mine ashore at the Quarantine [Station], which we found without much difficulty with the aid of a chart. A little before one o'clock we landed at the pier, where Mr. Loftie met us, and drove us to the Residency to lunch. It was a great treat to taste fresh bread and butter and cream once more, especially to me, for these are among the few things I am able to eat. After, several ladies and gentlemen came to call on us.

I was sorry to hear that a terrible epidemic of typhoid fever seems to be ravaging this little town. Built as it is on the side of a hill overlooking the sea, and with a deliciously invigorating air always blowing, Albany ought to be the most perfect sanatorium in the world. Later in the afternoon

I went for a drive with Mrs. Loftie all round the place, seeing the church, schools, and new town hall, as well as the best and worst parts of the town. It was no longer a mystery why the place should be unhealthy, for the water-supply seems very bad, although the hills above abound with pure springs. The drainage from stables, farm-buildings, poultry-yards, and various detached houses apparently has been so arranged as to fall into the wells which supply each house. The effect of this fatal mistake can easily be imagined, and it is sad to hear of the valuable young lives that have been cut off in their prime by this terrible illness.

In the course of our drive we passed near an encampment of Aborigines, but did not see any of the people themselves. We also passed several large heaps of whales' bones, collected, in the days when whales were numerous here, by a German, with the intention of burning or grinding them into manure. Formerly this part of the coast used to be a good ground for whalers, and there were always five or six vessels in or out of the harbour all the year round. But the crews, with their usual shortsightedness, not content with killing their prey in the ordinary manner, took to blowing them up with dynamite; the result being that they killed more than they could deal with, and frightened the remainder away.

The [yacht] steward's report on the resources of the place from a marketing point of view is more curious than encouraging. There is no fresh butter nor milk to be had, except through the kindness of a few private individuals. Mutton abounds, but there is very little beef or veal. Good York hams are to be procured from England only. Fruit and vegetables are brought down from Perth or come over from

Adelaide, and the most eatable salt butter is brought from Melbourne …

Tuesday, May 17th. A lovely morning, perfectly calm. Tom much better, and anxious to be off. Mails and farewell messages were accordingly sent on shore, and Mr. Loftie came off with parting words of kindness and farewell, and laden with flowers. Precisely at eleven o'clock, with signals of 'Good-Bye' and 'Thanks' hoisted at the main, we steamed out of the snug harbour where we have passed such a pleasant week and have received so much kindness. The pilot soon quitted us, and we were once more on the broad ocean … There are a good many invalids on board among the crew and servants, the symptoms in each case being very similar. This morning the two maids, two stewards, and three of the men had more or less succumbed to 'malarial colds' — nothing serious, the doctor says, but very uncomfortable. It is quite certain that many more are now laid up than we ever had on the sick-list in the tropics; but the sudden change from heat to cold may of course account for this state of things.

Wednesday, May 18th. Although the air was warm I remained in my cabin all the morning, feeling wretched and uncomfortable. The total distance now accomplished since we left England is 9,236 miles under sail, and 7,982 under steam, making a total of 17,218 miles.

Sunday, May 22nd. The state of things was wretched in the extreme. Sails flapping, the cry of the sailors continually heard above the howling of the wind, and much water on deck. Then I went to sleep, waking again at seven to find it blowing half a gale of wind, which rapidly increased to a whole gale.

We had service at 11.15 and again at four o'clock. In the morning there was no congregation; partly because of the rough weather, and partly because we had sailed so well that nobody realised how much faster the time was to-day than it had been yesterday, and we were therefore all behindhand. In the afternoon I went on deck for a short time, but found it so cold that I could not remain; for, although the wind was right aft, the gale blew fierce and strong. Tom had a very anxious time of it, literally flying along a strange coast, with on one hand the danger of being driven ashore if the weather should become at all thick, and on the other, the risk of getting pooped by the powerful following sea if sail was shortened. At 11 p.m. we met a large sailing-ship steering to the southward; which was felt to be very satisfactory, showing as it did that we were on the right track.

MONDAY, MAY 23RD. Precisely at 7 a.m. we made the lights of Cape Borda or Flinders, on Kangaroo Island, about twelve miles ahead, exactly where Tom expected to find it, which was a great relief to everybody on board, after our two days of discomfort and anxiety. At noon we had run 265 miles, and should have done much more had we not been obliged to shorten sail in the night.

In the afternoon the yacht passed between Kangaroo and Althorpe Islands, the coast of the former being very like the white cliffs between Dover and Folkestone. It was extremely cold, and after my night of neuralgic pains I did not dare to go out on deck, and had to content myself with observing everything through the windows of the deck-house. In the evening we made Troubridge [Point] and all the other lights on the way up to Glenelg, and after some deliberation Tom decided to heave-to for the night, instead of sailing on to the anchorage of Port Adelaide.

TUESDAY, MAY 24TH. By 6 a.m. we were on deck, endeavouring to ascertain our precise position, and about seven, a steam-launch came bustling towards us, whose occupants hailed us with cordial welcomes to South Australia. Directly they came alongside, our small deck-house was crowded with visitors, who presented us in the name of the Holdfast Bay Yacht Club with a beautifully illuminated and kindly worded address. So anxious had they been to give us a warm and early welcome, that they had been on the look-out for us all night while we had been waiting outside so as to arrive by daylight. It seems that the signalmen on Cape Borda had made out our number yesterday when we were more than seven miles off, so clear is the dry air of these regions. Our early guests were naturally hungry and cold; and a large party soon sat down to a hastily prepared breakfast. It was excellently supplemented, however — to us seafarers especially — by a large basket of splendid fruit which our friends had brought off with them. Presently the Mayor of Glenelg and his daughter arrived, full, like everybody else, of kindly plans for our amusement while here …

SATURDAY MAY 28TH. We had several visitors in the early morning, among whom was Brigadier-General Owen, who brought plans for the defences of Adelaide for Tom to examine. Mr. Millar also called to make arrangements about our projected trip to Silverton.

At half-past eleven we proceeded by train to Port Adelaide, where we were received by the Mayor and Corporation, and taken to see the new municipal buildings. Afterwards we had lunch in the town hall; and later on some of the party took a drive round the town and saw the museum, which, though small, is interesting, a large flourmill, and several other buildings. By the 2.50 train we left for Adelaide, and had to dress with unheard-of rapidity in order to be present at the Governor's reception, which was attended by several hundred people. Fortunately it was a lovely day, and we were able to take advantage of the mild spring-like temperature to stroll about the pretty garden and listen to the pleasant strains of the police bands.

SUNDAY, MAY 29TH. This morning we went to the Anglican [St Peter's] cathedral at half-past ten, and heard a most beautiful choral service, including a 'Te Deum' by Gounod. This being Whit Sunday, the interior of the church was prettily decorated. Service over, we drove to the residence of the Chief Justice, where zoology and botany are combined in a small space, for the semi-tropical garden in front of the house is lovely, while in the spacious grounds at the back much care is given to rare and curious pets.

WEDNESDAY, JUNE 1ST. A very agreeable luncheon at the Mayor of Adelaide's house, and afterwards to the town hall, where we received a formal welcome from the Adelaide Town Council. Kind speeches and warm acknowledgements, followed by an organ recital. The instrument superb and admirably played. By 4.45 train to Cockburn to visit the celebrated Broken Hill Silver Mine at Silverton.

THURSDAY, JUNE 2ND. Our special train reached Cockburn at eight o'clock this morning. We breakfasted at the running sheds and were afterwards driven over to Broken Hill, which we reached at two o'clock, and descended the mine both before and after luncheon …

SATURDAY, JUNE 4TH. On the return journey from Silverton to Adelaide I stopped during the early hours of this morning to see my cousin Herbert Woodgate, and thoroughly enjoyed, in spite of sleepiness and fatigue, the sight at his house of so many objects which brought back memories of old days … We were met at the station and carried off to luncheon at Government House, and afterwards had to dress as quickly as possible to go to the meet of the hounds. The day was fine and pleasant, and it was very enjoyable driving down in the Governor's mail-phaeton, and seeing the other vehicles of all sorts and kinds proceeding in the same direction. The drivers of these vehicles were so regardless of all considerations of time, place, and speed, that I began to think hunting on wheels, or even going to a meet on wheels, was far more dangerous than riding across country. I am not sure that I should enjoy my time in Australia so much if I had not a certain belief in kismet; for travelling out here is certainly very full of risk. What with unbroken horses, rickety carts, inexperienced drivers, rotten and ill-made harness put on the wrong way, bad roads, reckless driving, and a general total indifference to the safety of life and limb, a journey is always an exciting, and sometimes a risky, experience. A little excitement is all very well; but when it becomes absolutely dangerous, a little of it goes a long way. I dislike seeing a horse's hoofs quite close to my head, with a trace or two trailing in the dust, or to hear the ominous crack of splinter-bar or bolt; yet these are things of daily and hourly occurrence in our bush drives. I must say I was fully confirmed in my opinion that driving was more dangerous than riding when the hunt commenced. A man in scarlet went first with a little bag of aniseed, and was followed by about 150 people on foot, and as many more either on horseback or in vehicles. The drags were so arranged that many of the jumps could be seen from a ridge near. The clever way in which little horses of all sorts and kinds, well bred and underbred, with all sorts of weights on their backs, jumped high timber fences without touching them, was wonderful to behold. Some of the obstacles were even worse than timber, for they were made of four wires stretched between timber posts with a solid rail on top. The last fence of all, after a twenty minutes run through a fairly heavy country, measured four feet two; and yet not a horse out of the fifty or sixty who jumped it even touched it in the least. I noticed that one or two of the riders were very careless of the hounds, who had to crouch under the fences until the horses had jumped over them. Afterwards I drove with the children to 'The Olives', a pretty house with a lovely garden, full of fragrant violets, where a large party was assembled to meet us at [afternoon] tea …

TUESDAY, JUNE 7TH. … on our way to the [Adelaide] railway station we called in at the Lower House, and heard Mr. Playfair make his speech on the no confidence vote [denouncing government loans] ... two carriages had been reserved for us in the Melbourne Express ... we arrived at Murray Bridge soon after six, and all walked up to a snug hotel. I managed to keep up the fire of mallee roots all night, for it was bitterly cold.

WEDNESDAY, JUNE 8TH. I awoke at two, and as it proved impossible to get to sleep again, I wrote and read until daybreak. At a little before nine we went down to the bank of the river to meet Mr. Macfarlane and his daughters, who had come forty miles down the Murray in their pretty little steam-launch to take us to their station lodge, eight miles from Wellington ... we arrived at the landing pier, where we found one of the capacious trading-boats, of which we had met many on the river. It is a regular pedlar's store on a large scale, where one might buy dresses of the latest fashion, cloaks and bonnets, besides all sorts of medicines for man and beast, groceries, and stores of all kinds. A most useful institution it must be to isolated toilers on the banks of the Murray ... having dined [at Wellington Lodge] we returned to the railway, and took up our quarters in a boudoir-car attached to the express train, timed to arrive in Ballarat at six o'clock in the morning.

BALLARAT: THURSDAY, JUNE 9TH. After an excellent night in a luxurious sleeping-carriage I was called at seven. A little before eight the Mayor of Ballarat and others were announced, and I had to settle with them the programme for the day whilst the others were making their toilettes. At 8.30 we left the station for Craig's Hotel, where we found breakfast prepared in a comfortable room. Tom had parted from us at Port Adelaide on the 23rd instant, and had gone by sea in the *Sunbeam* to Melbourne, which they reached on the 6th, after a quick, but stormy passage.

SUNDAY, JUNE 12TH. The Government House of the colony of Victoria is an enormous building, surrounded by an extensive park, situated on the top of a small hill which commands a fine view over Melbourne and its suburbs. There is a complete suite of private apartments in the house, besides rooms for many guests, and splendid reception, banqueting and ball rooms.

MONDAY, JUNE 13TH. My cold is still bad; and although Tom is also far from well, he went to the town hall this morning to receive a deputation from the Victorian Branch of the Imperial Federation League ...

MONDAY, JUNE 20TH. The day of the grand volunteer review and the beginning of the festivities of the Queens' Jubilee dawned bitterly cold, as indeed one must expect in midwinter. I got leave from the Doctor, with great difficulty, for Tom to go to it in a closed carriage; for he was still suffering much from his eyes. Lady Loch [wife of the Governor, Sir Henry Loch] drove with me to the ground in an open carriage, and of course we had an excellent place close to the saluting-flag, and were able to admire the march past of the troops. They seemed an excellent and well-drilled body of men. The Lancers and the Royal Naval Brigade especially attracted attention. All the party went to the military tournament in the evening except Tom and I, who stayed at home with Lady Loch ...

FRIDAY, JUNE 24TH. Today a demonstration of school-children, said to be the largest gathering of the kind ever held in the colony, took place in the Exhibition building. Twenty thousand children must have been there; and as they each wore a rosette and carried a little flag, the scene looked gay as a summer garden. Of course there were the usual loyal anthems; and besides the cheers in the programme the children did a good deal of happy shouting on their own account. The Lord Bishop of Melbourne [The Rt. Revd. Field Flowers Goe] gave them an excellent address, and all the arrangements were admirable and carefully carried out.

SATURDAY, JUNE 25TH. Awoke early after a fairly good night, and set to work at once on my correspondence which accumulates terribly in spite of my efforts to answer every letter as it arrives. I made many futile attempts to write up my journal, but was interrupted by numerous interviewers, especially by secretaries of charitable societies, anxious to get some share of the proceeds derived from the showing the *Sunbeam*.

Precisely at twelve o'clock we started for the races at Caulfield. The road lay for several miles through prosperous looking suburbs consisting of villas and a multitude of small wooden houses with corrugated iron verandahs and roofs. However convenient this material may be for such purposes, it does not add to the beauty of the landscape. Bungalows in India, and indeed all over the East, look picturesque and pretty, with their deep wooden verandahs, which must surely be much cooler than these corrugated iron houses, said to be hot in summer and cold in winter.

We arrived at the racecourse at about a quarter to one. The heavy rain of last night had swamped the place, and though luckily the course was not flooded, it was very heavy going, and a great deal of the ground close to the course seemed quite under water. I heard a story of a lady having to swim her horse over a field during this morning's run! It was bitterly cold, and we all felt glad of the excitement caused by the appearance of the jockeys, mounted on nice-looking horses. I fixed my mind on horse number twelve on the card, and thought he looked extremely well as he cantered past the stand. The poor animal kept up bravely till near the end, when he caught his foot in a hurdle, while going at a pace, and fell, breaking his off-leg so badly he had to be shot on the spot … his jockey escaped with only a severe shaking. I had no idea until I came here what steeplechase riding was like in Australia. Today, just before the first race came off, an ambulance-carriage was driven into the centre of the ground and took up a central position so as to be able to quickly reach any part of the course. I was assured that it was not at all unusual for two or three jockeys to be injured in one race. Another significant and permanent adjunct of the Caulfield racecourse is the neat little hospital, provided with every possible medical and surgical appliance for remedying injuries to the human frame. There are eight beds in the hospital, and I was told that they had at times been all filled with serious cases.

It is not wonderful that these dreadful accidents happen, for some of the fences are truly fearful, consisting of a big tree cut into four or five pieces, nailed firmly one on top of the other to a height of four feet six inches. The arrangement precludes all possibility of the fence yielding if the horse touches it … The accidents, which are nearly as frequent and as bad in the flat races, occur generally from the tremendous number of starters. Today there were thirty-two in one race and forty-seven in another, and some of the worst casualties were caused by one horse falling and others stumbling over him …

THURSDAY, JUNE 30TH. We lunched at Government House. After bidding goodbye to H.E. and Lady Loch, from whom we have received so much kindness, we went to Menzie's Hotel, calling on our way at Cole's Book Arcade, which is one of the sights of Melbourne. A most curious place it is; consisting of a large arcade three stories high, about the length of the Burlington Arcade in London, though perhaps rather wider. The whole place from top to bottom is one mass of books, arranged in different styles, some according to price and some according to subject. It was crowded with intending purchasers, as well as with readers who apparently had not the slightest intention of purchasing, and who had only gone there to while a leisure hour, and to listen to the band, which discoursed sweet music to them whilst they read.

After strolling through this wonderful arcade, we collected the luggage from the hotel and sent it off to the station, following ourselves in time to catch the 4.55 train to Seymour.

FRIDAY, JULY 1ST. We left by the 9.30 train for Shepparton, in pouring rain, passing through a flat rich grazing country, which seemed well stocked with sheep. The grass looked luxuriant, and must be excellent for dairy produce. The fences were different from any we had seen before, made of felled trees laid lengthwise all round the paddocks. As may easily be imagined, they form a formidable obstacle for young horses, many of which were running in the paddocks. All this was interesting, but the beauties of the distant landscape were quite blotted out by the rain and mist. However, when we crossed the Goulburn, the sun began to try and peep through the clouds, which had hitherto hidden everything from our view. Shepparton is a rapidly growing township with 2000 inhabitants. A few years ago there was not a single house in the place.

Shepparton, like all Australian settlements, is arranged in square blocks, the houses consisting chiefly of four-or-six roomed cottages of one story, built of wood or corrugated iron. At present the whole place appears to be under water, but its habitants say that in summer it is beautiful, and the pastures certainly look excellent … we left by the 4.30 train for Seymour, reached at 6.30, just in time to change into the express, and at Albury we were again transferred, at 10.30 p.m., into Lord Carrington's [Governor of New South Wales] carriage, sent up from Sydney for us.

SATURDAY, JULY 2ND … Our train was late, and all were glad when Sydney was at last reached we found ourselves driving swiftly to Government House. The way lay through crowded streets resembling the Hammersmith Road beyond Kensington [London].

FRIDAY, JULY 15TH. An early start had to be made this morning in order to meet Sir Henry Parkes [Premier of New South Wales] at the station at nine o'clock. Tom, Baby, and I were the only members of the party who turned up, and we found that Mr. [Sir Julian] Salomons and the [visiting] Chinese Commissioners had been invited to accompany us. Precisely at nine we left the station in a comfortable saloon carriage, and, passing through the suburbs of Sydney, reached Parramatta at 9.30. This is one of the oldest townships in New South Wales ...

After passing Sir Alfred Stephen's magnificent place we reached Falconbridge, and by this time I felt so tired that I was truly glad of my carrying-chair. I do not think I could have walked even the short distance between the station and the house. Arrived there, I was obliged to ask leave to lie down instead of going to see the beautiful fern-glens with the rest of the party. It was a great disappointment. I was able, however, to enjoy the lovely distant view from the verandah as well as the closer view of the rocky sandstone cliffs and fern-clad gullies; and I could hear the mocking note of the rarely seen lyre-bird, the curious cachinnation of the laughing jackass, and the occasional distant note of the bell-bird. Even this brief rest amidst these pleasant surroundings refreshed me greatly, and I felt much better when later on we resumed our journey. The engine driver was told to go slowly round the sharp curves, and we were spared a repetition of the unpleasant experience of the morning. [Lady Brassey had complained the train was travelling too fast.] ... We arrived in Sydney a little after six, feeling much indebted to Sir Henry Parkes for his great kindliness ...

SATURDAY, JULY 16TH. I awoke feeling so tired that the doctor made me remain in bed till the middle of the day in order to keep quiet, though I contrived to get through much work with pen and pencil. Lunch was ordered early, and a little after two we went on board the yacht to receive the ladies of the Woollahra centre of the St. John Ambulance Association, to whom, according to previous arrangements, I presented certificates.

MONDAY, JULY 18TH. Went off to the *Sunbeam*, feeling quite sad that the moment of departure had at last arrived. The Admiral came on board at the last moment, bringing some violets as a farewell offering. Sailed slowly away, and gradually lost sight of the Heads in the darkness.

TUESDAY, JULY 19TH. At half-past twelve Tom came below to announce our arrival off the port of Newcastle. The wind had been so fresh and fair that we made a smart run of seven hours, sighting the lights at Nobby Head at about half-past ten. Our head was then put off the land, and we hove to, to wait for the tug. This is a process which to the old salt seems a pleasure nearly equal to that of going ashore, at all events to dropping anchor in a well-sheltered harbour. Though I certainly cannot call myself an inexperienced sailor, it appears to me to be the acme of discomfort. Even in a heavy gale it affords but slight relief from the storm-tossed motion of the ship. On the present occasion it was a change from pleasantly gliding along through the water at a speed of nine or ten knots an hour to a nasty pitching motion which made us all very wretched. Everything began to roll and tumble about in a most tiresome manner; doors commenced to bang, glasses to smash, books to tumble out of their shelves, and there was a general upset of the usually peaceful equilibrium of the yacht. So unpleasant was this, that I suggested to Tom that, instead of waiting outside for the reception tug, we should get up steam, and go into harbour at daylight so as to have a few hours rest. This we did, and glided into the harbour precisely at 5.30 a.m., anchoring just off the railway-pier, and quite taking the good people of Newcastle by surprise. The town presented a great contrast to its namesake at home, for the morning dawned bright and lovely, with hardly a smoke-wreath to intercept the charming view. We looked out on a noble river with a busy town on its banks and low hills in the background ...

All mines bear a greater or less resemblance to each other, whether they contain black diamonds, like the one in which we found ourselves, white diamonds, gold, silver, tin, copper, gypsum, or any other mineral. There is the same descent in a cage, the same walk through workings — higher or lower, as the case may be — or ride in a trolley or truck along lightly-laid rails, and the same universal darkness, griminess, and sloppiness about the whole affair, which render a visit, however interesting, somewhat of an undertaking. This mine seemed to contain a particularly good quality of coal, and the sides shone and glistened in the lamplight as we passed along them. Our walk through the levels of Pit 'B' was much longer than I had expected, and must have been quite half a mile. The temperature was always over 80°, the atmosphere sometimes very bad, and the walking rather uneven. Thousands, not to say millions, of cockroaches of portentous size enlivened if they did not add to the pleasure of the walk. We passed a great many horses, in good condition, going back to their stables for the night.

They are, it is said, very happy down in the pit; so much so, that when, during the Jubilee, they were taken up for three days holiday, there was the greatest difficulty in preventing them from returning to the pit's mouth, at which men had to be stationed to drive them back for fear they might try to put themselves into the cages and so tumble down the shaft. Horses very quickly adapt themselves to circumstances; and I dare say the garish light of day was painful to their eyes, and that they were anxious to return from the cold on the surface of the ground to the even temperature of 80 degrees in the pit.

Our walk was a long and weary one, and I felt thankful when we approached the pit's mouth and could breathe cooler and purer air. Our hosts were anxious that I should go a little further; but I could not do so, and sank down into a chair to rest. The others went on, as I thought, to see some other workings; but I afterwards heard that they soon reached a beautiful room hollowed out of the solid coal, with sides like ebony, and sparkling with black diamonds. The walls were decorated with arches and cleverly arranged geometrical patterns, formed of the fronds of various kinds of Adiantum [fern], an inscription with cordial words of welcome being traced in the same delicate greenery. In the centre stood a table with light refreshments of various kinds. The entertainment afforded the opportunity for speeches, in which the rapid development of the mining industry of this district was detailed in telling figures, and mutual sentiments of kindness were most cordially conveyed. At the pit's mouth crowds of women and children had assembled to see us, and a little further off a train was drawn up, filled by ladies and gentlemen who had preferred to wander about park-like glades, while their more energetic friends had made the descent into the coal-mine. The united party — numbering, I should think, nearly one hundred — next proceeded on board the *Sunbeam* for a very late five-o'clock tea and a hasty inspection of the vessel. At an early hour I retired to rest, utterly worn out

WEDNESDAY, JULY 20TH. Contrary to my usual habit of awaking between four and five o'clock, I was sound asleep when tea was brought at 5 a.m.; and I should dearly have liked to have slept for two or three hours longer, so completely was I exhausted by yesterday's hard work. But it could not be; and after a cup of tea, and a little chat over future plans, I set to work sorting papers, and putting names in books, to be given to our kind hosts of yesterday, in remembrance of our visit. At 7. 15 a.m. entered the boat which was waiting alongside, and proceeded to the shore, Tom, as usual, pulling an oar. Poor 'Sir Roger' [pet dog], who has been explosively happy during the past two days at having us on board again, made a desperate effort to stow himself away in the boat, which, unhappily, could not be allowed on account of the quarantine regulations. It seems very hard that the poor doggies can never have a run on shore whilst we are in Australian waters. Their only chance of change and exercise consists in being sent in a boat to some quarantine island for an hour or two.

The train started punctually at the time fixed, and passed through a dull but fertile-looking country, until we reached West Maitland, where I received a charming present of a basket of fragrant flowers. About twelve o'clock we were glad to have some lunch in the train. From Tamworth the country becomes prettier and the scenery more mountainous. At one station there was quite a typical colonial landscape: park-like ground heavily wooded with big gum trees, and a winding river with a little weir, where one felt it might be quite possible to catch trout. The country continued to improve in beauty, and we saw on all sides evidences of its excellence from a squatter's point of view. At one place a herd of splendid cattle were being driven along the road by a stockman, and we passed many large flocks of sheep. About eight, Armadale was reached.

The line from Armadale to Tenterfield is the highest in Australia, and is considered a good piece of engineering work. It is in that respect a great contrast to the line over the Blue Mountains, where the engineers had a comparatively easy task in following the tracks of the old bullock-road.

THURSDAY, JULY 21ST. The train reached Tenterfield about one o'clock this morning and we drove straight to the Commercial Hotel, where we found comfortable rooms and blazing fires. Everything looked clean and tidy, and a cold supper awaited belated travellers, of whom there were many besides ourselves. I was awakened at 7.30 a.m. by the sun shining gloriously through the windows of my room. The air felt delightfully fresh, reminding one of a lovely spring morning in England about April.

FRIDAY, JULY 22ND … at Wallangarra Station we left the train and stepped through the rail fence which divides New South Wales from Queensland. A walk of about two hundred yards brought us to the Queensland train, where we found a comfortable carriage prepared for our reception … I caught a severe cold on my arrival at Brisbane, and have been in bed for several days …

WEDNESDAY, JULY 27TH. We all rose early and started by the 9.30 train, with the Governor, Sir Samuel Griffith, the Mayor, and a large party, for the first Agricultural Show ever held at Marburg. The train ran through pretty country for about an hour, to Ipswich, an important town, near which there is a breeding establishment for first-class horses. On reaching the station we were received by a number of school children, who sang 'God save the Queen' and then presented us each with a lovely bouquet. After some little discussion over arrangements we were packed into various carriages and started off, the Governor's carriage of course leading the way. The horses of our carriage appeared somewhat erratic from the first, and soon we were nearly brought to a standstill against the trunk of a large tree. Fortunately the eucalyptus has so soft a bark that it tore off, and we did not break anything. We shaved the next big tree in our road by a hair's breadth, and then discovered that the reins were coupled in an extraordinary manner. Having rectified this mistake, we proceeded on our way rejoicing; but again we were on the point of colliding with a monarch of the forest, when one of our own sailors, who was on the box of the carriage, seized the reins and pulled the horses round. Tom remarked that it was rather stupid driving. The man who was driving (a German) said, 'Not at all, sir: the horses have never been in harness before.' When the other carriages came up we changed into a less pretentious vehicle, drawn by quieter horses …

The Show was duly opened by the Governor, and we waited to see some of the animals tried. Luncheon was served in a sort of half-house, half-tent, and some very good short speeches were made. We drove back by another road to Rosewood in order to enable us to see more of the scenery of this fine country. But our adventures were not over for the day. In going down a steep hill our driver did not allow quite enough room, and caught the back of one of the long low German waggons which are used in this district. The hind wheels came off, and a woman and child who were seated in the waggon were thrown into the road shrieking and screaming. Fortunately they proved to be more frightened than hurt, and the waggon having been repaired and the child and its mother comforted with pictures and sugar-plums which I happened to have with me, they went their way, and we reached the station a few minutes late, but picked up time before getting back to Brisbane.

FRIDAY, JULY 29TH. We were to have embarked in the *Sunbeam* today, with a fair fresh breeze; but there was a considerable roll, and having been on shore so long, we more or less felt the motion. During the night the question of stopping at Maryborough was definitely settled, and we sailed outside Sandy or Fraser Island instead of inside it. This prevented us from accepting the kind and hospitable invitation of the Mayor and inhabitants of the township. At noon we had run 204 knots, and were able to shape our course more towards land, the water becoming smoother with every knot we made. We saw Elliott Island, where if it had been calm it would have been very nice to stop. It swarms with turtle and seabirds of every kind, which are reported to be perfectly tame as the island is seldom visited. Cape Bustard was made later on, and we had a quieter evening; but about 10 p.m. the yacht began to roll again heavily, the wind having shifted a little, obliging us to alter our course.

Saturday, July 30th. At 5 a.m. we dropped anchor in Keppel Bay, but had to wait for the tide to rise. We landed in the course of the morning in the 'Gleam', the 'Flash', and the 'Mote' [the yacht's own boats] and made quite a large party, with dogs, monkey [pet], and photographic apparatus. We found a convenient little landing-place and looked over the telegraph station and post office, which are mainly managed by the wife of the signalman, Aird, an honest Scotchman, who knew me from my books, and was very anxious to give us a real hearty welcome to his comfortable little house. The first thing he offered us each was a tumbler of delicious frothy milk, the greatest possible treat. After sending off a telegram or two, and posting some letters, I was carried up to the lighthouse where the customs house officer lives, and from which there is a fine view over land and sea. When the tide rose we returned on board, and about half-past two all inhabitants of the station came onboard to see the yacht of which they had read and heard so much, and which they were glad to see, as they said, 'with their own eyes'. At half-past three our visitors returned ashore, and we had to start up the river. A little higher up, the harbour master of Rockhampton met us, bringing telegrams from various people in that town as well as Brisbane, all sent with the object of making our visit pleasant. We arrived at Rockhampton at 9.30 p.m. The cold I caught at the last Ambulance meeting has been gradually increasing, and became so bad today I was obliged to go to bed early and take some strong measures to try and stop it ...

MONDAY, AUGUST 1ST. A busy morning, as usual, before starting. We left at 10 a.m. in three waggonettes (or four-wheel buggies, as they are called here) for Mount Morgan, each vehicle being drawn by four horses. Our party occupied two of the waggonettes, and the sailors and luggage filled the third. After passing through the clean and tidy town of Rockhampton, the streets of which, though wide, cannot be called picturesque, we entered on a long stretch of road. I never saw anything so gorgeous as the Thunbergia venusta and Bougainvillea now in full bloom, which hid most of the verandahs with a perfect curtain of rich orange and glorious purple. The hospital is a fine building on the top of the hill; the grammar-school and several other good-sized public buildings give the whole place a well-to-do air. We crossed a bridge spanning an arm of a lagoon covered with a curious little red weed, out of which rose a splendid lotus lily, known as the Rockhampton Lily. The blossoms are blue, red, and white, and rear their graceful heads above the water in a conspicuous manner, growing sometimes as large as a breakfast-saucer. It was a beautiful morning, and had I not felt unwell with bronchitis, from which I have so long been suffering, I should have enjoyed the drive immensely. About seven miles out we came to a large poultry farm, but I am afraid the venture had not proved successful, for the farm looked neglected. Quite a little crowd had assembled in the verandahs of the inn and adjoining store, and the people had hoisted a Union Jack in our honour.

About half-way up the hill we were glad to pull up at a creek to water the horses and sit in the shade. This was just before reaching the 'Crocodile' inn, where several coaches were waiting to change horses. Soon afterwards we passed several mines, or rather reefs, with queer names, such as the 'Hit or Miss', the 'Chandler', and the 'Hopeless', arriving in due time at the Razor-Back Hill. It is indeed well named; for, steep as we had found the little pitches hitherto, this ascent was much more abrupt, and might well be likened to the side of a house. Everybody was turned out of the carriages except me, and even with the lightest buggies and four good strong horses, it seemed as if the leaders must tumble back into the carriage, so perpendicular was the ascent in some places. On one side of the road a deep precipice fell away, and when we passed a cart or met a heavily laden dray coming down from the mines we seemed to go dangerously near the side. Altogether, the drive would not have been a pleasant one for nervous people. Bad and steep as the present road is, however, it cuts off a great piece of the hill, and is quite a Queen's Highway compared to the old road. Having at last reached the summit of the hill and breathed our panting horses, we went on through a park-like country, more or less enclosed, which led to the Mount Morgan territory.

Here the most conspicuous building is the hotel, erected by the company for the convenience of the many visitors to the works. Although not yet finished, it is quite a pretty house, and will accommodate a large number of guests. It stands close to a dam across the mountain stream which flows through the valley, and has for a foreground a refreshing lake and bathing-place, formed by the arrested waters. We did not stop here, but crossed the creek and went up to the company's office, where we were warmly welcomed by the practical manager of the mines, Mr. Wesley Hall. The sun was now intensely hot, and it was quite a relief to retire into the shade. I felt very tired; but as they had kindly harnessed two fresh draught horses into the buggy on purpose to take me to the top of the hill, I considered myself bound to go; and off we started, passing enormous stacks of stone taken from the top of the mountain.

The township of Mount Morgan nestles in a pretty valley, and is enclosed by round-topped hills, which are covered with trees. A mile or two further we reached the foot of the steepest hill of all, where the rest of the party found trucks waiting for them, worked by an endless rope, going up and down. Into one of these they soon packed themselves, and were speedily drawn to the top of the hill, while we climbed slowly, and indeed painfully, up by a pretty country road, eventually arriving at the shoot, at the bottom of which three drays were standing. Into these, lumps of stone were being run as fast as possible, and when filled they were taken down to the works, to be quickly replaced by empty return drays. The stone looked exactly like old ironstone, but we were told that it was the richest native gold yet found ... the blacksmith's forge stood a little further on, and then we came to a very narrow woodland path, up which Tom and the sailors carried me in turns, as far as another platform on the hill.

... [We] returned slowly to the hotel, which we found clean and comfortable. While I was lying on the sofa, waiting for the others to arrive, a regular 'smash-up' took place outside. Five horses yoked in a timber-waggon (two and two abreast and one leading) were going down a steep bank into the creek below, when the timber suddenly lifted and came on the backs of the wheelers [horses nearest the front wheels]. The animals began kicking violently, getting their legs among the timber; it was extremely difficult to extricate them even with the help of a dozen powerful and willing hands, though everyone near ran to the assistance of the bewildered teamster, who seemed quite unable to cope with the emergency.

Presently an old man — a most picturesque individual — passed slowly by, surrounded by quite a pack of hounds, including lurchers, retrievers, and even curs, as well as some very good-looking, well-bred greyhounds and kangaroo-hounds. On inquiry I found that his business was to patrol the place all night, and prevent intruders coming to take away samples of Mount Morgan ore. The dogs are said to know their business thoroughly, and contrive to be a terror to the neighbourhood without seriously hurting anybody.

Australian up-country hotels are certainly not meant for rest. They are always either built of corrugated iron, which conveys every sound, or of wood, which is equally resonant. As a rule the partitions of the rooms do not reach to the top of the roof, so that the least noise can be heard from end to end of the building. There is always a door at one extremity, sometimes at both, besides a wide verandah, up and down which people stroll or lounge at pleasure. Every landlady appears to have half-a-dozen small children, who add their contribution to the day's noises in the shape of cries and shouts for 'mammy', who, poor soul, is far too busy to attend to them herself or to spare anyone else to do so.

TUESDAY, 2ND AUGUST. The day turned out lovely, and if my cough had not been so bad, I should have enjoyed the drive down from Mount Morgan. The pitches were just as steep, but they were nearly all downhill, which made our progress seem quicker and pleasanter. The country looked very pretty; the ferns were quite lovely, and the lilies in full bloom. The pleasure of the drive was further marred by the dreadful odours arising from the decaying carcasses of unfortunate bullocks which had been left by the roadside to die from exhaustion. Happily, there were no such horrors at the pretty place where we paused to bait our horses — the same at which we had stopped going up yesterday — and arrived at the railway hotel at Rockhampton at 2.5, and immediately went on board the *Sunbeam*.

WEDNESDAY, AUGUST 3RD. There was still a bright moon, and as we approached Emerald the country, seen by its light, looked most picturesque. At Emerald, the rail to Springsure branches off from the main line to Barcaldine. In the early morning, as we were passing Fernlee, where the Government line ends, our servants produced some welcome tea. From there we ran on to Springsure, where our arrival caused great excitement, for it was really the opening of the line, ours being the first passenger train to arrive at the township. By about half-past eight we were all dressed, and went to a comfortable inn, some on foot and some in waggonettes, where we breakfasted.

After watching experiments with various horses, to see which were best and quietest, we started in a couple of buggies for the opal-mines, or rather opal-fields, of Springsure. We had not driven far when we came to a fence right across the high road, and had to go some way round over rough ground and across a creek to avoid it. This did not excite any astonishment in the mind of the gentleman who drove us, and he seemed to think it was a casual alteration owing to the new line; but on a dark night the unexpected obstruction might prove inconvenient. When the top of the hill where the opals are to be found was reached, we all got out and set to work to pick up large and heavy stones with traces of opals in them, as well as some fragments of pumice, stone with the same glittering indications ... our search not proving very successful, we proceeded to the large sheep-station of Rainworth ...

THURSDAY, AUGUST 4TH ... we reached Rockhampton about 6 a.m., and were put into a quiet siding till eight, by which time we had dressed and were ready to go and breakfast at the comfortable railway hotel. There was just time for a satisfactory talk about arrangements for future movements before eleven o'clock, when the Mayor arrived to take us, in quite a procession of buggies, to the hospital. Here Doctor Macdonald met us, and I was put into a chair and carried through the various wards of an excellently planned and perfectly ventilated building. Everything looked scrupulously clean, and the patients appeared happy and well cared for. Several instances were pointed out to me by Doctor Macdonald in which the St. John Ambulance would have been of great use. I heard of one case of a man who had come down 200 miles with a broken leg, no attempt having been made to bandage it up. The poor fellow arrived, as may easily be imagined, with the edges of the bone all ground to powder and the tissues surrounding it much destroyed. Then there was another case of an arm broken in the bush, and the poor man lying all night in great agony; and again of another stockman who crushed his knee against a tree while riding an unbroken horse. The instances are too numerous to mention where the knowledge of how to make the best of the available means of relief and transport would have saved much needless suffering. There were some good rooms for convalescent patients, besides paying wards.

Everything looked bright, cheerful, and sunny except the ophthalmic wards, which, if I may use such an expression, displayed an agreeable gloom. Here, all was painted dark green, and the system of ventilation seemed quite perfect, for air without light was admitted and the temperature equalised, this being an important factor in bad cases. Ophthalmia appears to be quite a curse in Australia, as we have already found to our cost, through Tom's suffering from it. There were nice shady verandahs to this part of the hospital, and comfortable chairs for the patients to sit and lounge in, besides a pretty garden. Not far off, in the compound, stood the various quarters for the nurses and servants, and the dead-house, and dissecting-room, with other necessary though painful adjuncts to a hospital. The doctor's cheerful bungalow, also near, was surrounded by a pretty garden …

The sun became very hot, and I was glad to be carried back to the carriage and to drive straight to the boat, and so on board the yacht to rest, while the remainder of the party went shopping in the town. In the afternoon we all went in the steam-launch to see the Creek Meat Canning Factory — a concern which has lately changed hands, and holds some of the largest contracts in the world for supplying armies and navies with tinned meat. The quality is excellent. Mr. Bertram, the manager, met us at the pier, at which we had considerable difficulty in landing, for the tide was low. After a little time and trouble we managed to reach the shore, and went through the works, which are most interesting. The manufactory stands on the bank of the river close to a pretty lake embosomed amongst hills, and surrounded with paddocks, where the cattle rest after being driven in from distant stations.

We were all safe on board the yacht by 9 p.m., and at ten o'clock the anchor was weighed. The night was fine, and we only stopped at intervals to allow the pilot to reconnoitre, or to wait for a rise of tide. This is a most curious river, and might well be made the scene of a romance by some poetical person. It is only every ten or twelve days that craft drawing over ten feet can get up or down the river, and then only by the light of the moon. By day no large vessel can reach Rockhampton.

FRIDAY, AUGUST 5TH. At 1.30 a.m. we anchored off Johnson Point, and at 8 o'clock we hove anchor and proceeded to the mouth of the Fitzroy River. The pilot left us at 10.30, and we proceeded out to sea under sail ...

[Lady Brassey, now very ill, continued her cruise off the Queensland coast. She died on 14 September on board her yacht and was buried at sea at sunset.]

From Lady Anna Brassey & edited by Lady M.A. Broome, *The Last Voyage to India, and Australia in the* Sunbeam, London, 1889.

Martha

1887–1890

*Very little is known of this cheerful and independent
English domestic servant, who at eighteen years and quite
alone went out to Australia and managed to 'drop in' to
three very good jobs in some of the grandest houses in
Australia. On her return home to England to meet up with
her sailor brother, she eventually found a happy position
with a lady novelist [unknown] who lived next door to a
professor with whom she had been first employed. When he
moved away Martha became the novelist's cook.*

*The novelist, much intrigued by her, later wrote 'Martha
appeared in the Professor's garden next door. Her
comfortable figure, clad in pale blue, a white apron tied
about her middle, ambled down the path. It was my first
glimpse. From the upper window I watched her leisurely
progress. Noting the ease and propriety of her bearing, the
silver hair, brushed and screwed into a tight knot at the back
of her head, her comical profile, blunt nose and upturned
lips, I murmured: 'The Cook. That must be their cook.'*

*'... I rejoiced in Martha's gift of narrative. We sat
together as she polished silver, pewter and brass, her tongue
kept pace with her leather ... she had lived with writing*

ladies before ... 'I've often thought I'd like to write my life, ma'am, just for the fun of things, only I shouldn't know how to begin ...' Then the root I planted sprouted and the first instalment of her Memoirs appeared ... the publisher, to whom a few pages of the original memoirs had been shown, will keep our secret ... her name is neither Mary or Martha, for she insists on the strictest anonymity ... some of the manuscript, save for spelling and punctuation, is given verbatim, though much has been filled out and elucidated in the course of conversation ...'

O N Sunday evening I sat at the kitchen table reading *Lloyd's Weekly*, and I saw an advertisement: 'Free Emigration. Wanted for Australia, Young Men and Women. Must be over eighteen.' That did it. A free passage and only a pound to pay for kit. My mind was made up. What a stir it would make if I got the chance to go! It would never do to let any of them know till it was settled. The paper told me where to apply. In a few days a form came which had to be signed by a doctor, a clergyman, and my employer [Mrs. G]. I knew the missus would have been down on me like a ton of bricks, so I went to her husband. 'Oh, well, I don't see why you shouldn't get on,' he said, and signed the paper. The doctor was equally obliging. He examined me and signed too, and so did the curate at the Parish Church.

My next step was to gather a stock of clothes together. My wages were only twelve pounds a year and I'd been helping my brother. I still love him and look forward to meeting him again. He is now in the navy, which made me keener to get abroad, too.

Word came that I was accepted and was to sail in the S.S. *Roma*, leaving 12th December 1886. Everyone was horrified. Anyhow, I was determined to go. I told them I would be back in three years, and got laughed at for my pains. A year in Queensland was compulsory, but I meant to have one in New South Wales and one in Victoria and I stuck to that scheme, bar coming back a few months late on account of the weather.

Mrs. G. was far too angry to laugh. She sent me a rug, and said I was most ungrateful. When I went to bid them all goodbye at the big house, she gave me a letter for Canon Glennie in Brisbane, and asked me how much money I had.

'A pound, ma'am. Thank you very much for the rug.' 'Don't be silly, child, a pound won't move you from the wharf.' With that she gave me five shillings and a jawing, so I left her money on the hall table.

The day I went aboard was bitter cold. A drizzling rain made everywhere and everybody look very miserable, and the decks were dirty. Ropes, luggage and bundles, women and children crying, men trying to joke with one another. 'Gangway, please.' I moved hastily on one side to allow a man with a load of luggage to pass. He looked at me kindly, so I showed him my slip of paper and asked him where to go. He pointed to an officer standing by who exchanged my slip for another. Berth 47, Mess 19. I stared at the unfamiliar words. Berth? Mess? 'Pass on, please. Pass on.'

He bundled me downstairs. At the bottom, I was handed two blue blankets, one pair of unbleached sheets, two towels, one pillow slip, a large bar of soap, like lard, and again told to pass on. I stared helplessly round. I had my waterproof and umbrella and a very heavy box from Mrs. G. labelled: 'Not to be opened till Christmas Day.' My arms were aching, but I wouldn't let it out of my sight, and I and my belongings were getting trodden on. Luckily, the sailor

I'd spoken to above saw me and came to the rescue. He gathered up my goods and bid me follow him, which I thankfully did. I found myself in a huge compartment, the entire width of the boat and the length of a very long schoolroom. It was all partitioned into numbered sections. We got to Mess 19, and I found Berth 47 was the top one at the end of that block and nearest the port, so I had struck lucky ...

I took my tin hat box and returned to No. 19 where I was met by a tall middle-aged woman, a very good sort, called Susan Black, who told me she was taking charge of our party for the voyage. She showed me how to make my bed and how to stow all my luggage to the best advantage. One by one my mess-mates turned up, till we had got our number, twelve in all. Susan said she'd been told we should be classified, and the best put together. The roughs, and a rough lot they were, were all down nearer the companion. They fought like the dickens. Lowest kind of Irish women, and their language was something to remember, or, better still, forget. The matron was often sent for to separate them.

Our berths were in blocks of sixteen, four in a row, eight at the bottom, eight at the top. Our table ran along at the head; when let down, two pegs were put in like the blackboard at school. We were three decks down and the place was lit by swaying, smelly oil lamps. I wondered how I was going to stand nine weeks of it. The bunks were just a couple of iron laths and a ticking stuffed with what might have been seaweed. I slept like a top that night, and woke to the sound of a crowing cock. Where was I? I felt as if I were going in all directions. I sat up and lay down again, but I was determined to see what the day was like.

I tumbled into my clothes and went up on to the lower deck. It looked horrid. Pouring rain, just off the Scilly Isles, in what sailors call a dirty, choppy sea. We ploughed along through great troughs of water, and the waves looked as if they must swamp us, but I found they always broke up and we rode on. I hung on for a little while and ran a few steps at a time to my berth, thankful to get back to bed.

When we were in the Bay of Biscay, a passing steamer told us that a big emigrant vessel had foundered with all souls aboard about twelve miles ahead. Years after, I learned my friends and relatives made up their minds I was lost. Of course, it was just what they'd expected. Fortunately for us the storm was over. The swell was bad enough ...

We reached Malta on Christmas Day, but were not allowed to land. It looked a lovely place, with the streets all in layers on top of each other. We had roast meat and plum duff for dinner. I kept my box till the evening. That box was just like Mrs. G. Along with presents from every one were a plum cake, a plum pudding, jam, marmalade, German sausage, bon-bons, a packet of lemonade, dates, oranges, apples, nuts of all sorts, in every corner, and on to that a curt note with the two half crowns I had left on the hall table, saying I might be thankful for them yet. It was rude of me to leave that money, and I felt a little guilty, but I vowed to make no use of it. However, I decided to write and thank them all.

We left Malta and Mess 19 had a jolly evening. We were considered rather a cocky lot, keeping ourselves to ourselves. We palled in with two young married women and four sisters, and I don't suppose I spoke to half a dozen others all the way out. There were hundreds of women aboard, and I'm told a great many of them went on the streets later.

The boat only carried first class and us emigrants. The first class had their lower deck to themselves, and we had the other side. We shared the upper deck. Seats ran down the centre so we could see what went on on their side, and they our side. All sorts of games and sports, concerts, theatricals, minstrels, waxworks, kept us amused. We single girls were the best off of any on board, given better accommodation and better food than the married women and children — why, I don't know.

We came to Port Said, a very dirty hole, and just as we left and started up the Canal a baby died. A few hours after, a party went ashore and buried it in the sand. We never stopped, and they caught us up quite easily. I cried my eyes out to think of the little thing left to the mercy of stray dogs or birds of prey ...

Now, I must tell you, they gave us a pint of tea each for tea and breakfast, and a fair sized jug of water for the mess. As I never took tea, it meant I was short of water for the day. I told my quartermaster, so he brought me nearly a pint of water daily, and often slipped an apple or orange into my hand ... We always had pork on Fridays, and, if you're acquainted with ship's pork, you'll understand how I hated it. I used to slip up and eat my plum duff on deck, as I couldn't stand the smell of their pork ...

We reached Batavia, a queer little place it looked. We had to stand out as there was fever on shore. No one was allowed to land. The signals were all done with coloured lights and flags. We left during the night, and the ship settled down to the usual fire alarms and boat drills that kept us on the run.

We steamed on. We passed a smoking volcano; there were no flames, which was disappointing. I was always fond of colour. We all used to assemble to see the ship muster on Sunday mornings, when our friends appeared in their best snow white trousers. The lascars wore every colour of the rainbow: beautiful little sleeveless waistcoats, zouaves, braided in gold or silver, and some had little pill-box hats instead of their turbans. We all went to the first saloon for a Church of England service, there was a service for children in the afternoon, and anybody spoke at night.

We passed Thursday Island. I would have liked to land and stop there, but was not allowed, though several men came to the ship and asked for women 'house keepers', and a number of girls took the job, so I didn't see why they stopped me. We were now getting into Australian waters, and a lot of passengers were going off from the married quarters. The firing of a gun announced our arrival at Cooktown, then came Townsville, Rockhampton, Maryborough, etc., and six o'clock one evening in February saw us at the head of the Brisbane.

We were met by the news that the best part of Brisbane was under water and we saw a bungalow afloat upside down, a dog kennel with a kitten crying on top, a little dead baby under a bit of butter muslin, rabbits galore. It made us all feel a bit down. We got in about nine and landed in a great shed. There were seaweed beds stacked up against the wall ... One by one our passengers were collected by their friends. I was feeling lonesome. I found we all had to pig in together, men, women and children — anywhere, anyhow.

'Have you got any one to meet you?' I looked up, startled, to see a young gentleman. 'No.' 'Wouldn't you like my mother's home?' 'No,' I repeated. He asked if I knew any one out there, and I said I had a letter for Canon Glennie. 'Ho,' he said, 'you belong to the G.F.S. [Girls Friendly Society, a famous Anglican world wide society] 'My mother, Lady Musgrave, runs a home for young girls. She meets the boats, as a rule, but she is not well, so I'm here in her place. If I can get some of your shipmates to come, will you?' I agreed to that. About an hour later a dozen of us were packed into a covered waggonette and driven off to Petrie Bight. Every one there was in bed and asleep, but they all turned out to give the strangers a right royal welcome. We cleared up all the food in the house and turned into the beds, two in each, under muslin curtains.

Next morning, the matron told us all what we had better do and where to go. I had left England with a pound, of which I'd spent ten and six, and I still had those two half crowns, which I was determined to return in three years time, so I was off to look for work at once. At the registry office they sent me to a place in a compositor's family at South Brisbane, where I was to look after the children and do everything else needed in the house. I should have my work cut out!

The matron at Petrie Bight looked at me dubious. She didn't think I could manage it. After dinner she asked if there were any one who would take a note for her to Bishopsbourne. No one answered. We were all tired out. At last I volunteered. It was a sweltering day, and a two mile walk, with a parcel of books to carry into the bargain.

I walked up to the beautiful house of the Lord Bishop of Brisbane [The Rt. Revd. William Webber], little dreaming it was to be my home for a year. The housekeeper began immediately about the terrible floods. Not wanting her to know I was a new chum, I agreed with all she said until she put the question direct: 'Did you come in with the boatload last night?' Then how can you know about the floods? I could tell by your accent.' She had it all out of me: where I came from, who Mrs. G. was, my letter of introduction to Canon Glennie, and then she asked what clothes I had. I was none too pleased with her. 'You're very small,' she grumbled. That was a sore point, being almost as broad as I was high, and what business was it of hers, my clothes and my height? I think the Bishop will be interested in you, she winds up, thoughtful.

I couldn't think why, and when matron told me next morning the housekeeper wanted to see me again, I was in two minds about going. I was due at the compositor's next day and I wanted to look about me. It seemed as if I could never get free of folk bossing my life.

However, there was a note to be taken, so I decided to leave it at the lodge and slip off. The housekeeper was at the gates, waiting for me very friendly. It passed through my mind how lovely it would be in that big, white house, with its two storeys, built on a hill beyond the avenue. I thought of the green, sloping grounds and then of the compositor's little bungalow and his swarm of children, and the cooking, the washing, the housework.

You can guess what I felt when she said, 'Would you like to come and live here?'

Their housemaid was leaving in a few months to get married, and I could start in at once and learn the ropes. I was delighted, and quite ready now to brag of my nice outfit. They thought nothing out there of throwing up a job, but I was a bit took to thinking of the compositor.

'Remember to call him "My Lord", said the housekeeper, and pushed me into the study. It was a large, very untidy room, papers from one end of the floor to the other. The walls were all bookshelves, and there were square swivel bookcases stood about.

The Bishop was a fine handsome man, with a brown beard and kind eyes. He looked me up and down. 'Why, she's only a child, Mrs. Lamerty!' She argued I was getting older every day, so he told her to please herself, but he did not think I should suit. My luggage was sent for, and once more I had a job in a big house with religious people.

I was out of the frying-pan into the fire. We had our own chapel at Bishopsbourne and the household was obliged to attend morning and evening service. The bishop was a bachelor, but he had three chaplains; Mrs. Lamerty; her husband, the butler; the housemaid, Emily, who was marrying the coachman; a kitchenmaid, Lizzie; the stableboy, Frank, and myself. The laundry was under the house. The laundress lived at the lodge with her husband, the gardener …

I was always being chaffed for something or other. Only two Sundays before I had been lying on the terrace, outside the dining room, reading. The tea bell rang. I made to get up, and felt four legs clawing at me and a long tail wrapping round. I clutched the thing round the neck and screamed the place down. Everybody rushed to see what was the matter, but I wouldn't let any one come near me till one of the chaplains got behind me, held my arms, and the horrid creature fell down. It had got up between my skirt and the foundation [petticoat]. It was a frilled lizard, four inches across the back and ten inches long, a brownish green, all foaming at the mouth …

There was plenty of nasty, creepy things to put up with, and swarms of little green frogs. They called them Queensland canaries. When I laid the supper the next Sunday one flopped down off the fanlight. I got the broom, but could not find it. After I carried in the supper, the bell rang. I was not supposed to answer. However, Mrs. Lamerty didn't come and it rang again, so I went. The cheese dish stood on the corner of the table with half a Stilton on it. 'Will you please take it away?' said Mr. Power [chaplain]. I picked up the dish, looked in the cheese, there sat the frog! The dish went one way, the frog another, the cheese a third, and I tore out of the room. Mrs. Lamerty was vexed with me for being so silly.

Maggie Campbell, a friend from the *Roma*, who had a job in Brisbane, asked me to go with her to Toowoomba. 'Madness,' says Mrs. Lamerty. 'You two girls going up country. Australia's not like England.' I thought there wasn't too much difference. Always some one trying to crab you. I was set on it. Maggie had never been there herself, but, in the end, Mrs. Lamerty gave in and off we started without a word to say we were coming. The coach only took us to Esk. The country was flooded with the heavy rains, and the rest of the journey, about twelve miles, we had to ride. Neither her nor me had ever been on horseback. Two old shanks were lent us. When they trotted, we screamed, but they were steady goers and flip, flapped through all right.

I don't think I should care to live in the bush. You have to ride everywhere. The sheep shearing and branding was fun to watch. If the shears cut into an animal by mistake, it was daubed with tar and didn't seem to mind. In the evenings we played cards and had sing-songs.

I got back safe to Bishopsbourne, after nine days, instead of a week, being delayed by heavy rains. Nothing terrible happened to me, and I came to the conclusion that if I was to take any notice of my elders I'd go nowhere ...

Out in Australia they'd flock for thirty or forty miles [for church], without thinking about the weather. In they came on horseback, sometimes one behind the other on the same nag. Once there were three weddings and a number of children christened, and the people sang Moody and Sankey hymns at the tops of their voices, and enjoyed themselves no end ... and after one meeting, I had my first bush dinner. They cut a large Turk's head, a vegetable something like a pumpkin. The top was sliced off, all the pips scooped out; some rabbits were shot, skinned, cleaned, cut up and put inside with onions. A hole was dug and a pile of wood shoved in. When it was well alight a lot of stones were thrown in, then more wood, next the Turk's head which was covered and left till cooked. Some rabbits they roasted and they made some dampers — bushmen's bread — just flour and water cooked in ashes, and jolly nice they were, eaten as soon as cooked. Altogether, it was great fun, and made me feel as if I'd really travelled far from the little round at home.

So did the interesting visitors who came to Bishopsbourne.

Among them was Lord and Lady Brassey, in the yacht the *Sunbeam*. They put in to Brisbane for repairs for a couple of days, and the ship's officers and men used to come up to the house. We had some of them to tea, and in return were invited to tea on the yacht and to see all over her. How I should love to sail round the world in her, it was not long before Lady Brassey's tragic death …

My year there drew to an end. I wondered how I was going to get away. My heart was set on Sydney, and yet I was heavy at the thought of leaving a happy home and some very good friends. My chance came unexpected. The bishop was going home for the Lambeth Conference of Bishops. While he was away the household was to be reduced. It meant Maggie or me leaving, and I jumped at it, so it was goodbye to Bishopsbourne for me …

I had quite a crowd to see me off. Mrs. Lamerty packed me a nice basketful of fruit and sandwiches, so there was no need to stay below on the boat. I was used to boats now, and I put everything straight for the night and came up on deck prepared to enjoy myself, stowed in a nice cosy place with the basket. We puffed along up the river, me looking out for the scenery; but we'd barely started before we stopped, and at ten, when I turned in for the night, we were at a standstill. The weather had changed …

Nobody got any sleep Sunday night. We were terribly buffeted and knocked about, and were towed into Sydney Harbour at seven o'clock on Monday evening in a very bad way … Every one had cleared off my boat, bar one or two sailors. It was growing dark and there was I, once more in a strange land, with nowhere to go. I stepped ashore, feeling very low. Seeing a church steeple quite close, I asked a man its name. 'St. James's' [Parish Church of St. James King Street]. I took a hansom and told the driver to take me there. The pig charged me 2/6, and I could have walked it in ten minutes, but didn't dare say anything. On the church board I found out who the priest was, and so on to the vicarage, where I told the lady what had happened. She kept me for the night, and took me next day to the G.F.S. They had only a recreation room and one bedroom, so they boarded me with a caretaker of some offices, who became one of my closest friends.

Having no money to spare, I set about looking for a job. The good woman at the registry office gave me a card to go and see a lady who lived on the side of Rose Bay. I hailed a bus, and mounted on top just behind the driver and told him where I wanted to be put down. After a while, he made me feel wild, asking: 'You a new chum? I tell you how I know. Ladies never ride outside the bus here. It's not considered nice.' I thanked him, and we got chatting about my destination. 'Well, that place is no I good,' he said. 'They don't keep their maids more than a week very often. I know of a better job going. My girl used to live there. It's out at Vaucluse. They're jolly nice people and keep a lot of servants.' I thanked him, but thought it best to go where I'd been sent. He leaned over, persuasive, saying he could afford to wait, and if I didn't take it I could go on with him. It was a most beautiful house, but I took a dislike to the lady right away.

I told the friendly bus driver how I felt, so on top of the bus I got, and he drove on for an hour through lovely country to try my luck at the other place. We passed only two houses all the way, and never lost sight of the sea.

'You tell Miss Morton I sent you. I'll be going back at five,' he said. I was quite excited as I walked up to the big white house. Carrara it was called, and the large front hall was built of marble. The grounds were beautiful and beautifully kept. There were four gardeners, besides the coachman and the groom, and in the house a cook, lady's maid, two parlour maids, three housemaids, kitchen maid, laundry woman, and maid. I was to be Second Housemaid. Miss Morton engaged me straight away. They were a large family: father, three daughters and four sons at home, and an aunt. I was to come in on Saturday. The carriage would be sent for me, and I was to have 18 shillings a week. Miss Morton gave me my return fare to Sydney. Every fourth week I was to have a holiday from ten Saturday morning till six on Monday night. A change like that gives a girl a wonderful feeling of freedom and I was glad to think I shouldn't be watch-dogged all the time. They sent me into the hall for some dinner, and to make friends with my fellow servants.

On the way back, I thanked the bus driver, and asked him to slip a note in at the letter box to tell the other lady I shouldn't be coming. Mrs. Lamerty was very cross when I wrote to say what I'd done, and replied I must go at once to Bishopscourt, where the bishop's wife had a place for me. I never went.

Life at Carrara was very gay after my quiet time at Brisbane. I grew fond of the three young ladies. They entertained a great deal; but what I most enjoyed was hunting on the sands. Meantime, life went very happily at Carrara. I mostly gave satisfaction, but one of my duties was to prepare the old gentleman's shower bath, and I could never get it hot enough to please him. I was supposed to put boiling water into the cistern. It was a funny little bath, just room to stand up in it. You get in, tie the curtains together, pull the plug from the cistern and down the water showers.

One Sunday morning I went to call the young ladies, and found them all in tears. I wondered what was the matter. They told me Miss Morton had found some particular spider, which is a sure sign of death in the house, and the day before her father had come to breakfast wearing an opal ring he had found in a cabinet he had been turning out, and the week before that we'd had a dinner party for fourteen and one fell out. I had to get a schoolboy, who was staying with us, out of his bed to make up the number at the table, so that was three unlucky things to happen.

Well, whether it was that, or whether he caught cold going into that room, I don't know; but, sure enough, he fell ill and at the end of a month died. He was a dear old man, very wealthy. They were the owners of a wharf at Miller's Point. He was something in the seafaring line, and came out and settled in the early days. After his death, the property was sold and the family scattered, so as my time was up I decided to move on to Melbourne. I was even sorrier to leave Sydney than Brisbane … I don't know whether folk are more charitable nowadays, but the worst of Sydney in my time was the way people reminded you that it was a convict settlement. They couldn't forget Botany Bay, and they'd point to one fine house after another and say spitefully: 'Ah, he came over in chains.'

I said goodbye to all my friends, chief among them the caretaker with whom I had lodged, and she gave me an introduction to her nephew, who lived out at Toorak. Melbourne is quite different to either of the other places. Beautiful buildings, but ugly, very wide streets, with lovely shops. The river Yarra was very dirty. It wasn't nearly as pleasant as Sydney, and I missed the sea.

At the G.F.S. headquarters they made me very welcome. A day or two later, I came across the valet [from Brisbane], out with a girl from Government House. They were having a ball there on New Year's eve, and she asked me if I would come. Though longing to go, I would not say for certain. However, the housekeeper backed up their invitation with a nice little note, so I accepted, and had a lovely time. She asked me if I would go to live there as Kitchen Maid. I seemed to be going to a bigger place each time. At Carrara they could seat twenty five at lunch easily; but Government House, with its three hundred rooms!

I hated kitchen work, and hesitated; but of course it would be a good opening, and in the end I promised, so soon got suited with a job. As for the kitchen, I'd never seen such a barracks in my life. The afternoon the house keeper engaged me I only just peeped in and didn't take much notice, but I'll never forget my feelings that first morning. Why had I taken on the job? There was a skylight, a huge window on either side of a double glass door, and three as big facing them. On the same side as the glass door was the door into the scullery; beside it a wonderful contrivance they called a Banbury [bain-marie], a large copper case fitted with twelve of the dinkiest little copper saucepans for gravies and sauces, each in its place like a cruet. The range was enormous. You could lose a 20 pound turkey in the oven. Next came two vast gas ovens, as tall as myself. Then a large round tank, with a fireplace under it, all pipes, taps, and screws; a bunker holding five sacks of coal …

The waste there was shocking, and many a time I've seen whole legs of mutton thrown away. We had a sheep and a half daily. There were two long tables, about eighteen inches of wood and a steel plate running down the middle. They had sliding doors underneath and the dishes were kept hot inside. Next I saw a big deep sink. The fourth side of the kitchen held a great marble mortar, with a pestle attached through rings to the ceiling, I afterwards found that by the time I'd got the pestle up I'd no strength to bring it down.

There was a great butcher's block the size you see in a shop, and a long dresser, hung with copper stewpan lids and sauté pans, and in front were copper moulds and bombe ice bowls. Underneath was a row of stewpans and immense stock pots. I stared at them in dismay, wondering who had to clean them. At that end of the kitchen was a long deal table, where the kitchen folk had their meals.

The floor was dark tiles, covered with sawdust. No fenders. My work was to keep all the tables clean, get and clear all kitchen meals, sweep the kitchen twice a day; do all the kitchen washing up, mincing, pounding, sieving; make all sauces, clean all fruits, whisk all eggs, keep the chef supplied with clean basins and tools of all sorts, and cut and cook all fancy vegetables.

When the furnace was alight, it heated the tables with sliding doors and also the Banbury. In the scullery was a gas stove, a large furnace, which was never used, and a gas oven. On the other side were four large sinks, one filled with silver sand, one for washing up, one for rinsing, and one for vegetables. Two big baths for waste (that's where the mutton went).

The job I liked best was making ornaments for the supper tables and ballroom. We melted heaps of lovely wax candles; took out the wicks, and half filled the little bombes [culinary molds] bolted them together and shook them well; stood them in cold water, opened them and turned out lovely little fairies, angels, duck boats, birds, and most beautiful flowers and fruits, bunches of grapes, and all sorts. The tables looked grand. Once I heard a lady say she was afraid to help herself because she never knew which was real and which artificial ...

The new Governor [The Earl of Hopetown] ... brought out all his staff and we expected dismissal, but I was one of the ten to be kept on. I felt very pleased with myself, for I was given the job of Under Still Room Maid and a rise in my screw. It was much better than kitchen work. I had all the trays to prepare and clear, all the washing up, all the toast to make, get the teas and coffee, and all the washing up. My new mates were a lot nicer than the last.

The housekeeper was very different to any of the others, and she gave me different instructions from Mrs. Lamerty. No My Lording every five minutes. She told me to say it just once if I had to address the Governor, and that was enough. We were fifty five servants all told, including thirteen in the stables. Our Head Laundry Maid was taken ill with fever and sent off to hospital, where she died. Her poor sister is said to have smuggled some cake to her and it killed her. We were all sent off to Macedon, the country residence, for fear of the Governor's little boy catching the fever.

We went back to town in time for the Cup month, which meant we should not get outside the grounds for a month. In Melbourne, every thing is reckoned by the Cup. You say I'm going to do so and so after the Cup, the way we reckon by Christmas at home. The Governor had to drive in state to the racecourse, with postilions, and he didn't relish it. It was the custom to give two big Parliamentary dinners, two garden parties, two balls, and an evening reception each week. We worked like niggers. You can imagine the size of the ballroom. There were three great crystal chandeliers, with five hundred lights in each, besides all the side lights. It used to take three weeks each year to clean them. At the end of the room the orchestra played, up in a balcony, decorated with flags and ferns. A lot of naval men were told off for the job; getting to know them seemed to bring me nearer to my brother …

Everything comes to an end. I left Australia in May 1890, having been in Brisbane for the Jubilee, in Sydney for the Centenary, and in Melbourne for the Exhibition. I was sorry to go; but my brother was to be home on leave, and I hoped to have some time with him before he left England.

My passage was booked on the *Orient*. The housekeeper, kind to the last, had a box made to fit in my cabin, and packed it with all sort of tinned things, jam, marmalade, etc., so I was well off for food … My Australian days were drawing to a close … and I remember thinking if I lived to be an old woman I should never regret seeing that advertisement in *Lloyd's Weekly*. Sydney was nearest my heart.

Life at Bishopsbourne was too strict to give me a chance to sample the Queenslanders, and the Victorians were not in it with Sydney folk — still I made friends and met with kindness everywhere, and it was a great wrench when at last I bade goodbye to Australia, perhaps forever ...

From *Memoirs of Martha: An Autobiography. Elicited and Edited By Her Mistress*, London, 1933.

MARIAN ELLIS ROWAN

1891

Marian Ellis Rowan was married to Captain Charles Rowan who had an interest in botany and encouraged his wife to paint wild flowers. Consequently, Marian spent many years on painting tours, travelling around Australia, New Zealand and Europe. She is recorded as being 'small and fragile in appearance, she always dressed correctly in the fashion of the day for all her painting expeditions, no matter whether in the Australian bush or New Guinea jungle. Her skirts were worn full length, her blouse high-necked with long sleeves, her gloves, hat and umbrella just so.' She was tireless in her quest for subjects to paint and travelled considerable distances. Some of her best works, 947 items, are in the collection of the National Library of Australia.

Here I am, on my way to the celebrated Muldiva silver mines and the Chillagoe Caves [Queensland], and if this historical document is unusually stupid, I won't take any responsibility for its feebleness, for my energies have been almost spent on our two days journey to reach this place. To-night it is quite cold enough for a fire, although the heat in the middle of the day was almost unbearable. The noise and bustle in the street give one the idea of quite a large town; but it is only a small straggling mining village among hills, not unlike the township at Mount Morgan. At present it has a dry and barren look, and we are back among the gum trees again; poor stunted-looking ones, however, with a painfully grey, monotonous appearance.

I left Myola yesterday, at two o'clock, to catch the coach to this place; the country that we drove through for many miles was beautiful. We passed over the Cairns range and through tropical scrub, with here and there glimpses of the sea shining below us, and, in the far distance, the dim, blue mountains; but once over the coastal ranges, a feature of these northern latitudes, the belts of jungle become less frequent, and the country assumes a dull and uninteresting aspect, mile after mile of shadeless, grey, sombre-looking gum trees, poor and scantily clothed, stretch away in indefinite monotony. Here and there along the roads we passed teams of bullocks carrying stores, and the inevitable swagman, with all his earthly possessions on his back, tramping away to the land of silver and of gold. The road was a very up-and-down one, but Joe, the driver, a regular Australian bush boy, was such a splendid whip that even I was not nervous; not even when night came on, and we got off the track, and the seven horses went as hard as they could through the gum trees, crashing down young saplings, and grazing stumps by a hair's breadth, but never once coming in contact with anything.

As the night became darker and the road rougher, we could sometimes, through the dust, barely distinguish even the wheelers, and I held on more and more tightly, and wondered if it was instinct or sight that guided Joe. Suddenly, crash went one of the bars; everyone had to get down, and it was an hour before it was patched up and we went on. We crossed the Barron River, where the fording place is a rocky ledge, so narrow, that an inch one way or the other would set the horses swimming. 'It was just here,' said Joe, by way of encouraging me, 'that the coach went over into deep water not many months ago, and we had a rare old swim.' However, we splashed through with a dash, and up the bank, at the top of which we heard the welcome sound of dogs barking, while here and there the lights of the township showed up. In the pitch darkness it seemed to consist only of two hotels.

Here I had my first experience of what is called an up-country inn; we all had our supper together in one long room. Joe sat at the head of the table, the cloth of which bore traces of many meals; the other convives [fellow diners] here a miscellaneous collection — diggers in their shirt-sleeves, mothers with their babies, etc. There was a furious click of knives and forks, resolutely bent on making up for lost time, and scrimmaging their best for the unsavoury looking compounds on the table. I was very hungry, but I could not stand these 'fag ends'; and the pangs of hunger were only a secondary consideration to those of my bed. The house was so full that I could not get a room to myself, but at last they consented to make me up a bed on an upstairs verandah. Here I fought until daylight with mosquitoes, and, finally, submitting myself to circumstances, hailed dawn with inexpressible relief.

By five o'clock we were well on our way again: it was a most uninteresting drive; here and there we passed through a shady bit of jungle, but the rest of the journey lay through dry and stunted gum trees. We passed many piled-up stacks of magnificent cedar logs which have been lying there for some years, waiting for the railway to be finished. The road for the last few miles before reaching Herberton was a great pull for the horses, and the heat was almost unbearable; indeed, even on the verandah of the hotel, I had to sit with an umbrella up, for there was no protection from the sun under the corrugated iron roof.

I went off at once to the Post Office where I had ordered my letters to be sent, but some one (they did not know who) had called for them the day before, and taken them away. Then I felt furious, and told them that they had no right to have given them up without an order from me; the man only smiled, and was so profuse in his apologies that I couldn't say anything more. They all turned up in the evening, papers, magazines, and all …

I had visitors all the afternoon, all doing their utmost to

persuade me not to attempt the rough journey to the Caves. But how could I turn back after coming so far, notwithstanding that I have met with a great disappointment, as I had a half promise that a lady companion would go on with me from here, and I found that the idea of the journey had frightened her. The prospect does not look promising; a coach drive to-morrow (for I have determined to go on at once) from five in the morning until half-past eleven at night, when we ought to reach Muldiva, and then a rather indefinite Beyond. How I am to get to the Caves from there I have yet to find out, but I am armed with three or four letters which will help me on the way …

I AM GRADUALLY NEARING THE CAVES, but what a journey it has been! In spite of the many warnings I received I was determined to come, and here I am, sitting now, as I write, in a corrugated iron house in the principal street of this newly-formed mining town of Muldiva. I am only too glad to have been lent this retreat to come to for the day, away from the noise of the hotel, which is only a few doors off. Opposite me is the police station, which fact is painted in red letters on a piece of canvas. This place consists of two diggers' tents and a sort of verandah made out of branches of gum trees. The general store is a tent on forked sticks with a wall of branches on all sides, the proprietor's name is written in huge letters upon it, and a counter with glasses and an array of tins proclaim his calling. The thermometer is 120° in the shade.

Next comes a real bush bark hut, of which many are studded about in every direction, then another tent, a bakehouse, one or two more stores, and two shelters that call themselves hotels. A man sits under an awning in the principal street (which is still full of felled trees and stumps) with the air of an Indian potentate, guarding a keg of beer, tumblers, matches, tobacco, pipes, etc. Here and there a native goes by, more or less in a state of intoxication. The butcher's shop is a green arbour of boughs. Stores just now are 'out', and a pound of flour for the time costs a shilling.

Everything is full of life and activity. The new chum that you meet is reticent, the old hand communicative. Above, below, and around, are miners with thews and sinews, wresting the precious metal from beds of rock, burrows in hill-sides, and along the beds of an apology for a stream, whose waters are so full of lime that everything becomes encrusted with it, and even your clothes from the wash are powdered. John Chinaman goes by with his pack-horse, for already he is pioneering with his garden stuff. Where his garden is I do not know: everything seems baked and parched up, and the poor miserable gum trees do not look as if they could cast a yard of shade. All around the bare rocky hills, and just behind the town is the great Muldiva mine which at present shows every sign of a prosperous future. A bullock-team goes by, and more natives, gins carrying water, about the only thing they are good for.

It is Sunday, and the day seems as if it would never come to an end, not a breath of cool air anywhere, not a book to read; bottling up my self-imprisoned thoughts, I sat on the doorstep, I sat on the table, then under it, but still I could not get away from that fierce heat; then I went back to the hotel and into a little hut next door, where I sat and fanned a child dying of fever; there it was slightly cooler, and I had something besides my own worries to think of. Evening came at last, and I went for a walk with the housemaid from the hotel up to a hill overlooking the town. She gave me a most ghastly description of life in a mining town, and already I long for the night to be over, though the thought of that journey back hangs over me like a hideous nightmare.

I have had many rough drives, but they all pale in comparison with that which brought me here; the five horses had literally to climb up and down hills and rough tracks for miles after leaving Herberton (they say it is the roughest road in Australia), dragging that great heavy Cobb's coach behind them. It needs to be strong, and so must, I suppose, be heavy; here and there, where the track was unusually steep, and the coach going down literally had to drop from one boulder to another, all the passengers excepting myself got out. I begged leave to remain, not because I was not a coward, but because I preferred terror to that walk over the hot stones.

In the grey dawn of the morning the temperature was just bearable, but as the day wore on the heat and dust became intolerable, and by ten a.m. we were only too glad to stop while they changed our horses, and get a quarter of an hour's rest and a cup of tea at Montalbion, one of the barest and most miserable-looking places I have ever seen. Thence we went on in what they called a 'Buckboard', a four-wheeled, low, hoodless sort of buggy, in which we got the full benefit of the sunshine and dust; such clouds of the latter there were that no one could possibly have distinguished the colour of anything we had on. From Montalbion to our destination we passed over the same endless, rocky, gum-tree-dotted hills, one of which they call the 'Featherbed', because it consists of huge round boulders, of which a few only have been removed from the track, and here again everyone had to get out.

We changed horses once more, thirty miles from Montalbion, at a little hut, rough but very clean, where I quenched my thirst with some lime-juice and water, the only drinkable liquid I could get. Here we changed into a coach again. At the next stopping I asked, 'Had they any soda-water, or, lemonade, or gingerbeer, etc.?' 'No, they had none of them fancy drinks; but would I like some sarsaparilla?' When we started again night was coming on, and we had only one lamp available, the heat of the sun having melted the candle in the other, and, too tired at last to keep awake any longer, and the coachman having put a strap round me and fastened me to the coach, I fell asleep; for how long I don't know, but I was suddenly awakened by a bump and a crash: we were off the track, the leader was over a log, and the others trying to follow; they were all hopelessly mixed up together among broken harness; I have only an indistinct recollection of their bolting, but it is all so hazy that I cannot tell you more. We were patched up somehow or other.

A second time, when we picked up a log in the wheel, they bolted, but this time I did not care what happened. Finally, to my unspeakable joy, at two in the morning we reached this hotel. I was taken to my room where I fell asleep while undressing, and awoke at four a.m. to find myself sitting on the floor, resting my head against the bed. The whole house shook at six that morning with the tread of heavy feet, so that there was no more rest to be had, and indeed, in any case, the heat of the sun would soon have driven me out, so I got up, scooped the dust out of my bag, and finally had the luxury of a bath (though it was about the colour of pea-soup) and breakfast in my own room.

A few days ago the journey to the Caves was described word for word in a letter to me thus: 'It is almost an impossible journey for a lady unless you camp out. The whole way the heat and flies are unbearable, the country lies very low, and on account of the heavy thunderstorms just now you are liable to be flooded out. The whole district is totally uninhabited,' and so on; but now good-bye for the present ... for a post goes tomorrow, and, as they are not every-day occurrences here, I cannot afford to miss this chance.

From 'Ellis Rowan: A Flower Hunter in Queensland', *The Town & Country Journal*, Sydney, 1891, 1892.

Flora Shaw

1893

Flora Louisa Shaw, author and journalist, later Dame Flora Lugard, was a great Empire traveller. She was the first woman Special Correspondent and Head of the Colonial Department at The Times *in London and visited Australia in that capacity, sending back well-informed and lengthy 'Letters from Australia' which appeared in* The Times *during 1892 and 1893. Later she undertook special commissions for* The Times *in South Africa and Canada. She married Sir Frederick Lugard of the British Foreign Office in 1902 and was joint founder of the War Refugees Committee in Britain, and in 1918 was appointed a Dame of the British Empire. She died in 1929.*

THE FIRST IMPRESSION WHICH IS GAINED of Australia in a long train journey from Melbourne to Brisbane is one of extraordinary monotony. I am told that this is partly due to the circumstances that the railway line has been laid through a poor belt of country, and partly due to the accident of passing the least interesting portion of the landscape. However it came about, the effect produced is a scarcely broken tract of grass and gum trees. From Melbourne to Sydney, from Sydney to the Queensland border, grass and gum trees stretch on every side. Day after day the eyes open on the same unvaried tints of grey and green; one acre is like an another, one mile is like the last.

Hundreds of miles are left behind, and there is nothing to show that the end of the journey is any nearer. The river and forest scenery of Tasmania, with its farms and orchards, its hedgerows of sweetbriar and yellow gorse, and the familiar English aspect of its gardens, fade in the distance like a dream. The tropical vegetation of the north has not yet become a reality. Between the two the immense extent of gum trees stretches indefinitely, blotting out the conception of anything but its own lightly-timbered pasture. It has not even the gloom and impressiveness which we associated in England with the name of forest land, for the trees are thinly scattered, their long leaves hang vertically from the branches and sunlight filters through with sufficient force to promote the growth of the tussocked grass beneath. The whole would be indescribably commonplace, but that the vastness becomes at last by its own force impressive. Here, again, you feel, as you feel in Africa, the immense size of the physical problem.

The areas are so wide, the distances to be got over are so great, that even the preliminary network of civilisation, which the train you are travelling in and the towns you have stopped at represent, contains subjects for marvel, and the first sensation of weariness is lost in admiration for the patience and the energy that have, as it were, lassoed the wilderness and brought its resources within the limits of the Empire …

In the wood clearings on either side of the train where the practice of 'ring barking' to kill trees is in extensive use, there stand patches of timber from which the bark and leaves have dropped, and of which the dead white trunks and branches are waiting only to be felled. Sometimes an entire hill side will be white with such a ghostly forest. The habit is not to fell them at the level of the ground, but at heights varying, according to convenience, from one foot to two or three above the root. Grass spaces in which the stumps still remain form a constant feature of the landscape …

It is difficult to imagine a more absolute antidote for too much London than a five hundred miles drive through the Queensland bush with the thermometer hovering round 100 degrees in the shade, and breezes, scented by their passage over half a continent of grass, cooling the otherwise unendurable heat. The buggy in which you drive has an awning, a station hand canters after you with horses to select a change from when yours are tired, and for yourself there is nothing to do but to jog quietly over the mileage from sunrise to sunset with the assurance of station hospitality at the end of the day. The stages are long, for the stations are wide apart and there is nowhere to stop midway, but the roads here are not like South African roads. They are tracks that run smooth and firm over rolling plains, where at any moment you might, with a small stretch of imagination, fancy yourself in the heart of a big English park. The country does not in the English sense of the words resemble either 'bush' or 'downs'. It is simply rich pasture land, which sweeps away in fine open breaths on all sides and carries timber enough to redeem it from the monotony of mere fodder. In the summer of a good season, cattle stand sometimes shoulder deep in the long grass ... The timber, of course, when seen close at hand is strange. Boree and gidyah, coolibar and white wood, briggelow, mulgah, and myall are the unfamiliar names by which you learn to recognise the commonest varieties ...

The state of the temperature scarcely disturbs any illusion [of English forestland], a hundred degrees of fahrenheit does not mean the same thing in this high and generally dry atmosphere that it would mean in England or in low lands of the coast. You are permeated with sunshine, soaked with it through and through in a way which must, you feel, be supremely wholesome. The invigorating smell of the earth is always in your nostrils; you are frankly hot, but you are not overpowered. A hundred is far from being the limit to which the thermometer rises; 110 degrees is common and during the summer it has been known to reach 125 degrees in the shade.

When you ask, what shade? you are answered that it was the only shade there was, and therefore represented the temperature at which people had to live. Houses differ very much. A well planned verandah, painted white and covered with a vine, which is not allowed to exclude air, will be as much as 10 degrees cooler than one upon which the sun's ray are allowed to beat; and the temperature taken at one station may vary proportionately from the temperature taken on the same day at another.

My own experience did not go above 105 degrees, registered on the verandah of a station at which I spent the night, and I drove 75 miles on that day without special discomfort. Still, the heat is fierce. Not only does your face burn to a colour which is scarcely human, but the protection of clothing does not prevent arms, wrists, and ankles from peeling. This ardour of climate has probably more effect than is altogether recognised upon persons who are constantly exposed to it, and the alternation from summer heat to the frosts of winter, which is bracing to man, is distinctly trying to vegetation.

The amenities of life generally are hard to procure in the bush. Existence is wholesome, uncomplicated, large, and free; it is lacking in daily pleasantness.

Four iron walls and a mud floor; instead of a window, an aperture which could be closed at will by a rough hinged plank; a partition, behind which there were two beds and some furniture converted from old packing cases, represents the home of a fairly well-to-do working man at the first mail change at which we stopped. No enclosure, no garden. In dry weather dust, in wet weather mud, up to — I cannot call it the threshold, for there was none, but to the uncertain line at which bush ended and house began. The inside of a big tin biscuit-box could not have been simpler, and it might easily have had the advantage of being cleaner. And this may be taken as fairly representative of the home which a poor man out in the bush thinks good enough for himself. On the stations the cottages which are provided for the permanent hands are sometimes as good as can be desired, but it is on the whole an exception. The isolation and constant association with the extremes of external nature seem to have a roughening tendency, of which the limits are hard to fix. Food is plentiful to an extent unknown in England. Wages are high, and the man who is content to have a home little better than an animal's lair will expect and get three solid meals a day, nor know what means in a material sense. But throughout the West [of Queensland] one is struck by the absence of pleasure and its civilising influences ... the universal relaxation is to drink and gamble ...

The owners and managers are the men who are laying the foundation of the future landed gentry of Australia, but at present they are few and far between and the population is so sparse that for a time the toughest of men scarcely present themselves.

One is occupied merely with the external scene, and there are other conditions besides the heat, which by degrees serve to bring home the fact that after all this is not England, but Australia ... Of these none is stranger than the mirage, which, even when you are close enough to trace the reflections and to count the animals browsing on the imaginary shore, will represent a sheet of water so absolutely real in appearance that, in country which is unknown to them, it is impossible for the most experienced bushmen to recognise the deception. When my companion first drew my attention to one, I thought he was amusing himself with hoaxing a stranger. After he had convinced me by driving me into the middle of the place where the water appeared to be, he had my life in his hands if he cared to take it, for I was quite prepared to drive into the next real sheet of water under the impression that it was mirage. Or you may chance to meet a travelling whirlwind. In the distance it looks like the smoke of a grass fire. But it travels along, those that I have seen generally moving at the rather leisurely rate of a slow locomotive. As it comes nearer you perceive that the rate of progress bears an infinitesimal proportion to the rate of revolution, and that it carries a column of dust, thickened by all stray bits of wood, grass, or foliage which it has stripped from the country in its passage. If it chances to pass by a wool-drying floor where wool is exposed, a couple of bales are swept up in a moment, after which prank it dances sedately away like a mischievous ghost over the plains. The circumference of the column it makes may be not more than 30 or 40 feet, but the carrying power is very great, and even a side blow, when you think that you have given it a pretty wide berth, may chance to overturn buggy and horse.

Rain is not frequent, but if it comes you begin to understand the important part which the wet weather filled in the records of the shearers' strike [of that year]. That it plays on your person and horses for short intervals with the volume and force of a hose of a fire-engine is, comparatively speaking, nothing; you are quit of that at the price of a shower bath. But it renders locomotion absolutely impossible. The soil appears to be mixed with cobblers' wax and sticks to the horses' feet and wheels of the buggy till the wheels refuse altogether to go around. There is nothing then to be done but to get out, pack the luggage as best you can under the waterproof apron, and ride the horses bare-backed to your destination. Struggling with thoroughly willing draught horses to get the vehicle on has been known to result in pulling the front half out of the buggy while the wheels stuck fast; and progress on foot is scarcely more possible, for the weight and the stickiness of the mud which accumulates on your boots makes the struggle between them and you seem nearly as desperate as the struggle between the horse and buggy.

You are lucky if a river has not risen between you and your night's shelter. In two or three hours a stream which was almost dry will become an impassable flood, and in that case the only alternative is to go back — if you can get back — to the place you started from in the morning, and wait patiently for the rain to cease, roads to dry, and rivers to return to their beds.

What the scale [of properties] is may be partly realised from the size of the first station upon which I was received. It had an extent of 1500 square miles and carried nearly half a million sheep. In the course of a drive of between four and five hundred miles, though the whole of the ground covered was taken up and fenced, I passed altogether only 12 stations.

When it is a question of getting the wool off the sheep's back and into the London market, then shearers are wanted and factory life in the bush begins. But it only lasts on each station for a period varying from a fortnight to two months, according to the state of the weather and the number of sheep to be shorn. The hardships entailed by this condition of the industry are, I believe, at the bottom of all the discontent expressed by the shearers and their associates, who are known under the more generally accepted generic term of 'roustabouts' … when one shed 'cut out' another must be found. Men hardly count upon getting more than four or five months employment in the year. The remaining time is spent either in the little townships or in going from one station to another asking for work …

The roughness of the existence in the intervals of work is probably unknown and unimagined by any one who has not endured it. From time to time some boundary rider comes across a blanket and a few scattered human bones, picked clean by kites, bleached white by the consuming sun. Murdered? Dead of thirst? Dropped from exhaustion here by himself, with no means of leaving a record of his name? Nobody knows. His name probably was not worth recording, except, it may be to someone somewhere, who at times still considers whether Jim, or George, or Dick is yet alive. Ninety per cent of this wandering population is unmarried, and they may die hungry, thirsty and homeless in the bush without greatly affecting any other human lives. You learn in this country what dying like sheep really means, and more men do probably so die than are entered upon any district register. In driving through the bush, men upon the tramp, carrying their swags in a rolled blanket upon their backs, are to be frequently met. But pity for them would be keener if it were possible to forget that, at the end of each shearing job, they leave the station on which they have been employed with cheques for twenty, thirty, fifty pounds in their pockets and that the common custom is to go to the nearest township, hand the cheque over to the owner of the local tavern, with instructions, 'When it's done, let me know', and proceed to indulge in every available form of dissipation till the money is finished. There are innkeepers who will grimly joke of the number whom they have buried. This is the gruesome side of the bush, and it is, I believe, in large measure attributable to that lack of wholesome pleasure in the natural conditions of which I have spoken. The life is so rough that the slip across the line into brutality is half unconscious.

I should not leave this side of the subject without mentioning that no wanderer in the bush who keeps to the beaten tracks need ever starve. Station hospitality is extended to every one who claims it. How large the number are who profit by the custom may be judged by the lists of rations distributed to sundowners ... the rations consist usually of meat, flour, tea, and sugar, but anyone who is in need of soap, tobacco, or currants does not hesitate to ask for them. The recipient camps out of doors, makes a fire and cooks for himself.

I was first introduced to shearers on a station where, rain having fallen, work was temporarily suspended. I was taken to their quarters, where they were at their evening meal. About seventy of them, bare armed and dirty, were gathered round a table under a shed roof, out of doors. They were eating copiously of joints, stews, bread, pickles, jams, and cakes. Intoxicating liquor is not, I believe, allowed upon the stations. In any case, it is not introduced, and tea is the universal beverage. They have tin plates and mugs; the knife generally served all purposes; there was no table cloth. It was a hugger-mugger of food on dirty boards, just one step removed from the well-filled troughs of swill I have seen pigs crowd at home. The wastefully-heaped masses of food only added to the unpleasantness of a scene, the disorder and ugliness of which could hardly have been surpassed. If a man did not like what was on his plate he threw it over his shoulder and began again. I am told that the amount of waste food daily collected in the shearers' and roustabouts' camps, and burnt as a sanitary precaution, would suffice to keep as many men again as are employed ...

The quarters provided for shearers and roustabouts are, like shearing sheds, big constructions of corrugated iron. The sleeping and dining sheds contain nothing but wooden bunks, tables and benches. The kitchen sheds are provided with good cooking ranges. There is much grumbling among the men at the roughness of this accommodation. But the quarters of any given station are occupied, it must be remembered, for a few weeks only of each year; judging by my own experience of a shearers' supper, and that of the homes which the men think good enough when they are free to house themselves, there seems little in this complaint for which the remedy does not lie in their own hands.

The shearing camp is usually in the heart of a station, isolated by, perhaps, 20 or 30 miles of bush on every side, and it may easily be conceived that the conditions of life of a hundred or so men of the roughest type gathered together under the circumstances, and without women, without home occupations, and with absolutely nothing to do for nearly half the day, are neither edifying nor agreeable. Respectable men often prefer camping out to occupying the bunk allotted to them in the shed. The better ones spend their leisure in reading socialistic and other literature, the others play cards, and appear to find an outlet for their energies in the abundant use of foul language ...

During my visit as a comparative stranger [I was] helped in the kindest and most cordial manner by all sections of Australian society ...

From 'Letters from Australia: From Our Special Correspondent',
The Times, London, 1893.

Lady Ida Poore

1908–1910

Lady Ida Margaret Poore, daughter of the Lord Bishop of Limerick, married Sir Richard Poore, Bt. RN., who later became the Royal Naval Commander-in-Chief of the Australian Station between 1908 and 1911. From her home at Admiralty house in Sydney, Lady Poore followed official and social life. Her reminiscences are full of racy and interesting observations of the few years spent in Sydney and visiting in the country.

Jt was on the 30th of August, 1903, that I became the wife of an Admiral ... He was far from being elated by his promotion, which was automatic, although the fact that he had become a rear-admiral at the age of fifty was due to two special promotions for war service and three years as commander of the Royal Yacht, *Victoria & Albert*. He had been thirteen years a captain, but for an admiral he was young ... early in December 1907 my husband was offered the Australian Station ...

Lieutenant F. C. Fisher, R.N. was appointed flag-lieutenant to my husband, and before they sailed in January he and I had many a consultation about footmen's liveries, stamping of note-paper and all the details which had to be thought of and executed quickly and finally. When one is going to the Antipodes for three years it is almost like dying, for one's home, one's garden, one's prospective tenants and one's pensioners (down to the thrushes and robins) must be meticulously arranged for if one is to start on one's long journey free from anxiety as to all one leaves behind. And then there was Roger [Lady Poore's son], who had decided to be a planter in Ceylon, and 'shoved off' shortly before I did.

Before my husband left England, the Austral Club entertained us at dinner at the Ritz, where we met a number of Australians, all as friendly and helpful as could be. Lord Jersey — once Governor of New South Wales, and with Lady Jersey deservedly beloved and remembered in that State — took me in to dinner, and both he and Sir Fowell Buxton (once Governor of South Australia), told me much that was of interest then and of service later. In a letter I received shortly afterwards from Lord Jersey, he said: 'I hope you and the Admiral will have a great time … You will find the Australians open-hearted and generous, devoted to those who carry out the naval duties of the Empire and desirous of making every visitor to their land happy and at home.'

I was really thankful to be off when the moment arrived, and clutching a bunch of lily of the valley and duplicate copies of Mr. [William] Locke's latest novel — all farewell offerings — I stepped into the boat-train for Marseilles. The knowledge that all I best loved was ahead of me (like the proverbial carrot hung before an unwilling donkey's nose), enabled me to start in good heart upon what, of all things, inspires me with loathing — a long sea voyage.

There was a capital cabin for me on board the Orient liner *Omrah* at Marseilles, and a warm welcome from my maid, who had come alive, but not unscathed, through the Bay … The voyage would have been like any other long illness but for the fact that we had on board a most attractive and entertaining theatrical company bound for Melbourne …

At Colombo I had a few hours to spend with my boy. We lunched together at Mount Lavinia, drove about in rickshaws and parted at sunset on the coaly deck of the *Omrah*. One 'carrot' had been devoured all too quickly, and the poor donkey felt very forlorn with the weary ten days run to Fremantle, and the dreaded passage of the Bight still to be won through before she could secure the second.

At Fremantle I had only time to find out how good Australian grapes are and how treacherous and inadequate are sea-legs when first ashore, and after a hot walk through the flat streets with the Acting Governor and his A.D.C. (both possessing very long and useful land-legs) I was almost glad to return to the ship.

As we rolled round Cape Leeuwin I longed to make a joke about the 'Bight being worse than the barque', but, though I had time and seclusion in abundance for this mental exercise, I reached Port Adelaide without succeeding. There I was met by Captain Boddam-Whetham, the Governor's A.D.C., who conveyed me to Government House, and I was so glad to see Sir George and Lady Le Hunte that I never curtseyed to His Excellency!! I think it was Lady Le Hunte's fault for welcoming me so warmly that I forgot for the moment Sir George was the King's representative in South Australia. It is so nice to be welcomed by an old friend after spending several weeks among strangers, however friendly. That afternoon I left Adelaide for Melbourne ...

About noon next day, our train being very late, I found my second 'carrot' on the platform at Melbourne. He had not promised to meet me there, for he has always disliked making promises which may never get beyond the abortive stage of good intentions, so it was something of a surprise. Together we drove off to Federal Government House where I curtseyed accurately, and most willingly, to the Governor-General and Lady Northcote and had a peaceful hour's tête-à-tête with my husband before lunch. Lord Jersey had been good enough to write and ask Lord Northcote to befriend us, and from that day to the moment of their leaving Australia, some six months later, no one could have been more kind and helpful; and the staff were equally so. As for Lady Northcote, no novice ever had a more admirable Mother Superior (in status, not age) than I found in her. Both she and the Governor-General were as just and wise as they were generous, and though I sometimes heard them criticised for keeping up too much state, I always maintained my view that a viceroy must be *plus royal que le roi*. Kings and Queens can unbend when and where they choose; a viceroy must play the kingly part on every occasion unless he obtains a special dispensation to relax ceremonial …

I resumed my journey to Sydney the same afternoon, and saw by moonlight for the first time the pallid, ghost-like stumps of gum trees, ringbarked and dead, on either side of the railway line. My maid took them for tombstones until their number made such a theory untenable; for there were miles of them. They are to my mind one of the most depressing evidences of civilisation. Past suburban stations with Scotch and English names which confuse the newcomer by their strange juxtaposition we ran through the early hours of a sunshiny morning into Sydney. There my old friends, Captain and Mrs. C. L. Napier, met and welcomed me, and together we crossed the narrow strait separating Sydney proper from North Sydney and landed at the bottom of the garden of Admiralty House.

As we walked up the steep path we met a big black and white 'willy wagtail', my first bird friend in a garden full of birds. He was a delightful personage who flirted his tail and piped 'Sweet pretty creature' from the far side of a bed of scarlet salvia, and my cup overflowed.

It was five days before the flagship [H.M.S. *Powerful*] came into harbour, so I had time to learn the names of the footmen (luxuries who had hitherto been strangers within my modest gates) and to lose my awe of the chef whom we had inherited from our predecessors — a piece of good luck for which I can never be too thankful — before the house filled up ...

Our first appearance in public was made on Easter Eve at the great Autumn Agricultural Show. My husband lunched with the president and committee at the show ground, and Lady Northcote very thoughtfully asked me to Government House so that I should go with her party. The show itself was excellent and the exhibitions of horsemanship (and horsewomanship) thrilling. No wise man finding himself for the first time in Australia will call himself a horseman until he has seen what the bushman can do.

But even more interesting to me than the show itself were the spectators. The smart gowns and pretty faces of the women, the lean, bronzed men from 'out-back', the gay crowd generally — all were worth looking at, especially by such an ignorant stranger as I felt myself to be. If I had had the least notion of the burning interest taken in the new Commander-in-Chief's wife I should have been unbearably nervous, but in spite of some hints I was far from being fully alive to my new importance, and when I had been presented to that fine old sailor, Admiral Sir Harry Rawson (Governor of New South Wales), who had already welcomed me by letter, I entered the arena feeling pretty comfortable and quite unconscious that no detail of my personal appearance, my unpretentious white garments and doubtfully successful hat would escape the sharp-eyed ladies of the Press.

But they were generous to a fault, and indeed from that day till the moment when I bade good-bye to Australia nearly three years later, the Press was far kinder to me than I deserved. One paper only, so far as I know, was thoroughly nasty ... Even the *Sydney Bulletin*. whose bitter cleverness I had been taught to dread before I set foot in Australia, gave me no such shock; indeed, it went so far as to say that I looked like a seagull at the first Government House Ball I attended — a compliment — which gratified me extremely.

Those first weeks in Sydney were full to overflowing. The Randwick Autumn Races and three big balls all took place in Easter-week, and I made some dreadful blunders by speaking to people to whom I had not been introduced and calling others by names that were not theirs. But I did try very hard to cultivate a memory for both names and faces and was thankful to anyone who was unmistakable through some peculiarity in appearance. But freaks, frights and frumps are very rare in Australia, and pretty girls and women very common, so my memory was most severely tried ...

Dinners, small garden-parties, tea-parties and dances at Admiralty House punctuated our first four months at Sydney, and I enjoyed them all. A husband who never shirked, a competent and experienced flag-lieutenant, a friendly and helpful flagship, and a staff of servants all willing to do their best, reduced my responsibility to nil. I pressed the button and the machinery worked. The guests themselves did the rest. I will not say we had no failures, but Australians are rarely bored, and the ugly habit of posing as superior beings is practically unknown among them, so they are easy to entertain …

Of course there were cliques and circles outside which our official position placed us.

Australians are not specially interested in grand or smart folk unless these possess attractions beyond grandeur or smartness. In Australian society nobody is more popular, no one more freely entertained, than the girl or woman who earns her own living, whether as an artist, a nurse, a masseuse, a teacher or a tradeswoman. But here I must observe that the working lady of Australia possesses the gift of putting off her business face along with her business gown the moment she 'downs tools', and that she plays as hard as she works; hence her social acceptability and it is not because she is ashamed of her trade or profession that she so swiftly lays aside its insignia, including such traces of fatigue and worry as are effaceable. She possesses the capacity, rare among women, for doing one thing at a time and doing it thoroughly.

The superior practicalness of the Australian woman is, no doubt, greatly due to inherited powers, as well as the conditions of her life, for her mother and grandmother had to use both brain and fingers to provide substitutes for such articles as were in their time unpurchasable or unattainable for her house and her wardrobe, and even now in the great cities good servants are hard to get and keep, while the standard of wages is so high that people of comfortable means have only three maids where five would be considered necessary by an English family of equal position. In the Bush it is almost impossible to get trained servants. Ladies' maids are few and far between even in such places as

Sydney, and the capacity of Australian women for cutting out, sewing and contriving, and for turning themselves out fresh and smart from the top of their shining heads to the toes of their small and well-shod feet never failed to excite my admiration and envy ... In my opinion, which I offer knowing full well my temerity, they have still a good deal to learn as regards the decoration and furnishing of their houses. Better colour-schemes and more unencumbered floor-space would make their rooms more attractive; but as practical housekeepers, not directors of a corps of well-drilled servants, they are far ahead of us.

... Australian ladies are house-proud. They cherish the antique, and even elderly, furniture brought out from home by their fathers and grandfathers, many of whom would charter a small ship and carry with them all their household goods; and beautiful china, old-fashioned glass and plate and valuable books and pictures are to be found in many Australian homes as well as in the salerooms of the great cities. Their houses are usually smaller in proportion to their income than ours, but there are fine specimens of the old 'colonial' style among the villas on the shores of Sydney harbour, and their colonnaded verandahs, spacious four-cornered rooms and tall French windows are beautiful as well as suitable to the climate; far more attractive, in short, than the fantastic, many-bowed irregularities which can render a perfectly well-meaning house grotesque.

I once heard an English girl, both clever and original, who was travelling in New South Wales, find fault with Australian women living in the Bush because they were beautifully dressed for dinner every evening! To me it seemed only a very admirable evidence of self-respect. Their critic dressed abominably herself, and as she spoke in disparagement of the 'too smart' Australians, I could not help taking a mental inventory of her own apparel. She wore a shabby, shapeless, old straw hat; a coat both stained and frayed; her gloves had holes in them and her hair hung about her ears in little lustreless wisps. It is fair to say we were out on the harbour in the barge and the weather was showery. Still she might have looked fresh and tidy …

My first acquaintance with the Bush was made at Tuggeranong, near Queanbeyan, and as first impressions have a certain value owing to their freshness I will record them here. The impression above all others which the Englishman new to the Bush receives is one of stillness and space. The stillness is such that he can hear, or thinks he can hear, every revolution and pulsation of his own internal machinery; the space makes him feel as insignificant as a solitary midge in St. Paul's Cathedral. The Bushman's heritage is one of wide horizons; of far-stretching landscapes uncut by macadamised roads, unscored by walls and hedges, unspoilt by cities; and over his head a high dome of clear air, unsullied by coal smoke and untainted by the exhalations and emanations too common in the well-thumbed, dog's-eared little Mother-country …

At Tuggeranong the sensation of aloofness is almost disconcerting. We might have been dropped from an airship on to a spare planet among a folk so little given to speech that they might well be of another race than ours. Shearing is in full swing, and fifty men and boys — shearers, musterers, and rouseabouts — work, eat, and rest within a hundred yards of the homestead, and yet neither by day nor by night does any noise of shouting, singing, or angry voices reach our ears. The lonely stillness of the Bush engenders in its sons an astonishing power, habit — call it what you will — of silence. Messengers ride into the yard, do their business and go about their business, and we look on as though at a cinematographic display. In the shearing-shed only the whirring of the sixteen machines is to be heard. The sheep before their shearers are dumb; and but for the occasional call of 'tar' from a shearer who has drawn blood and summons the 'tar-boy' with his pot of antiseptic, the eight-hours day might pass undisturbed by the sound of a human voice.

The very children at the homestead are quieter than ours. Barefooted and bareheaded they steal about the garden and orchard, and never seem to shout and quarrel at their play. Half the day they spend among the gnarled branches of the big almond trees that shade the flower-filled courtyard from the morning sun, as much at home there as the red and blue parrots who share the fruit with them. And then, when the lamps are lighted, they creep into the central hall, to bury their small persons in armchairs and sofas and their minds in books …

At daybreak there is silence in the sheepyards, and the musical jangle of the magpies down at the creek first wakes, and then lulls us back to sleep until such time as the bare feet of Bolton, Unity, and Pax [servants], pattering on the boards of the long verandah, announce that another day has fairly begun …

The distinction between the Australian of the towns and the Australians of the Bush is one so marked that the most casual visitor cannot fail to notice it. A far wider gulf separates the man bred and employed in an Australian city from the Bushman than that which lies between our cockney and his bucolic brother, for nowhere in these islands can one find the utter isolation which characterises the Australian 'back-blocks'. It produces splendid men, silent, self-reliant and thoughtful; possessed of a natural dignity, and showing a quite peculiar courtesy and gentleness towards women and children. Few men afraid of their own thoughts could long survive such an utter severance from the means to stifle them as long solitary months in the Bush entail, just as few sailors who can live for weeks with no more than a plank between themselves and eternity can be wholly bad.

Nearly every real man, however, has something tough and insensitive in his fibre which enables him to enjoy a solitude not unmixed with danger; few women do more than endure these conditions. The wives of Australian pioneers were for the most part heroines born or made, since in their day to the fear of bushrangers and the discipline of exile was added the oft-recurring trial of bearing children where no skilled woman, much less a doctor, was within reach. And can anything be more harrowing than the spectacle of a mother whose baby had died while its father had gone two hundred miles to fetch a doctor, nailing down the coffin of that baby with her own hands because the carpenter who had fashioned the rough box was so drunk that he was driving the nails in at random and piercing the little body inside? This is a thing that really happened …

Here and there will be found a woman of stiffer mould who actually enjoys the glorious freedom of the Bush oblivious of its loneliness and risk. With the use of her head and hands and the society of her husband and children, she can make as fine a thing — perhaps a finer — of her life than many of her sisters in Melbourne or Sydney. She is the 'mistress' of the station, a little community numbering from ten to fifty souls, for whom she provides and by whom she is looked up to. I have been on one such station, not 'outback', but poor in neighbours and many miles from an unimportant railway station, and if one dare apply such an adjective as patriarchal to the atmosphere of any spot in Australia, that of X. was patriarchal; but in the best sense. Every soul on the station was to the mistress a friend as well as an employee, for every soul was befriended as well as employed. The maidservants married the boundary-riders, or other station hands, and their children when old enough found employment about the place. When the first of the great bullock-wagons piled high with bales of wool started for the railway station (I was there at shearing time) young Mahony was in charge of the leading team. With the second wagon came old Mahony, blue-eyed and white-haired, with a tie to match his eyes and an incongruous band of rusty crape round his battered billy-cock; and little Mahony of the third generation brought up the rear on a half-broken pony. The shearers, transitory hands, the shearers' cook (a most important functionary), the casual 'sundowner' in search of a night's lodging, all saluted the mistress, not because she expected or exacted the tribute, but because she was well known and well liked. It was an unconscious acceptance of the patriarchal system; the result of wise and kind management, not by a manager but by a master.

The absence of companionship for both children and their parents in the less accessible parts of the Bush is an evil and a hardship which only closer settlement can mitigate, but the difficulty of educating isolated children has been courageously met by the responsible authorities. There are now travelling schoolmasters who go their long rounds among the scattered settlers, taking care that no child, however remotely placed, can grow up without education. This opportunity is frequently taken advantage of by the parents, to the great improvement of their own characters and of their usefulness as citizens …

We had been warned that the offer of higher wages would tempt our English servants to desert us in Australia, so it was, we thought, something of an achievement to bring back every one of those who went out with us — eleven, counting the flag-lieutenant's and secretary's servants who lived at Admiralty House. Of the men-servants who came home with us, no less than three have found their way back again to Australia, where they are — unless they have enlisted — in civil employ but not in domestic service. Thus strongly does that big new country appeal to those who have once known it.

There is no doubt that the conditions of life at Sydney proved extremely pleasant to all our servants, and the two maids who went out with us readily adapted themselves to their surroundings, and were so kindly and cordially welcomed by hitherto unknown relations, and the friends of those relations, that their outings were made very enjoyable. In addition to this the excellent steamer-service on the harbour made it possible for them to get plenty of fresh air in the hottest weather at a negligible cost. But they had no desire to remain in Australia. There women-servants can rarely confine their duties to the exact limits laid down in an English household. With us a carefully-trained cook or housemaid is a specialist, and does not easily expand into the bonne a toutfaire who will wash, or wait at table, or act as maid, without considering whether it is 'her place' to do so or not. It is the bonne a toutfaire, the 'cook-general' of the advertisement sheet, who is chiefly needed in those parts of the Empire where wages are almost double those given in England. Such a servant welcomes the help of her mistress in the kitchen and elsewhere, whereas the specialist resents or suspects it. One hears it said that Australian mistresses expect too much of their servants and give them only indifferent accommodation. There may well be mistresses answering to this description, since there are everywhere careless or exacting employers, but in Australia, where the demand so greatly exceeds the supply, a mistress would be extraordinarily shortsighted were she to overdrive or underfeed her servants. But the State, which leaves very little to chance in these matters, has recently ordered an investigation respecting the housing of servants …

As a rule a spell of three days of hot and searing westerly wind is followed at Sydney by a cold and boisterous 'southerly buster', which sweeps the cobwebs from every brain and procures for over strung nerves and aching eyes the luxury of a long night of refreshing sleep. My husband and I had adopted the Australian practice of sleeping out on the verandah, a practice so pleasant and healthful that we regretted it should be impossible of continuance when we returned to England to confront the memorable heat of the summer of 1910. But verandahs in this country are such thieves of the light and sunshine we cannot afford to waste, that our houses are better without them, even though at first I thought our windows looked like lidless eyes, flat and fishy, unshaded by these picturesque additions …

Even in a mean street, narrow and densely populated, the outer air is preferable to that inside its houses, but where a garden of any size surrounds a house and the garden is in turn bounded by the sea, sleeping out is a positive delight, and a delight incomparable, since it provides a sensation unlike any other …

Close to the verandah where my bed was placed stands a Norfolk pine some seventy feet in height, which possesses about fifteen neatly arranged tiers of branches, ten of which were visible to me as I lay at my ease watching the birds whose playground I commanded … But of all the birds that frequent the tree the most dear to me are the 'Willy Wagtails', as they are called in Australia. They are the handsomest, the friendliest and the most entertaining in this aviary of volunteers. The glossy black head, large bright eye, creamy white breast, and coal-black wings and tail belong to a beautifully proportioned bird, strong and graceful, and not quite like anything in the old country, either in marking or shape. He wags his tail, not up and down, but from side to side like a dog, and this is long and full enough to embarrass him seriously on a windy day as he runs about, an unconscious weathercock, picking up grubs on lawn or midden. These wagtails have more power of expressing themselves in song than most Australian birds, for not only can they screech like a parakeet, but they can whistle a pretty appoggiatura of three notes, execute variations on the theme of 'sweet pretty creature' in a most engagingly melodious chuckle, and in early spring warble a short song not unlike that of a thrush …

There are some disadvantages connected with sleeping out on the shores of this great harbour. In thick weather steam-whistles, foghorns, ships' bells, and blood-curdling sirens effectually prevent sleep at both ends of the eight hours devoted to it; in the summer belated excursion steamers, filled with festive singers of 'Auld Lang Syne' or 'God Save the King' (the most popular barcarolle on the harbour), pass close inshore, and cargo-boats with shrieking winches and derricks, load or unload early and late when time presses. But there is no such thing as a nuit blanche, for the sleeper-out. A peace, serene and benignant, pervading mind and body alike, descends upon him in the small and quiet hours. The soft wash of the water against the rocks below, the sighing of the light breeze in pines and gum trees, lull him to rest, and as he drifts into the haven of unconsciousness he feels himself specially and supremely blest — blest with the triple benison of earth and sky and sea …

From Lady Ida Poore, *Recollections of an Admiral's Wife 1903–1916*, London, 1916.

Rosita Forbes

1917

Rosita Forbes was a serious wanderer and explorer, and became a travel writer for The Times, The Daily Telegraph, Pearson's, The Illustrated London News, The Sphere *and* The Saturday Evening Post. *Weary of the Great War, Rosita made her first trip with her friend Undine. They embarked on an Atlantic liner in England while submarines were still prowling about, and stopped in New York on their way to the South Pacific and the Far East. Then they journeyed south, and after a short time in Sydney, sailed for the Australian Territory of Papua where tourists were rare, more especially two women tourists. Rosita was slight of stature, very pretty, and proved an intrepid traveller, later touring extensively in Africa, India, Afghanistan and South America. Her experiences provided the raw material for all her well-received books. She was awarded medals by the Dutch and French geographical societies and from the Royal Society of Arts in London where she was elected a Fellow of the Royal Geographical Society.*

FROM FIJI WE WENT SOUTH, past pine-clad Norfolk Island with its ruins of the old convict prisons, to the land of the Wattle and the Waratah. Australia broke upon us with a line of dazzling golden sand ...

We spent Christmas Day on a glassy sea somewhere within the Great Barrier Reef. It was torridly hot, but we ate plum-pudding with the delightful captain of an ancient tub which wandered slowly round the Solomon Islands and dreary little Queensland ports, and heard stories of the Sydney strikes when every labour man, butcher, baker, railwayman, tram-driver, sailor, engineer stopped work, and for seven weeks all the business of the town was done by volunteers. Women managed the bakeries, squatters with large bank balances ran the trams, farm-hands signed on as able-bodied seamen. The captain said it was a nightmare, as all the stewards were sea-sick and the men at the wheel never could realise that a ship was not run on the principle of a watch ...

It was a quaint voyage. We were the only women on board. The rest of the dozen passengers were flotsam from the hemp and tobacco plantations of the ruthless isles. They vied with each other in telling us strange tales, and sometimes slipped by accident into relating the simple truth, because the things they had seen and done under the

Southern Cross were so much stranger than the stories they could invent! They talked glibly of vanilla and coco and copra as we lay limply on the thirty-foot deck, while the scorching sun crept slowly under the tattered awning and licked worn canvas shoes, and glasses that had held 'Doctor Funk' cocktails and, as the boat rolled on the oily sea, crept up to the white anaemic faces of those who earn their bread — and drink — in the tropics.

We slipped into Port Moresby harbour one grey wet morning, and all my preconceived ideas of savage Papua 'slowly and silently vanished away'. I had dreamed of a tangle of orchids drooping over dark fever-haunted rivers, with alligators lying on mud banks, great scented forests where cannibals performed their horrid rites, green snakes slipping into blazing masses of tropical flowers, birds of Paradise flitting like living jewels above huge painted creepers, honey sweet! Alas, we landed in the 'dry belt'. Port Moresby consists of a handful of red-roofed, corrugated iron shanties flung down pell-mell on a sandy hillside amidst a few stunted blue gum trees. Its roads are mere wandering trails with many a pitfall to the unwary, but its inhabitants point out with pride two excellent street lamps which shed a murky ray over various ant-hills and sand-heaps.

The hotel caused us infinite delight. It was like a large barn divided by sheets of galvanised iron into dim cubicles, which resounded with the sayings of every lodger under the spider-haunted roof. We began to realise the defects of such a system when we were wakened at 3 a.m. by a violent altercation between two tearful individuals in the next compartment as to which should take off the boots of the other. Undine forcibly prevented me from issuing forth in great wrath and a pink 'crepe de chine' nightgown to offer to remove all their boots if only they would be quiet. Port Moresby is hospitable, and it is cheerful, in spite of the heat which reduces every one to the consistency of oozing syrup, but it could scarcely be called quiet. It is too prone to settle its small differences with the aid of a revolver, or, taking an extreme view of the undesirability of human life, try to end it with a blunt razor outside the hotel dining-room.

One day we went along the coast for about an hour in a Government launch to inspect a hemp plantation. We were met by the overseer at the jetty, requested to seat ourselves on a couple of packing-cases on a tiny trolley and pushed along an uneven log track by a 'bunch of boys'. It was slow work, as the little line wound uphill all the time through endless blue gum trees and tree-ferns, but, luckily, the overseer was a talkative young man, and entertained us with stories of the hundred and fifty boys working on the plantation. Labour is generally recruited from very remote districts, and from the smaller islands of the Archipelago. The boys sign on for one to three years at the munificent wage of 10 shillings a month and their food. They go back to their villages with a few knives and belts and strips of bright calico, and are regarded with exaggerated respect and awe for the rest of their lives, which are not unduly prolonged, as they are generally killed and eaten when they are too old to work or even to look after themselves.

The Papuans do not seem to have much family affection. On one occasion we wished to see a feast on a certain far-off plantation, which we understood was in honour of the recent birth of a child. We found this was altogether a mistake, as the child in question formed the chief dish at the feast! Needless to say, this was only discovered later when, severe questions being asked as to the disappearance of various children duly registered on the plantation books, the only answer forthcoming was, 'We eat him kai-kai!' These Guri-Bari boys are unpleasant-looking creatures, with their coal-black skins, broad repulsive features, and short woolly hair. They wear gleaming white bones stuck through their nostrils, enormous shell earrings, and huge knives stuck in the pieces of string which form at the same time their belts and their only clothing. They cheerfully eat raw toads and rats or anything else they can get hold of. You see them sometimes with a live bird or small rodent tied to their belts waiting till they have time to devour it, with or without cooking it. They have a great fear of horses, being utterly ignorant of what species of animal they are. When they first came to that plantation they said, 'The big white man rides a large pig. Let us kill it or it will eat us'; so they tried to murder the unfortunate beast with stones and spears.

Civilisation, of course, is much retarded by the quantity of different languages spoken. A boy from the coast can't understand the talk of a village twenty miles inland, and sometimes two villages separated by a river or a narrow valley speak entirely different tongues. The white men have invented a sort of pigeon 'Motu' which is understood a certain distance along the coast; otherwise it is like the Tower of Babel.

To return to the hemp plantation, the manager's house of red corrugated iron was set on a slight rise in the midst of two thousand acres of hemp, which looks like rows and rows of tall, smooth-leaved cactus. After an excellent tinned lunch — everything in Papua comes out of a tin, except when a rare steamer arrives with Australian meat in cold storage — we were mounted on the usual raw-boned, hard-mouthed quadrupeds and taken round the estate. We saw the boys cutting and stacking the long pointed leaves, piling them on trucks and pushing them down to the shed where an engine tore off the outer green sheath, and shredded the inner pulp into white, juicy fibre. We saw the latter drying, like tangled white clouds fallen out of a summer sky, on long lines of wire, and, finally, we saw the dried product packed into bales ready for transport to the coast. Then we rode back to our launch and chugged through the winding harbour, broken up into so many bays, and dotted with so many islands that once the whole Australian fleet lay hidden there, and no one in Port Moresby knew there was a single warship in their harbour.

We passed some picturesque Water Villages, built high on piles above the sea so that they are protected from attack on three sides. They are only joined to the land by a few ladders and rough wooden gangways. The first sight of Elevara or Hanumabana is utterly bewildering: straw and reed houses perched up in the air, the family pig seated placidly in a rudely constructed style just above the waves, brown babies hanging in plaited fibre bags from any convenient post, the next meal cooking on a tiny charcoal fire on a wooden shelf projecting in front of the house door; long boats, piled with bananas and sago, poled swiftly through the water streets by tall ebony figures devoid of other covering than a few shells or feathers, their massive mop of hair standing out like a bushy halo round their heads. One is struck by the grace and poise of the women in their short, swinging petticoats of straw, sometimes dyed orange or red, barely sweeping their slender knees, open at one side so that the whole of an elaborately tattooed limb is visible. Generally the rest of their shapely persons, even their faces, is stained or tattooed in bright blue, and they wear armlets of shell rings, and perhaps a lobster's claw or two in their hair. Add to this a nose bone and a scarlet lip-ring and the effect is startling.

Unfortunately, they all chew betel-nut, so their teeth are stained scarlet with the juice, and generally pushed forward almost out of their mouths by perpetually sucking the large nut. On shore, under the palm trees, one sees women molding the great clay-pots which, at a certain season of the year, they take down the coast on a big double-sailed lakatoi — which is made by fastening together many of their flat, fishing boats — and barter for sago.

When a lakatoi returns laden with grain there is a great dance in the village, always at night. We saw one on a very dark night, when no moon threw dancing shadows of palms across the beach. Out of the heavy blackness came the beating of a drum. The light of a few far-off torches flickered occasionally across the two lines of dancers who, linked closely together, man and maid alternately, moved slowly and rhythmically up and down. Sometimes the lines met and, joining, came down the centre two and two, till they swung apart in a slowly swaying circle. Some of the men beat together clicking white bones, and all drummed monotonously with their feet. It was silent, restrained, and sinister, akin to the windless night, the dull booming of the surf on the reef, and the sickly sweet scent of oil and flowers. Sometimes a torch flared up and disclosed the fantastic head-dresses, whole skins of beasts, rows of waving birds of paradise, or grinning masks of painted wood and clay as well as long chains of seeds and plaited grasses, rings and anklets of white bones, ropes of shells, necklaces of dogs' teeth wrenched from the living animal that they may retain their lustre. There was no shouting, no laughter.

The drum was like the earth's pulse beating, the thrumming of the feet was her coursing blood. There was something relentless, cruel, passionate about that dance, yet it was slow, quiet, and almost sleepy! One felt an undercurrent that one could not understand, and my vision of strange, deathless rites, age-old as the earth, came back to me there in the darkness!

When kangaroo meat and mangoes began to pall on us and we had learned to distinguish from his harmless brethren the vicious malaria mosquito who bites one standing on his head and waving his hind-legs in the air; ... when we'd grown grey hairs in the heads of the powers that be with our thirst for information, we decided to go inland. With the temperature that of a hot bath we started cheerfully off on a buckboard, which, as the initiated well know, is harder than the hearts of the Huns, or than the rocks on which one falls from one's pet Parnassian heights! It was drawn by two world-worn and weary horses, who fell over the trace-chains and their own noses at every second step. I nearly upset the whole thing driving it down the main street of Port Moresby, as I could not find the brake, so we went down the hill at a hard gallop, missing the only tree and several heaps of stones by a hair breadth, and plunging round the corner on one wheel and an eyelash!

From ten till three we bumped perilously through sanddrifts and creeks, over rock-strewn rutted roads, between desolate blue gum trees athirst for their native Australia and huge white anthills. Then, when we began to feel that our aching bones were indissolubly part of that rattling, jolting buckboard, we saw a big tobacco plantation dipping down to a muddy river, so we turned into an even worse road and jerked up to a wide verandahed bungalow with wicked, spotted orchids climbing up the pillars. The planter was, as usual, extraordinarily kind and devoted to us his last tin of Marie biscuits and a omelet which two fuzzy-headed creatures cooked with breathless interest. Then he showed us a short cut between neat rows of tiny tobacco plants under sheltering straw mats, over a bridge which might have shaken the nerve of the youngest and maddest aviator, for it was only a few strands of wire plaited with willow thongs, slung from two sagging cables sixty feet above a grey river where snouts of greedy alligators poked out of the water.

Then came more jolting down a long bush road, and towards dusk we came to a Government rest-house made of galvanised iron and straw, from whence the most energetic woman I've ever met rushed forth to meet us. Between snatches of ribald song and violent bursts of abuse of things in general, she conjured hot baths out of the river, roast pork out of the primitive oven, and horses out of the bush, so that we stumbled over the creek in darkness, and, as the Southern Cross swung up into a sapphire sky, we started up the Bluff. It was a wonderful ride in the starlight, with the great crag looming above our heads, and long tentacles of hanging creeper clutching at us as we passed, but my most vivid memory is of the tin hut perched among rows of pineapple just over the ridge, where a mighty native, attired in a magnificent feather crown and a piece of string, produced cocoa and eggs and bacon under the direction of the sleepy manager.

We woke to a world of drifting violet shadows on the soaring Owen Stanley Range, whose northern slopes guard the untrodden country, happy hunting-ground of cannibals and head hunters. The last intrepid planter who penetrated to an inhospitable village was eaten with his clothes and everything else. The punitive expedition recovered his boots after they had been cooked for many days to make them tender. I gather, however, that the Papuans are careful to kill their dinner before they cook it, and it is generally a swift end beneath battle-axes and spears ... Curiously enough, there is no actual law against cannibalism in New Guinea or Papua. I mean if A commits a murder and B devours the corpse, the latter has committed no legal offence. This worried intensely the lawyers of the coast until they decided that the act could justifiably be punished under the heading of 'indecent behaviour to a corpse'. In some of the inland villages all the warriors live together in a high straw house, perhaps one hundred feet long. It is divided into cubicles, and over the door of his own particular compartment each warrior hangs the skulls of his defeated enemies ... No woman is allowed to enter such houses, and in certain districts all boys of sixteen are taken from their homes, and kept shut up in one of these 'dongas' for several weeks or even months. The missionaries have tried hard to break this custom, as the boys are supposed to undergo certain rites of initiation during this period of rigorous seclusion.

However, I should imagine the sullen, suspicious Papuan of the interior is difficult to convert to new ideas, as witness this delicious story told me by a Roman Catholic priest. A would-be Christian arrived at his house one day and said he wished to be baptised. As he had attended a mission school for some time the priest consented, but finding that he answered to the name of 'Snowball', he decided to re-christen him Patrick. The boy was duly immersed in the nearest pool and told that his name was now Pat, and that it behoved him most particularly not to eat meat on Fridays. Unfortunately, the very next Friday the priest discovered his latest convert devouring a large piece of kangaroo. 'Oh, Pat, don't you know that this is Friday, and I told you only to eat fish on that day?' he reproved sternly. 'Me no eat meat. Me eat fish,' said the erstwhile 'Snowball' eagerly. 'But I can see it is meat. It is very wrong to tell me lies,' was the indignant answer. 'But this no meat,' insisted Patrick. 'I put him in the water and I christen him fish!'

Very little is really known about the strange folk who inhabit the wild forest country of the interior. Some of the villages are entirely built in the trees, and their only approach from the solid earth is a long ladder that can be pulled up at the approach of an enemy tribe. These glorified dovecotes are often of two stories with an admirably constructed platform in front of the door, on which all cooking is done. It was once officially reported that the natives of a certain district north of the Owen Stanley range had tails! This was because the long ends of their tapa cloth belts flew out behind them as they ran. The tapa cloth is made out of inner bark fibre and painted with juices brown and red.

It was a day of dreaming peace and curly snowflake clouds when we left our tin hut and rode along the ridge, our destination a big rubber plantation beyond the dry belt. We rode some time through exquisite long grass country in which tall feathery fronds reached above our waists, then we dropped into gloomy mangrove swamps haunted by swarms of mosquitoes, which literally blackened our clothes as we scuttled through them. There were alligators, which the natives like to eat, in the rivers, and orange and white orchids hanging in clumps from dripping tree branches. Occasionally a hornbill with a jarring screech flew clumsily across the trail. They are the ugliest birds I've ever seen in spite of their gorgeous tawny orange and black plumage, for their quaint, curved, razor-edged bills are literally a third of their length. There were flights of sulphur-crested cockatoos in the blue gum country, but we didn't see our first bird of paradise till we left the dry belt behind us and plunged into luxurious forest, steamy and dark beneath the tangled wealth of creeper. These gorgeous flame-red birds with exquisite panoply of shimmering tails are of the crow species and are as common as the homely rook in England. The pale yellow variety comes from German New Guinea and is rarely found in Papua, but the red ones do much damage to the crops, and every planter regrets the Government fine for shooting them.

It is a severely punishable offence to export them, but rare specimens find their way out of the country hidden in hat linings, or folded between the pages of local newspapers, or forming part of the stuffing of innocent travelling cushions. I knew one ingenious woman who marched on to the ship with a complete petticoat of the precious birds under her fashionably voluminous skirt, and she confided to me afterwards that she had suffered agonies of terror, it being a windy day, lest a fluttering orange frond should detach itself and float gently down to the inspector's feet. On the self-same occasion one of the male passengers was seen jauntily walking up the gangway with a delicate swaying feather protruding from his coat collar. We left it to the harassed customs official to discover where the rest of the bird was!

Goura pigeons are other lovely inhabitants of Papua. They are deep smoke-blue in colour, and carry most exquisite upstanding crests on their heads. I remember I once bought thirteen for two bottles of whisky from a bleary-eyed settler who assured me he badly needed the spirit for his neuralgia! The natives kill, with their bows and arrows, the glorious goura pigeons for food, and use quantities of birds of paradise to make the enormous head-dresses used in their dances, though really I should have thought their immense shocks of hair would be sufficiently exotic ornamentation. The only reason they mind going to prison is because their hair is cut off there, and they are not allowed to join in the dances unless they are shock-headed.

Long before we reached our destination we fell in with a heated and damp surveyor jogging along on an old brown pony and suitably attired in open-work grey flannel trousers and an ancient pyjama coat from which most of the buttons were missing. His boys almost fled at our approach. They evidently considered us a new specimen of mankind, and we heard them asking: 'Are these a new kind of Sinabada?' [chieftainess] We joined forces with the surveyor for a time, and he took us through trackless blue gum country to the edge of a mighty ravine, where a torrent thundered down over a great precipice, and a strange bird village clung to the top of the opposite cliff. I don't think we ever reached that particular township, but we came to one cluster of rough straw huts in a clearing of the primeval jungle where we saw a most interesting bird dance.

The broad-featured women, darkly tattooed, huddled round a charcoal pan and giggled, while the old men inhaled smoke from long hollow bamboo pipes, burnt with intricate black designs. The young men fetched long tapering spears and their mightiest head-dresses, and squabbled for some time over their most precious decoration — a long and very old woollen stocking! With infinite pride the winner drew on the coveted prize, and it reefed itself half-way down his leg and considerably impeded his movements.

It is difficult to describe the bird dance, but it is exactly like the alternately grotesque and dignified posturings of Great Bustards on a Scottish moor in the mating season. Then it changed and the performers used the springing, swaying steps of the dancing cranes, hopping, gesticulating with such grace and agility that one could almost see fluttering wings spreading out from their ebony bodies, and imagine their whistling calls really proceeded from the throats of a love-sick bird piping to its mate in the spring-time!

I imagine that the Papuans are a very low and degraded type of native, as they have scarcely any tribal law; they acknowledge no hereditary chief, and certainly age receives no veneration, as it merely provides meals for the younger generation! In many districts one comes across a clearly Jewish type with a very hooked nose. In fact, substitute a white skin and you would not hesitate to claim the result as of Hebrew parentage! They are nomads who rarely live in one place for more than a few months. One week there is a prosperous straw village deep in the shade of some scarlet flame-trees, the next, most of the houses are destroyed, and the whole tribe has migrated many miles away. This is one of the difficulties the missionaries have to contend with — their scholars and their congregation may vanish in a night …

We went on one long expedition down the coast in the Governor's delightful yacht. We started very early and slipped along inside the reef for many sunlit, lazy hours, the only unfortunate episode being when the native butler, contented in the knowledge that his fluffy hair stood out almost as wide as the cabin door, reflectively combed back the woolly mass with a loaf of bread, which he afterwards calmly placed on the table. I looked with horror at the immaculate private secretary who was doing host to see if he had noticed the contretemps, but he was contentedly immersed in salmon mayonnaise, so I left him to the old adage, 'What the eye does not see, the mind does not trouble about!' …

The destination of His Excellency's white yacht was a village built nearly a quarter of a mile out on the coral reef. We got into the dinghy and rowed through the main street, followed by a train of hollow log canoes, poled by slim, laughing girls, of the island far-famed for the beauty of its maidens. Indeed, they were weirdly and wonderfully tattooed: we saw one symmetrical goddess attired in an intricate design of black snakes painted on her own firm brown skin. We climbed laboriously up one of the rickety wooden ladders, stooped through a low entrance, and found ourselves in an immaculately clean and unexpectedly large interior, the floor made of smooth wood beams and the walls of elaborately plaited reeds. In the centre was a blackened circle in which smoldered a few charcoal embers. Of furniture or even mats there was not a trace. A large calabash full of water stood in one corner, and some strings of certain bright-coloured seeds and shells, amulets against witchcraft, hung from the roof beams, while rows of turtle skulls were ranged along the walls. Otherwise it was utterly empty ...

That was almost our last day in Papau, and always I shall have a memory of steaming into the beautiful harbour with the crowded hills purple against a blazing sunset, and seeing the customs house flag flying at half-mast. A man with whom we had dined the night before was dead. Life and death go hand in hand in the ruthless islands of the southern seas. One of the gymnastic Papuan mosquitoes must have accomplished his nefarious design, for the instant we arrived at Cairns — a desolate, galvanised iron township surrounded by blue gums and banana trees — I collapsed with dengue fever. However, Undine nursed me so strenuously that, in self-defence, I found it necessary to recover in spite of a delightful toy which she borrowed from the only chemist one hot, dry day when I was babbling cheerfully of cannibals and caterpillars! It was called a Home Thermometer, and one's temperature either ran out altogether at one end past a scarlet notice which said, 'Call a doctor at once,' or sank despairingly to about 60 where 'No danger' was written in sulphur yellow.

A dilatory steamer finally picked us up in the middle of a cyclone, carried us for three peaceful days north to Thursday Island, ringed with its fleet of pearl fishers, and forthwith plunged headlong with us into the North-West monsoon. For unnumbered days we lay in wet deck-chairs, lashed to any convenient rail, while the fo'c'sle plunged down into great breakers which broke right over the deck, covering the bridge in spray, and the propeller sailed triumphantly out of the water, and pretended it was an aeroplane. When I wasn't falling downstairs to the hermetically sealed saloon to have soup upset in my lap, and potatoes dribbled in my hair, I remember I chased elusive but very strong smells through cockroach-haunted passages, with a tin of Keating's powder, to the infinite fury of the chief steward, who generally followed with a broom …

How glad we were to reach Java, in spite of some delightful Australians, wounded in the war, who cheered our dripping hours on the unsteady decks with stories of Gallipoli as seen through the rose-coloured spectacles of the cheerful Anzacs! One, who had contributed a hand to the tragedy and the glory of Suvla Bay, reduced us to helpless mirth with his description of the kindly soul who visited him in hospital, and exclaimed in impulsive pity, 'Oh, my dear man, have you lost your hand for good?' …

From Rosita Forbes, *Unconducted Wanderers*, London, 1919.

Philippa Bridges
1923

Philippa Beatrice Bridges, author and traveller, wrote for Blackwood's Magazine, Cornhill Magazine, Queen and Gentlewoman, *all popular periodicals of the time in London. After a family visit in Adelaide she organised a trip to Darwin accompanied by her Aboriginal helpers Macumba Jack and his wife Topsy, together with four camels — Ladybone, Snowy, Barley and The Oont.*

A LONG ENJOYABLE VISIT TO MY BROTHER [Lieut-General Sir Tom Bridges, Governor of South Australia] and sister-in-law at Adelaide was drawing to a close when the idea occurred to me of overlanding across the Continent and taking a homeward bound ship from Darwin. Central Australia has not so far attracted the woman traveller very much. The first lady to cross the Continent was Mrs. Dutton, who motored to Darwin from Adelaide with her husband a few years ago; and last year the Governor of Victoria and Lady Stradbroke followed the same route. I intended to travel unhurriedly in the same fashion as the dwellers themselves did. I had a great wish to see the Never-never, and possibly a flicker of the nomadic instinct may also have urged me, for I know that the thought of the long northward march, which extended practically from the Great Australian Bight to the Arafura Sea, made a strong appeal.

Before starting I talked with several people who had travelled in Central Australia, notably the Hon. Walter Duncan [a pastoralist], who had recently returned from Darwin by motor, and Samuel A. White, ornithologist and anthropologist, who has made several journeys into the heart of Australia, and whose wife has travelled farther by camel than any other white woman. It was from their conversation, coupled with my brother's account of his visit to the Northern Territory the year before, that I made my first mental picture of Central Australia.

Mr. Duncan's advice was … 'Remember on which side of the telegraph line you are, and if you meet with any real difficulty, make for it and damage it as much as you can. Then sit down under a telegraph pole and wait; somebody will be sure to come along.'

I left Adelaide on a cold spring day in August for Oodnadatta; by the fortnightly mail train, a thirty-six hours run of 686 miles. I found my fellow passengers congratulating themselves on having a through train, for until lately it was necessary to spend two nights on the way. Quorn Station was in darkness. We groped about after our baggage (for it is necessary to change carriages three times on the through train, partly on account of difference in gauge), one lantern among many, and partook of strong tea and meat pies, which seemed to be the only form of refreshment available. Presently a comfortable sleeping car was put on, in which one could have got a good night's rest had it not been for the incredible amount of bumping, which the other passengers accounted for by saying that cattle trucks had been coupled between the carriages, rendering the air-brakes useless …

Several fellow-passengers had introduced themselves, among them a retired sergeant of the fourth Dragoon Guards, who had made his home comfortably in Australia, and also a young police 'trooper', who asked me to send a message to the Governor, who had helped him in his career, and he wished His Excellency to know how well he was getting on. He was now on his way from Port Augusta to Oodnadatta to bring back some 'wild blacks', who had burgled a store somewhere out in the Never-never, the idea being that the man who was robbed was the first white man these natives had ever seen.

Somebody said that 'George' would give us tea. George was the railway-gang cook at a halt. At 'train-time' he was always ready with a plentiful supply of tea and pasties. 'You'll taste George's pasties,' I was told, in a tone that made me think that a visit to Australia would not be complete without this experience. The train pulled up beside a low stone cottage, towards which there was a general exodus. I remained where I was, and presently a man came along with a simple invitation. 'He says, will you come?' The courteous and hospitable cook and two or three of his friends were waiting at the door. They ushered me into the stone kitchen. A long table and forms were dimly lit by a swinging lamp that cast gleams, and glooms on tired, good-humoured faces. The pasties and tea were really excellent.

An hour later, in the pitch dark, we ran into Oodnadatta, and stopped at the platformless station, where the inhabitants were standing in a row two deep, awaiting the fortnightly excitement of the train. I spent two or three days at Oodnadatta very pleasantly, thanks to the kindness and hospitality of Doctor and Mrs. Shanahan. They have lived here for many years, and I found their conversation of unfailing interest. There is no church at Oodnadatta or Anglican priest, but a Roman Catholic priest came by train for an annual three days visit, and my hostess's drawing-room was turned into a chapel for Mass, confession, and a Christening.

Nominally the doctor's practice runs south, for it chiefly concerns the railway, but virtually it extends wherever a doctor is needed, and includes any sick person within reach, and several who might be considered out of reach. To the north there is no other medical man nearer than Darwin (about 1,300 miles).

Some years ago the telegraph brought news of a man hurrying doctorwards with lockjaw. He travelled by buggy with a herd of spare horses from a station 600 miles away, and was accompanied by two Aborigines. His complaint made it impossible for him to eat, but his servants contrived in some fashion to make him swallow liquid food and orange juice. At night they camped and looked after him to the best of their ability, and in the process of time — six weeks — they arrived at Oodnadatta. The Doctor, who had had news of him from the telegraph stations on the way, felt puzzled at the nature of the complaint, for he said that tetanus would have carried him off in about two days. He discovered that the jaws were locked owing to poison from a decayed tooth, and a cure was effected by chiselling away part of the bone. The patient made a good recovery, and then set off again with his natives on his 600 mile journey home …

Oodnadatta holds a dance in the Memorial Hall on 'train nights' … Two buckets of clear, cold water stood on a table for the refreshment of the dancers. Here linger dances that have been forgotten in English ballrooms: the polka, schottische, valeta, and mazurka waltzes. The Master of Ceremonies stepped forward saying, 'Gents, select your partners for the Alberts,' and I watched a quadrille-like measure that I suppose Queen Victoria must have trod with the Prince Consort.

A day or two later I went on to the Macumba, one of the

cattle stations of Sir Sidney Kidman, who had very kindly offered to help me on my journey ... Mr. Kempe, the manager, made the preparations for the first part of my journey, with the result that I had a very compact little 'plant', efficient and easy to handle. The four camels were in charge of a native boy called Macumba Jack, whose lubra (wife), Topsy, came as my maid. There were the necessary saddles, harness, camel boxes, and other gear. Mrs. Kempe packed a capacious and well-filled tucker-box, and Mr. Kempe saw to it that I had a new, strong, and comfortable saddle.

Having said good-bye to the Macumba party, and thanked my host and hostess most heartily for their hospitality and kindness in making such careful arrangements, I mounted my camel, was heaved aloft, and set off, Mrs. Kempe's parting advice being, 'Whish down well before sunset, and get a comfortable camp before dark.' Rain had been threatening all day, and postponed my departure until after dinner, so the first stage was a short one of about twelve miles. We camped at Ross's Hole, and though I got in before nightfall, nothing could have made it a comfortable camp, for the wind rose, bringing the dust, which smothered everything, and nearly scattered the fire. Most of the creeks and holes had dried up, for this season bade fair to be the worst for forty years, which in this country means — within the memory of man. I settled down under the lee of my tent, opened the excellent tucker-box, and ate my evening meal. Macumba Jack and Topsy, their work in camp finished, had settled down under a break-wind of branches, and were cheerfully making the best of things. On the other side of the muddy water-hole the camels were vigorously breaking off branches of the gum trees and eating the leaves …

At the Ten Mile I dismounted to look at the Bore, and found scalding hot water tumbling out of a pipe, making a small lake with its outrush, the cooler end of which harboured a splendid flock of waterfowl. An iron hut, the only building for many miles, appeared to be a store, for it was full of tinned oysters; and a white man whom Macumba Jack called Ole Ike Hervey shook my dusty hand in his dusty hand, and wished me the best of luck. The only other living thing that I saw that day was an emu, which would not wait to be photographed, but raced away with enormous strides faster than a horse can gallop. We camped about sunset at Aldnagowra, and during the night the wind abated.

In the morning we met the camel mail that plies between Oodnadatta and Horse Shoe Bend on its return journey. The mailman, Mr. Bromley, whished down his camel, and the string came to a standstill. He told me that there was no feed within six miles of Hamilton Bore, for it had all been eaten out by cattle. The camel mail struck me as being a strange and picturesque survival. Probably its days are numbered, for as soon as the heavy sandy creek called the Alberga is bridged for motors, a car will be able to run all the way to Alice Springs, with little fear of getting 'bogged' in the sand. At present, the mail service of Central Australia is not very adequate. Alice Springs gets a fortnightly camel mail from Oodnadatta, the 'rail head', but the stations beyond are served once in six weeks, which, of course, means that they only have regular communication with the outer world eight times in the year.

A few hours later, when the lubra and I were riding along,

the boy making a circuit through the woods in search of game, we came upon a lost bull camel, and Topsy cried, 'I frightened he go for us.' So we took the string into the Bush, whished down and dismounted, and when he came towards us I flapped a big cloak at him, and Topsy waved a long pole, and though he returned again and again, our united wavings and flappings persuaded him at last to depart. He had a broken hobble on his leg, and looked a very derelict ship of the desert; but he was dangerous as well as pathetic ... We had dinner in a little dry creek near the road, and a black boy on a trotting camel swung into view, looking for the bull, which he said had got away from the mail two days ago. He had dinner with my blacks, and then, though they told him that the camel was not far off, he departed the way he had come, saying he would 'send nother black fellah.'

At Hamilton Bore, which we reached about 4 o'clock, there was a large Afghan encampment with about a hundred camels, and the land was as bare of grass as if it had been ploughed and harrowed. There was a dead cow in the water, but nobody seemed to mind, and as Macumba Jack did not see his way to pulling it out, we left it there.

Our four camels were all strong animals individually, but they did not make a good string, camels being more difficult to match than pearls, for the excellence of the string lies not in the equal or graduated size of the units, but in their ability to walk at a regulation pace. Barley and Snowy, the lead and baggage camels, could do a steady three miles an hour all day long, and my riding camel and The Oont were both good trotters, though slow walkers. Barley had suffered rough handling at some time in her life, for part of her nostril had been torn away, and a new place pierced for the stud. On the afternoon march she carried the baggage, and Snowy, released from the load and made leader, began to walk too quickly, with the result that I noticed Barley's nose was bleeding, and called a halt … Next day we did only a short stage, and I chose to walk. The camels had all recovered, and were in good form, though the stony country had yielded a feed of dry stalks.

Blood's Creek, called after a Doctor Blood who once travelled this way, proved a hospitable spot in spite of its and surrounding and uneuphonious name. Mr. and Mrs. Roper, who have a hotel and store here, came out to meet me with a hearty reception. I had a comfortable rest and a pleasant chat with Mrs. Roper, who gave me several hints on Bush travel, and also remarked, 'I think you will feel you have had enough of it by the time you get to Alice Springs.' We watered the camels, filled up the canteens, and started off again in the burning heat, across the sand and the gibbah …

One afternoon I came upon the boy dismounted, hat in hand, looking down at a little heap of stones. 'He bin perish,' he said. 'Some man bin perish. Dunno who. Dunno when, but he planted there,' I would not have known that the place was a grave, and asked if there was a white man buried there, and the boy said yes, he knew by the stones. To 'perish', in these parts, means to die of thirst. The boy mounted again with a sigh, as if of regret that anyone should perish in a place where life is as scarce as it is here. Next day we crossed the undefined border of the Northern Territory, and arrived at Charlotte Waters …

The telegraph station is built of solid blocks of stone, with a walled courtyard, designed for defence; relic of the old troublous days when the natives still hoped to exterminate the white men. Indeed, it was not until some of the Aborigines had paid visits to the cities of the south that they gave up the hope of doing so, the population of the cities convincing them that the white man had come to stay.

Mr. Hocking, the station master, said that he had expected me to dinner. 'I had a hot roast waiting for you until two,' he said. I asked him how he knew that I was coming, and he said that Mrs. Roper had told him on the telephone that at the pace I was travelling I should be at Charlotte Waters in time for dinner. It was refreshing to sit in a cool room and drink tea, for there was not a particle of shade on the road.

Then I crossed the hot dry creek that I suppose in the wet season is Charlotte Waters, to see Mrs. Johnson, whose husband was just completing the new well. They were living in a tent, and Mrs. Johnson told me that tent-life was quite comfortable until the wind began to blow, when the dust distracted her. In that little canvas home she seemed to have everything necessary to civilised life.

She asked me if I was not lonely travelling with only black servants, and seemed surprised when I told her that I had not felt at all lonely so far, but might have been so if I had not had a good lubra with me. She asked me to camp beside her, but this I was not able to do, for there was no feed for several miles round the well, and I thought it wiser to stay with the camels. There were several people working here, and the big iron tank and engine and rigging gave an air of progress that I had not seen before on the journey.

It was now dark, and we had four miles on heavy sand before we could find anything that the camels could eat … Dead bullocks, a frequent roadside feature, had begun to appear again, and I dreaded that in the dark we should camp upon their bones. The boy and lubra, though anxious to get to their supper and rest, were very patient. They lit the lantern and searched over the ground, reporting, 'No bones here, no dead bullock. Good clean camp.'

I saw several kinds of hawks, which are beautiful, graceful birds in spite of their bad reputation, large flocks of galah parrots and sulphur-crested cockatoos, and occasionally a pair of Major Mitchells. Live rabbits were scarce, but we frequently came upon dead ones, stuck in the lower branches of trees, whither they must have climbed in search of food only to get entangled and perish.

We reached New Crown, one of Sir Sidney Kidman's stations, during the afternoon ... Mr. King, the manager, showed me the garden and well and some fascinating little dingo pups, the first I had ever seen, and gave me good counsel regarding my journey, advising me, since I was 'travelling happily' with my present plant, not to change it at Alice Springs, but to take it on as far as possible. He also remarked that there was no such thing as accuracy in the Bush. 'If you ask ten Bushmen the same question, you will get ten different answers.'

Most of the wells in the Dead Heart are leased to settlers who undertake to keep them in repair and charge stockmen a small sum per head for mobs of cattle and horses watering there. All the country round the Old Crown Station was terribly parched. The horses were too weak to work, and only camels and donkeys were now being used. Mr. Summerfield at the Old Crown Well is said to have the best camels in Australia. They certainly looked in excellent condition, and reflected great credit upon their owner. The difficulties of life in these parts can be a little imagined when one hears of donkey teams being sent several miles for firewood, and one knows that every sort of foodstuff, save meat alone, must be brought by pack animal from Oodnadatta. Mr. and Mrs. Summerfield kindly invited me to dinner, talked about the problems of life in the country, and showed me strange pebbles and 'rubies' found on the hillsides near by ...

I was never afraid of losing myself on my little excursions, for the Australian Aboriginal is a tracker above all else — I believe he can see a footprint on a bare rock — and I felt sure that Jack and Topsy would always have found me. Tracking is part of an infant's early education. As soon as a child can crawl its mother takes a paw of wallaby or 'possum, and gives him lessons in reading footprints in the dry sand. Topsy sometimes amazed me by looking down from the height of the camel-saddle and remarking, 'Dingo, three days old', 'Kangaroo, last night', 'Snake, this morning'. I once hoped to floor her by asking which way did the snake go, but she answered promptly, 'That way.' I learnt to know the track of a snake, but never got to the pitch of being able to tell in which direction it was travelling ...

I camped on Paddy's Plain after darkness had fallen. Topsy had to make damper and flap-jack, which she did very neatly. Her pastry board was a sack sprinkled with flour, on which she kneaded the dough made of flour, baking-powder and water. Meanwhile, the boy had got a good hot wood fire, and Topsy beat the charcoal into tiny pieces, and mixed it with earth to lessen the heat, then she threw on the damper, and covered it carefully with a mixture of charcoal and earth, putting embers on the top.

She baked the flap-jacks on the embers without covering them. They were done in a few minutes, but the damper took two hours to bake ...

The Finke Creek was scorchingly hot when we watered the camels, and I was glad to leave the glare of the white sand and get on to the Hugh River, where there are lovely gum trees, and as the afternoon waned, we reached the Depot Sand-Hills, camping about four miles south of Rocky Hill. The sand was as red as brick dust, and the camels floundered about in it. We went up and down some steep rises. Topsy alighted and caught a sand-devil, a little animal that looked like a large toad, but walked like a lizard, and was clothed in a patchwork of small squares, each with a soft but prickly spine ... Later we saw others sitting at the mouths of their tunnels, waiting for us to go by. They all seemed ridiculously tame ...

At Alice Well Constable Mackay at the police station gave me dinner, talked about the country and native life, and cleverly mended the camera, which had been jolted out of action. The constable has an excellent garden, and he gave me some fresh eggs and lettuces, both great luxuries.

Macumba Jack advised me to follow a 'black-fellah road', which he said would take us a short cut through the Bush, saving twenty-two miles, or about a day's travelling, and this I decided to do, partly because time was a considera-tion, but also out of curiosity to know what a 'black-fellah road' was like. As a matter of fact, there was no road at all, we just struggled along through the Bush for eight hours, and I am sure that both camels and riders found it much more tiring than the proper road would have been. Camels like a pad along which they can follow each other dreamily, and the Bush seemed to make them all nervous; the rider had to be on the alert the whole time. I rode The Oont, which was quite a good little camel and a fine trotter, but when it came to getting through a thicket, instead of letting me choose the place, he would rush at it, put his head down, and scrape through somehow. Of course, I got scratched and torn. Upon the road The Oont would never have dreamt of jumping a gutter across the pad, but out in the Bush he leapt these gutters in an amazing fashion, and he would rush at a wash away, and scramble through it in a manner quite different from his usual cautious behaviour. Then he would tear on until we came to another obstacle, which he would negotiate with a rush or a scramble or a leap. It was late in the afternoon when we emerged from the thickets on to the proper track.

I camped early, feeling that I had had enough exercise. Topsy, who was a most industrious lubra, made the damper, and then cut out and began stitching a new dress that she intended to make … Though I seldom felt lonely, either during the day's march or the solitary evenings in camp, it was, of course, always a pleasure and an event to arrive at a homestead. After the day's skirmishing about the camels were quite ready for a good drink of water at Deep Well the next morning, and here I found news from Adelaide, to which I was able to reply, Deep Well being in telephone communication with the telegraph station.

Topsy was a picture of industry, perched upon her camel, stitching away at her new dress to be 'flash' to enter Alice Springs. I had run out of meat, and told the boy to try to shoot a bird. But we saw nothing edible. After a sudden halt, however, and a race round a bush with a stick, he came running with a lizard that he had caught. He carried it along in a kerosene tin, and cooked it in the ashes of the fire for dinner. It was very tender, and tasted like chicken. I think it was the species they call iguana.

The blacks eat a great deal of meat. For their morning lunch they would share a lump of beef about as big as a football, dispatching it without any bread. Their dinner was always a serious matter, and I never knew that human beings could eat so much, for when they had finished a large ration of beef, they would turn their attention to three or four rabbits and half a dozen galahs that they had killed on the morning's march. We frequently killed snakes, but all of one variety — the alinga. If there was a chance of cooking a snake immediately, the natives would always enjoy eating it, but they would never eat one that had been killed for more than about an hour.

I got the idea that we were losing time, and decided upon a night march, so we camped from 5.30 to 7.30, and I had a supper of parrots. Though not a good shot, the boy was an excellent hunter. I used to watch him stalking game. He got quite close to it before risking a shot from his short-barrelled gun. If he got three parrots for the expending of one cartridge it was all the better, though I always felt a little compunction at killing these beautiful little birds for food, especially as they did not make a very satisfactory meal.

It was beautiful riding along under the stars. The camels watched the road intently, every hair on the alert, and picked their way with care over the shadows even of twigs. Macumba Jack preferred to walk, so he tied his camel to the tail of Snowy, and set off into the Bush. I think he had an idea of hunting, but about an hour later he returned to the string, and said he would lead. Both he and Topsy slept while they were riding, and I felt so drowsy that I kept 'dropping off' also, but waking with a sudden start as Ladybone skipped over a dark shadow. I suddenly realised that I might be in danger of dropping off in another fashion, and after that I kept watch. The Bush was such a place of beauty and interest under the faint light of the stars that I was loth to call a halt at all, but about midnight fatigue compelled me to do so, and we whished down, unloaded, hobbled the camels with all swiftness, and sent them off to graze, I helping with the work. The boy searched the ground with tufts of lighted grass, reporting, 'No snake — all clean.' Topsy threw my sleeping-bag on to the ground, and the next instant I was asleep. I do not think, however, that we saved much time by the night march, for my retainers were very dull and slow in the morning.

Wire Creek Soakage, to which Macumba Jack had often alluded, proved to be an unimpressive hole in a mud bank. Nevertheless, if we had been short of water, it would have been of the utmost importance, for we could have procured it here by digging. The day grew hotter and hotter; there was no shade whatever, only hot brown earth and a few brown rusty trees. The distant rim of hills towards which we were travelling lost their morning blueness and became barren and arid. They were the MacDonnell Ranges, and presently the boy pointed out Emily Gap to the east, and the conical hill that appears to block the passage through the Ranges to Alice Springs …

During the afternoon a Myall suddenly stepped out of the Bush in front of us, and it was so long since The Oont had seen a passer-by that he went off at full gallop. He raced along for about half a mile, and as it would have been very difficult to pull him up without pulling out the nose stud, by which means alone the Australian camel is controlled, I let him go, and made the discovery that a camel's fast gallop is a far easier pace than his walk. Animals that are used to travelling through the Bush get very shy, and will look with deep suspicion upon anyone else who has the assurance to use His Majesty's highway!! …

Apparently we were nearing Alice Springs … Another half-hour and the silver grey dots that are the iron roofs of the houses, and some green trees, came in sight. We whished down in front of the solid stone-built police station, whose doors opened hospitably, and Sergeant and Mrs. Stott came out to receive me. This brought the first part of the camel journey to an end, a distance of three hundred and twenty-five miles, which had taken me a fortnight to cover. The mailmen do it in twelve days.

Mrs. Stott took me for a picnic to Simpson's Gap, a 'black tracker' (native policeman) driving us through the Bush. All the horses were poor, shadowy things, and the state of all animals was truly pitiable … The water in the Gap was black with dirt, and the animals had tried to make a soak for themselves before they would drink it.

With heads and hoofs they bored holes in the ground into which the water would sometimes filter, but many dry holes testified to their vain efforts. We came upon a tunnel about four feet long, with a little water at the end, which the tracker said a cow had scooped out with her horns. All the waterholes were places of tragedy. At Emily Gap the water was shallow and black. Bush horses came down to drink, whinnied to the buggy horses in friendly fashion, and went to the water, but they did not seem able to touch it. Dead horses and bullocks were lying at the edge, and cattle coming to the water would not pass them, but made a wide detour. A lovely mare and foal came down, saw the dead horses, shied, and rushed away. Presently they returned, found the water undrinkable, and went away again thirsty into the Bush.

The black tracker made a soak with his hands, and thus got some fairly clean water to fill the quart pots, and in spite of all the surrounding tragedies, we had a pleasant little picnic. In a country where the conservation of water is of such vital importance, I was surprised to find no precautions at all taken to ensure its cleanliness. It appears to be nobody's business to see that carcasses are burnt or buried. A dead dingo added to the dangers already existing. Dingoes are killed by means of poisoned baits, which take effect when they drink water.

Sergeant Stott, who had lived for forty years in the Northern Territory, and whose advice was therefore of great assistance to me, arranged the next stage of my journey.

It can be no easy task to hold the scales of justice in a sparsely populated slice of country about ten times the size of England when the claims of the retreating black man and the invading white man happen to clash, and clear-headedness and initiative characterise the Police Sergeant, whose authority has been all but absolute.

The laws are simple, and within the comprehension of the natives. They are based on the live-and-let-live principle, it being understood that the black man shall do no harm to the white man, his servants, or his property. There are still many natives who have not yet come under the white man's influence — protective or otherwise — and with these the law does not concern itself, their affairs being settled by their own tribal law. They are therefore free to go their own way, even to the extent of eating their babies, without interference from their enlightened brothers.

Cattle-spearing, or robbery of any kind, is quickly put down, and the small gaol at Alice Springs receives the offender, after he has been dealt with by a Justice, who may be a telegraph operator or a station manager, but is always a responsible person, properly sworn in. Serious crimes necessitate a march to Darwin, some eight hundred miles away, the constable, locally called the 'trooper', and escort travelling on horseback, the prisoners linked together, and footing it all the way at the rate of twenty-five miles a day.

There are some lonely spots. One white man rode into Alice Springs the other day remarking that he had not seen a white woman for four years ... The need for white women in the Northern Territory is proved by the relative numbers of white children and half-caste, for while there were only eight white children of school age, nearly forty little half-castes were being maintained in a refuge called the Bungalow at the Government's expense. Here, apparently, they looked after themselves. All slept in the same room at night, and the girls at the age of twelve and the boys at fourteen were drafted off into the service of anyone who had no prejudice against them. They seemed bright children. I saw them at work in the school, and was rather impressed by their neat writing, correct reading, and good memory.

Probably a resident doctor in Alice Springs would make life easier for parents of young families. I met a man there who had just bought a station some miles out, and intended to live there with his wife and eight children. He said that if the doctors in the south once visited the place, they would be quite willing to take up their abode there, for the interesting study that the natives afforded from a medical point of view.

There were thirty-six white people in Alice Springs, and they seemed a very united little community. The need of a church and a dispensary is probably felt either consciously or unconsciously by all. Across the road from the police station stood a partly built hostel of the Australian Inland Mission, which the Government intended to finish building and 'equip' with two nurses. The dwellers in the Dead Heart have little recreation, but I was pleased to find a tennis club being opened and I enjoyed a good game on the opening day. The court was beautifully made of a substance called ant-bed, from the abandoned ants' nests in the neighbour-hood, than which material there is nothing better for a hard court in a hot climate … plans for the remainder of the journey were now practically settled. Sergeant Stott arranged for me to take Sir Sidney's plant as far as Tennant's Creek, beyond which point there would be no camel transport on account of the dangers of the ironwood tree.

The postal authorities in Adelaide, upon hearing that I was travelling north, kindly arranged to run a buggy from the Tennant to Powell's Creek, for which I was very grateful to them. Otherwise it would have been difficult to get enough horses for the baggage owing to the dry season. The stage from Powell's Creek to the Katherine River (about three hundred and seventy miles) remained doubtful for several days.

The letters in that district go by 'contract mail', the mailman owning the plant and merely, as the term suggests, contracting to carry the mails, and at liberty to take or decline a passenger as he chooses. We could not, however, get into touch with the mailman, communication being particularly difficult because the Katherine Races 'were on', but the telegraph station master at the Katherine River telegraphed to Mr. Allchurch, at Stuart, near Alice Springs, that he thought it would be all right. This verbal 'all right' from a third, or rather from a fourth party, may seem slender assurance in view of the length and description of the journey I was about to undertake. But the experience that I had already had of the Bush showed me the hearty fashion in which travellers are assisted and sped on their way, and I had no intention of giving up the journey, unless some calamity made it quite impossible to proceed. So I regarded the matter as comfortably arranged. And kindly messages came over the telephone that the North would be pleased to meet me when I arrived, and would give me a welcome.

I was glad to continue with the same plant, for I felt that I understood these particular natives, and they had got used to me. All natives will not go beyond their own district, even when travelling with white people, for the tribes look upon strangers with suspicion, especially when feed and water are scarce. But Tennant's Creek was Macumba Jack's own country, and Topsy had been part of the way, travelling with a camel-string, when she was a girl. The same language — Arunta — carried them all the way, and from time to time they met friends ...

I bade good-bye to Sergeant Stott and his capable wife,

who had taken so much trouble on my behalf, mounted my camel, and rode out under the gateway. I stopped at the telegraph station at Stuart, about two miles away, to say farewell to the Allchurch family, who gave me a very hearty send-off. My last sight of them was a hat waved aloft on a stick as I made my way among the rocks. The camels seemed very tired and weakly, and on coming to a beautiful gidgea tree in full bloom we cut it down relentlessly, and they devoured every blossom. The country was so badly eaten out that even a camel found it hard to pick up a living ...

As we got nearer to the Poison Belt I began to get a little anxious about the future, for I had not yet decided upon any definite course of action. There were two ways of proceeding, firstly by tying up the camels at night, and feeding them with cut branches, when they would be safe only as long as they were tied, and in imminent danger later, for when released hungry they would eat the first greenstuff they saw, which might happen to be gastrolobium or indigo bush; or they must be left to feed as usual on the chance of coming upon the poison at any time. The boy was so long in bringing in the camels that morning that I began to wonder whether the poison bush had not made its way further south than is recorded. And then I remembered having seen him going off under the stars with his gun under his arm, and the camel cords in his hand, and I hoped that he was hunting. When the stars paled the birds began to sing. There is a common little bird that wakes in the morning, faces the heat of noon with a song, and sings the sun to sleep. I have never seen him. The natives call him 'Hevalaval', and told me that he was 'all same wren', but this only meant that he was a small brown bird. Then a wagtail flitted into a mulga bush, sluing his tail to left and right, not up and down in the English mode. The hour of dawn is always interesting in the Bush, particularly when one has camped in the dark the night before ...

At Connor's Well two natives were drawing water with a 'whip', and a big mixed mob of animals was crowding and panicking by turns round the short trough. Poor thirsty beasts, with their eyes nearly dropping out of their heads, would just get a mouthful of water, and then be pushed aside on to the edge of the crowd, and have to wait their turn again, queue fashion. A great raw-boned draught horse kicked mightily, letting fly to right and left, making it known that he was going to have a satisfactory drink before all the water was gone, and a little thin mare, who had several times essayed to get to the water, lost her foal in a sudden scatter, and the tiny thing went about questing for her. Cows and calves, nearly dropping with weakness, tried to find a place at the trough, but they only seemed to get a mouthful before they were pushed away. Then a big spent bull, in such poor condition that he was hardly able to walk, took a few steps forward and rested, bellowed to the others to make room for him, walked on a little farther, and stood helpless, and then pawed the ground as if impatient at his own weakness.

While the camels were drinking the boy surprised me by reporting a mob of motor-cars on the road. I could see nothing, but presently some little dots came into sight, and he discovered that they were not motor-cars, but horses, and 'one white man, two black fellah.' The white man was the one who had passed me near Stuart. 'You do travel,' he said.

'I camped three miles behind you last night. You have already done pretty well this morning.' ...

Almost as soon as we had left him the big tin basin fell off the top of the load, and away went Barley at a canter, pulling the poor baggage camel along after her, so fast that she got a sore nose in the process. The other two also 'got the hump' promptly, and everything was in commotion. The load had tipped sideways, so we had to whish down, unload, and load up again. The affair took over half an hour, and I was afraid that the man whom we had left at the well would pass by before I had got things tidied up, and would alter his opinion about my being a fast traveller. But as a matter of fact he did not catch us up at all, and I never saw him again ...

Mr. and Mrs. Nicker of Glen Maggie, at Ryan's Well, easily persuaded me to stay the night, and I heard a good deal from them of the difficulties and disappointments of the people who live in the Dead Heart ... Eugene Nicker, the youngest son, had lately done a long camel ride alone, with only one camel, and said that he had managed quite comfortably by tying up his mount at night, and feeding it with branches. It is, of course, too risky for a solitary traveller to let his animal loose to graze, in case he should not find it again. I listened to all advice as I went upon my way, and reflected upon it in camp in the evening. It certainly was a good idea to tie up the camels, hobbling them as loosely as possible, and fastening the tether to the hobble chain ...

Hanson's Well was as bare a place as I had yet seen. The only living thing in sight was a poor horse hanging round the empty water trough in the hopes that someone would turn up to draw a bucket of water for him before he perished. The water from the well was very bad, but the camels did not object to it, and after we had left I saw the poor old horse making his painful way towards the well. I think it was his last drink. I have seen many sad sights. Sometimes very far from water or feed we passed a few cattle standing with lowered heads. They did not move off at the approach of the camels. Often they did not even turn their heads, but sometimes they would look at me, or so I thought, with *Ora pro nobis* in their eyes. Of course, they were doomed. To-morrow their heads would be lower. Then they would sink down. I saw them in every stage.

For several miles a little party of Bush camels had been following us, and we could not shake them off. At the Stirling homestead Mr. Ross yarded them, for he said that though they appeared to be harmless, they might stampede my camels in the night, and as I am not fond of night alarms, I was grateful to him.

I had been expecting to meet an Afghan called Allah Mahomed, coming south with a camel string, who would give me information about the poisons. One evening we heard camel bells about a mile to the north, and early in the morning I walked out to find his camp. He greeted me with the dignified, 'Salaam, memsahib', of his country, followed by an Australian handshake. He had only lost two camels out of a string of sixty-three, and one of them had died of old age, and the other had wandered into the Bush to calve, and would probably return to the string later.

He told me that it would be unwise to tie up the camels at night and feed them with branches as I had meant to do, but advised grazing them in the ordinary way, hurrying over stony places and 'gaps' where the weed was thickest, and halting beside the ashes of his own camp-fires, as these stopping-places had proved to be safe ones.

That evening I met with the sage-bush that I had believed to be a camel poison. To say that we camped warily gives a poor idea of the extreme caution with which Macumba Jack and I led along two of the camels, Topsy holding the other two, and gingerly allowed them to graze. We held them on very short strings, ready to pull the weed out of their mouths if necessary. When we found that they did not touch the sage-bush, but nosed in and out among it, eating other weeds, we hobbled them and let them go as usual.

I was soon, however, to see the effect of noxious weeds upon cattle. Near Taylor's Well we came upon the carcasses of about fifteen hundred poisoned beasts that the crows would not touch, lying in twos and threes, and sometimes in heaps. We could hardly get the camels to go forward. I can give no idea of the sinister effect of the bright sunshine and foul atmosphere, nor can I describe the feeling of loneliness that came over me when I found myself in the midst of the devastation, riding along with compressed lips, reins tied to saddle, a stout mulga switch in each hand, working with these and my heels to urge my unwilling camel on. It was a relief to reach clean country and get into camp, which we did a little way north of Limestone Hill.

The next watering-place was at Wycliffe Well, which remote spot has been the home of Mrs. Crooke and her husband and daughters for many years. Their nearest woman neighbour in the south was Mrs. Nicker, a hundred and twenty-five miles away, and to the north a family named Bohning, one hundred and eighty-five miles away.

One of the daughters told me that when the Bohning family passed their home with a mob of cattle and goats a few months before, she had not seen a white woman for three and a half years. They entertained me very kindly to dinner, and the girls were so prettily dressed that one would not have imagined they led such an isolated life. I parted from Mrs. Crooke with real regret that I could not make a longer stay. Among those women who face life in the wilds and separation from the society of friends I thought Mrs. Crooke was the bravest …

Macumba Jack proved himself a good pilot. He walked on ahead, weeding the gastrolobium from the path and threw it aside. The camels were 'tied short', nose-cord to crupper, so that they could not stretch their long necks: out very far. Under the shadow of a Marble Rock a solitary pedestrian was boiling himself a billy-can of tea. He said that in another two hours we should be out of the danger zone, and added, 'but over there, two miles to the eastward, a friend of mine lost fifteen of his thirty camels in a night.' He was Mr. McHugh on his way to Wycliffe Well, 'foot-walking'.

Next morning, when all should have been easy and the Poison Zone a thing of the past, the lead camel suddenly began to 'sing out', lay down and rolled. The boy did not wish me to try the remedy. 'Might be hungry, might be tired. Mulga over there,' he said. We loaded her with the baggage to discourage further rolling, and rushed the string along to the mulga, and all four camels were soon feeding contentedly, but if Barley had wanted to make my flesh creep, she could have found no surer way of doing it.

My friends at Barrow Creek had warned me not to camp within two miles of Kelly Well, because big black ants of the kind that bite, had taken up a four-mile block in that locality and populated it densely … It was no use camping in the domain of the black ants, so we pilgrimaged still farther in order to get beyond the two-mile limit. The camels stamped their feet and began dancing about when the ants bit them. Finally, after searching the ground with lights, we found a place that seemed clean enough to camp, and I for one felt glad when the day's march was over.

In the morning, though the boy had made an early start to fetch the camels, it was long ere he arrived, and even at 8.30 there was no sign of him. Dawn showed us open country, red earth, and a low scrub. As time went on Topsy kept on going out to look for him and coming back. She was afraid that he had had an accident, and I was afraid that he had found all the camels dead or dying. It was no good trying to follow him, for we did not know what direction he had gone … at ten o'clock a tired black fellah, sitting on the hump of the first of four camels, came slowly into camp. He said they went ten miles, which means that he must have gone about twenty miles.

He sat down to his breakfast with a resigned air while Topsy loaded up. The camels had evidently stampeded, for all had broken their hobble straps, and I suppose they had passed all the way through the black ants' territory without having had any rest or feed during the night. For myself, I had awakened with a headache, so strange an occurrence that I searched my memory for any possible cause, and presently remembered that during the varied incidents of the preceding day, while I was trying to identify a new bird by means of Mr. Leach's 'Bird Book', my eyes on the page instead of on the road, The Oont had suddenly rushed off into the Bush, and carried me under the low branch of a tree; and it was well for me that I was wearing a pith hat (though, of course, it was rather bad for the pith hat) …

My little party had conscientiously observed Sergeant Stott's instructions to put out the campfire before moving on; but ahead of us we saw the smoke of five different Bush fires, which probably had their origin in smoke-signals, the native method of sending news through the Bush. No white man has yet solved the mystery of the native 'wireless', and the extraordinary way in which natives, isolated from their fellows, are able to receive news of them. Many people think this must be due to telepathy, because smoke could not bring news in detail. This, of course, was quite different from the mulga wire gossip that entertains, with its extravagant scandals, the white people who are linked together by the telephone. I was told it would shock me if I could have heard the flights of fancy to which the gossips attain. But it supplies the want of an evening paper, and assures at least some people having a cheery hour, and probably does more good than harm.

We were in no danger from the Bush fires, because they had already crossed our path, but a north wind, which continued for two days to cover us with dust and nearly suffocate us with smoke, was rather trying; also the heat was intense.

After the quiet of the Bush, Tennant's Creek seemed bustlingly active. Besides the telegraph station master, Mr. Rabbitt, and his assistant, who gave me a very kind reception, the line party had come in for their stores, making a total of six white men. The line party travels beside the Overland Telegraph at the rate of five miles a day, keeping it in repair, and cutting away the Bush. An important part of their work is the tautening of the two wires after a few hundred parrots have perched upon them and suddenly taken flight. I heard again that the last resource of an overlander, who falls sick or cannot get to water, is to make for the telegraph line and damage it, certain that the slightest interruption to messages will bring repairing parties from the nearest stations, and though such interference is punishable by law, people have been known to take the risk in the hope that indulgent telegraph officers will report that the damage was done by parrots. I had a feeling for the line, having day after day watched the short metal poles coming rhythmically to meet me at the rate of one a minute, by which I could gauge the camels' pace at three miles an hour …

The pack-horse mail arrived from the south in charge of mailman Sam Lynch, who had ridden thirty-seven thousand miles during his seven years service without ever being late or losing a parcel. With him came Mr. Phillips, the new station master for Powell's Creek, one hundred and twenty miles north, who had never been in the saddle until he left Oodnadatta on the seven hundred and seventy mile ride to take up his new duties.

I now sent the plant so kindly lent me by Sir Sidney Kidman back to the Macumba station. It had brought me along safely for six hundred and fifty miles. Topsy reiterated her little farewell, 'Goo'bye, I lose you. I lonely.' Both she and the boy proved trustworthy and efficient, and I think that they were particularly good types of their race. I arranged that on their return journey the boy and lubra should be provided with food and money when they were half-way home, which seemed a necessary precaution in view of their socialistic instincts and gambling tendencies, for I am sure that they would have shared their last crust with their fellows as readily as they would have gambled away their only coat; but it was not reassuring to be told by a man who knew the natives well that they would probably arrive at their own station quite destitute ...

The night before we started, the man who had been overhauling the buggy sought me out and advised me to keep on the camels and continue the journey with them because, he said, though he had put two days work into the buggy, he was still afraid that the wheels would 'turn inside out' ... I decided to take the buggy and trust my luck; and it carried us through quite safely, though we were not without moments of anxiety about it.

We watered the horses that afternoon at the Carryman Lagoon (which seemed to be chiefly mud), and had a dry camp that night at Gibson's Creek, choosing a bit of hard ground to avoid snakes. My camp was pitched beside the buggy, and the black boy, who rode in charge of the eleven spare horses, made me a bed of fragrant gum leaves that was softer than any mattress ... I felt truly sorry for our animals; the second pair of horses could hardly do any work, and one of them had to be left behind to be picked up later when the mail returned. The next pair were in little better case. They stood still and endured a very futile flogging, apparently unable to move, and it was only when the men put their shoulders to the wheels that the poor, half-starved creatures could start.

The buggy held out pretty well (the tires had been padded with greenhide), but it needed a little attention with a hammer from time to time. Also a bolt, fastening the swingle bar to the front carriage, jolted out, and the whole concern began to sway and rattle and the pole to swing against the horses' legs in rather an alarming manner. The boy was sent to search beneath the telegraph line for a piece of discarded wire, and as he was fortunate in finding one the repair was quickly done.

At one point we overtook a travelling blacksmith encamped by the roadside, journeying alone with a buggy and two horses. He had come from Queensland, and was looking for work in the Northern Territory.

We passed Wildguard Creek, Mucadi, Prentice's Lagoon (dry), the North and South Tonkinsons (also dry), and on to Helen Springs. About six miles before we reached the homestead the five Bohning children, who were all born in the Northern Territory, came cantering out to meet us. It was eleven days since I had seen a white woman, and Mrs. Bohning gave me a kindly welcome. There is a very interesting garden here, where various experiments were being tried, and Cape gooseberries, peanuts, and a pleasant-flavoured fruit called the Austral berry were successfully grown. They also had large flocks of goats, which are a great feature of life in the north. They are kept literally by the thousand, and thrive where cattle would starve. Mrs. Bohning told me that she had tried the experiment of giving a goat a sprig of gastrolobium to eat, and the animal instantly fainted, but recovered after a teaspoonful of Condy's Crystals had been poured down its throat.

The Bohning family run their station without any black labour. Both the boys and girls are very much at home on horseback, helping in the work of droving, cattle mustering, etc. They showed me an orphaned camel two years old that had been brought up by a goat which grew so attached to it that though she had had two sets of kids since she adopted it, she neglected them in its favour.

One of the drawbacks to life in the north is the limitation of the parcel post to three pounds weight. I heard how one boot arrived alone, and its fellow was delivered by the next mail six weeks later; of a saddle forwarded in three-pound parcels to be remade by the purchaser; of sheets and dress lengths cut to fit the exigencies of the parcel post. Part of the mailman's work is to keep an eye on the telegraph line and report if he sees anything wrong. He can do simple repairs, such as putting on a new insulator, and takes a repairing outfit with him. He told me of the difficulty of travelling in the 'wet', one district, called the Gluepot, having a particularly bad reputation for bogging horses unawares ...

Mr. and Mrs. Bohning had arrived, bringing a horse that was to travel to Darwin by the mail. I found her conversation about matters connected with native life of the greatest interest. The Womra and the Lepi tribes of this district have not yet forsaken their cannibal habits, the old men, as usual, being the worst offenders in this direction. The Womra are baby-eaters, but it would seem as if they had an uneasy conscience in the matter, for they knock out two of their front teeth when they first begin this horrible custom, to let the child's spirit escape lest it should haunt them. They have many children, but the husband will only let the lubra keep two; the firstborn is always killed at birth, because the mother, who is generally about fourteen years old, is considered too young to bring it up. A few years ago, in the

Powell's Creek district, there was a Massacre of Innocents; the young men, tired of taking their elder brothers' cast-off wives, and the young women tired of being married to old men, took the law into their own hands, and ran away together, so that the old people were left to starve. The elder men of the tribe (who rule the women absolutely) decreed that the male babies should die. An 'old' man of perhaps forty will take all the daughters of a family and 'grow' them (bring them up), and he has them as wives, passing them on in turn to his younger brother.

A white woman told me a very harrowing story of a lubra in her employ who went back to her husband's camp on a holiday with her child, aged about four years, which she was trying to bring up with particular care under her mistress's guidance. She went out hunting in the traditional fashion for her husband's food, and on her return the child was nowhere to be found. The woman in whose care it had been left could only shake her head, and would not utter a word. When pressed for a reply she had to own up that in the mother's absence the child's father and his fellows had taken the child from her, and cooked and eaten it. The poor mother returned to her mistress in a state of grief and disappointment, which was rendered more pathetic by the fact that she could speak a little English, and told her the story brokenly, ending with, 'You should a heard me cry.'

There were so many people at Powell's Creek, what with the Bohning couple, the northern mailman and southern mailman, the two telegraph masters, the lineman, two men who were camped in the Creek, and myself, that it was supposed that there had never been so many white people there before. The evening passed cheerily ...

I was prepared to start the next morning with mailman MacGregor on the three-hundred-mile journey to the Katherine River, doing the first sixty miles on horseback, for it had been impossible for the mailman to bring his buggy south of Newcastle Waters. Just as I was setting out, however, the Government contractor, Mr. Peacock, who was sinking a well in those parts, telephoned to say he was sending a car over the next day, and would be glad if I would make use of it. I had intended to do the whole journey in a leisurely fashion that would allow me to make observations of bird life, etc., on the way, but Mr. Peacock's kind offer was not to be declined, so the sixty miles to Newcastle Waters, which would have taken two days with the mail. was accomplished in a few hours ...

Our next night was spent at Milliner's, another bore with windmill, trough and tank, where a leakage had nurtured a patch of grass upon which the horses crowded. The mailman, the only regular passer-by, regulates the flow of water. A day of great heat followed, and the scrubby trees, lancewood, bullwaddy and the picturesque quinine bush, gave no shade at all ... Farther on we saw a native's grave up in a tree, like an enormous bird's-nest. This was just before sunset, and there was still light enough to take a photograph. I did not need the mailman's advice not to go too near. One of the terrible rites of the natives in these parts is to light a fire under a corpse that has been 'buried' in a tree, and sit round until moisture drips from the body above them, and with this they anoint themselves, rubbing vigorously in the belief that the courage and strength of the dead will thus become their own.

I could not help thinking that the presence of white women in the Northern Territory would do a great deal towards making the natives abandon their dangerous and disgusting customs. All the telegraph stations would make good homes, and if the Government would let land and cattle rights freely to a married stockmaster who undertook to provide the telegraph station with beef and the horse transport necessary for repairing the line, there would very soon be a useful little colony of white men and women and probably children, who would keep up the proper traditions of the Empire.

Just after sunset the buildings of Daly Waters came in sight, and Mr. Holtze offered me the hospitality of the telegraph station. A surveying party numbering seventeen was encamped here, giving the impression of a dense population.

We made our dinner camp next day at Ironstone, where I could watch the birds clamouring round the water trough; and at sunset Roderick's Bore was like an aviary, hundreds of little birds of several different kinds — greenbacks, doublebars, redhearts, diamond-birds, and those lovely little beings called Java sparrows — were skimming over the trough and taking a drink on the wing, or holding on to the edge and twisting their necks round to reach the water; and the fluttering and warbling and joyousness of these tiny, pretty creatures, after a long day spent in the dry, parching Bush, was truly lovely ...

We started off again with fresh horses and a passenger from Queensland on the last two days of our journey through the Bush. After a twenty-four-mile run we camped at Rockhole, a pretty spot where the water lies under a cliff, and a flock of pigeons came down under the rock to drink. There was another camper here, on his way south from Emungalan, who sent us over a large bag of lemons, a gift that was generous, as well as refreshing, as citrus fruits have to come by sea. We made an early start, and crossed Maude's Creek and the Bullock's Head, where we saw gorgeous parrots in large flocks. Twice we met men travelling with buggies, and once a team of thirty-seven donkeys hauling a six-ton load from the railway to a remote cattle station, a journey that they accomplished twice a year. The little animals all looked in fine condition. They had neither rein nor bridle, but responded to the voices and whip-crack of their white master and his black helper. A group of natives approached, to pass the time of day. One of them was known as a rain-maker. On being chaffed upon the futility of his profession he told us his method. He got a bowl of clean water, put a clean white stone in it, poured some more water over it, and sat down and waited for the rain. But this time the rain had not come, and he was at a loss to account for his failure. He was now begging the mailman for a 'bit of flour and a bit of meat', for he, his little brother, and his blind friend were all very hungry. 'All true,' he remarked, 'I not gammon mailman' ...

The Queensland passenger proved himself an acquisition, for the five horses, which had pulled the buggy over fallen tree-trunks and up and down rocks as a matter of course, took fright at a sheet of bark lying in the road and bolted. They had some cause for fear, for the near leader trotted over its edge and it upped and slapped him. They raced into the Bush at full gallop, and tore through the scrub. Our safety depended on whether they could be got back to the road before they reached a tree that stood at the edge of a thickly wooded bit of country. The mailman handed one of the ribbons to the Queenslander, and they each wrapped a rein round their hands and pulled. We returned to the road again without anyone being hurt, but there was time for a good thrill before the horses could be persuaded to return and work off their excitement in a safer place. The little incident gave rise to some excellent stories of runaways and other adventures.

Small holdings of land were being taken up on the banks of the Katherine, and the district looked prosperous and settled ... The waters of the river were clear and beautiful, and must have been appreciated by the horses, which for many days had drunk only of the dregs of water-holes and billabongs. We stopped at the post office with the mails, and the postmaster handed me telegrams, and gave me tea in his cool verandah looking over the river. Mrs. Morris had asked me to stay with her until 'train day', which, owing to the increase of traffic caused by the bridge works, was now once a week instead of fortnightly. So I said farewell to the mailman and my fellow-passengers, trusty friends of the road ...

At the Edith River and Ferguson white men were working on the railway, and I was surprised, in such a climate, to see a white stoker on the engine of the train. Passengers were set down to spend the night at Pine Creek, flourishing little township with a hospital and hotel, which miners and prospectors seemed chiefly to inhabit ... An early start was made, and the train meandered on its way through varying country: occasionally we saw a waterhole belonging to a station and then came gradually past infrequent grey roofs to clusters of buildings and flowering trees, until, as we neared the outskirts of Darwin, a gap in the landscape gave me my first view of the sea — a stretch of blue dancing water under the hot, milky white sky. And I realised that the life of wide spaces, open sky, patriarchal simplicity — all that the word 'Bush' had meant to me — were things of the past, and the journey was over.

Now that I can look back upon the journey as a whole, the things that stand out are the wide spaces and baking heat; the small tearing sound with which the gum trees strip off slivers of their bark in the hot silence of noon; the glamour of the sunset, and the benison of the evening breeze; the sudden meetings with men and occasionally women who, by no means rendered either dull-witted or nervous by their isolation, were, on the contrary, frequently well-read and versed in the affairs of the day. Their hospitality, of course, is proverbial, but I found besides that an unfailing friendliness, which alone made it possible for a stranger to travel across the continent from sea to sea, and to arrive with so many pleasant memories.

My wayside friends entertained just a tired traveller, but I was meeting staunch, loyal types of the sons of the Empire, keenly alive, thinkers and men of action. I felt the bond that united us at the first handclasp, and when I found, as I very frequently did find, that they had fought in the War, of course the bond was doubly strong.

This account of various journeys is necessarily both slight and incomplete, for I did not set out with the idea of writing about them, but of travelling for my own pleasure and education, glad to have an opportunity of gaining a little first-hand knowledge of this very important part of the Empire. Yet the writing of it has been a pleasure, for to some extent I have lived these journeys over again, and met again — if only in the realms of memory — men and women whose friendship I shall always prize. I owe them my thanks, not only for their kindness to me, but for what they taught me. Hands across the sea!

From Philippa Bridges, *A Walk-About in Australia*, London, 1925.

Lady Violet Apsley

1925

Lady Violet Apsley, together with Lady Leighton, her experienced travelling companion, made an unusual journey under the strangest circumstances, from Darwin to the north-west of Western Australia, eventually meeting up with her husband, Major Lord Apsley (a Home Office minister in the British Government), before flying south to Perth. Lord and Lady Apsley travelled in the Northern Territory officially and incognito as Mr. and Mrs. George Bott with Lady Leighton. The reason for the subterfuge was that Lord and Lady Apsley were later to investigate the living conditions of the Group Settlements in the south-west of Western Australia for the British and Australian governments and they wanted to be afforded the same treatment as any married couple newly arrived from the United Kingdom. The enterprising project was kept secret and they compiled a satisfactory report and published a book of their journey.

WHEN MY HUSBAND FIRST TOLD ME of his plan to visit Australia under the guise of an emigrant settler, I was living a happy and care-free life with enough work to be busy and enough hunting and parties to be ready for more, and it came as a bombshell, to shatter everything. I did not like it ... However, to serve the best purpose, my husband had to do the first part of the plan as a single man. Preparations were quietly made and, to the last moment, life went on exactly as before. In the early hours of March 7th we packed an old suit-case and a second-hand bag with suitable clothes for 'Mr. Bott' — a strong pair of breeches, boots, a pair of corduroy trousers, a few shirts for all occasions, a thick sweater, handkerchiefs marked 'G.B.', a few comforts and clothes for wearing on the voyage out! ...

I went to Singapore by the Blue Funnel S.S. *Patroclus*, which was a delightful boat, and took only twenty-four days to Singapore, none of which were dull. Lady Leighton came with me. Besides being a splendid companion, she had travelled much in various parts of the world, and I knew that she and I could do together what would be impossible for a lone female ... On July 7th we arrived at Darwin ... The town of Darwin has rather a temporary appearance and consists of a number of corrugated iron bungalows placed on a rocky, sandy peninsula, with a population of about 1,200 at the height of the season. It was nobly planned, with wide streets, a public park, several churches, a Government House, railway station and the port … The imposingly designed main street, is unfortunately mostly thick dust and long-grass, as traffic in its one main street does not come up to the expectations of the original town-planners. Few of the houses can be said to be suitable for tropical conditions. Most of them are Government owned, have not been repainted for years, and barely keep out the sun, let alone the rain. Reliable domestic help is almost impossible to obtain. There are no electric fans in Darwin, in spite of the fact that during the wet season climatic conditions are similar to those in Singapore!

However, appearances are more than made up for by the warmth of greeting to strangers on the part of the people of Darwin. Mr. [F.C.] Urquhart, Administrator and Chief Advisor to the Commonwealth on Territory affairs, most kindly offered us hospitality all the time we were there, and many people invited us out to picnics, parties and a gala entertainment at the town hall, where I, unwittingly, made history as the first lady who had ever made even the tiniest speech in Darwin.

Owing to a shipping strike Mr. [Michael] Terry [explorer] was late, so the start of his expedition was considerably delayed. It had been intended that we should see the party start, and go round the coast to Western Australia to meet them after they had done some 1000 miles of their journey. We found, however, that there was no means of doing so by sea, as there were no coastal boats due for another six weeks and all the available pearl luggers leaked. By this time I had become wild to see part of the Northern Territory, but neither Australians whom we had met on the way out, nor the people of Darwin, had encouraged the idea of women tourists going into the inland; no one could be hired to take us overland under any form of conveyance. There were no horses to be obtained in the coastal area. People talked of 'wild blacks', 'mosquitoes', 'snakes', 'pests', 'dying of thirst', and disasters of all kinds. But by patient inquiry, these vague statements were proved to have been made by people who had not been there themselves.

Becoming aware of our desire to go inland, Mr. David Conacher, the managing director of the Frozen Meat Works in Darwin, and therefore the largest employer of labour in the Territory, interested himself on our behalf and introduced Mr. A. E. Moray, the Chief Pastoral Inspector for his company, which controls most of the cattle country in the Northern Territory and in the Kimberley District of West Australia. Mr. Moray offered to take Lady Leighton and myself with him on the customary tour of inspection upon which he was about to start in his car. His route would be from station to station, and along much the same route as my husband would be going with the Terry cars, so we gladly accepted his invitation and the hospitality of the Bush, where all visitors are wholeheartedly welcomed.

After arranging for our luggage to be dispersed by various means to various parts of Australia, and with a small amount of hand-baggage, we left Darwin on July 17th, everyone from Mr. and Mrs. Urquhart, Mr. and Mrs. Conacher, and the police downwards, being characteristically Australian — helpful, kind and hospitable beyond all words. We kept the train waiting half an hour saying good-byes. The station master laconically offered us return tickets!

We knew that everyone expected to see us back again very soon, and that a few days in the Bush would make us keen to reach the comforts of Sydney, one of the two great Meccas for all good Australians. As loyal Australians they did not like to see English visitors gaining their first impressions of Australia in the worst part. It was like entering a palace by the meat-larder! They did not appreciate our desire to see wild country.

This is the only railway line in the whole of northern Australia, an area twenty-seven times the size of England. It wanders 240 miles across the continent in the direction of Adelaide, and it is believed that some day the 2000 miles gap intervening between South Australia will be bridged by the continuation of this light single-track railway to meet lines coming up from the south. The train runs at infrequent intervals on a single line, and has the boast of never leaving a passenger behind. It is a friendly little affair and stops at every little wayside hut. It holds the proud record of never having run to time, and of once attaining the extraordinary speed of 40 miles per hour after a race meeting dinner!!

Romance does live in Australia, and part of the charm of travelling through the undeveloped part of the country is to see it with the magic eyes of the 'May-be-one-day'. In the meanwhile, one may note that the railway track laid by imported Chinese labour cost a shilling a yard, and fifteen shillings a yard when continued by white labour. Labour is scarce and dear in the Territory and experiments are often costly failures, so at present there is nothing to see from the train between Darwin and Pine Creek — where the train stops at the end of the day — but dense, small

Bush timber stretching relentlessly flat on either hand, with here and there a little clearing where some brave soul is trying to make a living. It was hot and dusty, but with pleasant company all the way it was an agreeable journey, and, we thought, much more comfortable than travelling in Java.

We spent the night at Pine Creek, a tiny place boasting a station master, a policeman, an hotel, a store, and one or two other residents with a few prospectors and miners searching for a lost vein of gold in the surrounding hills. There used to be a comparatively large amount of gold found around Pine Creek but that which was easily found has long since gone.

The hotel was kept by a Mrs. Gordon, kindest of hostesses, and one of the first white women to come to the Northern Territory from West Australia after the Kimberley gold rush. Thirty years ago, she trekked alone with her men folk and bullock wagons across really unknown and unmapped country, with wild blacks roaming everywhere and water holes very uncertain. Some day, when there is a history of the Northern Territory to be written, her name and others like her ought to go down the Ages among the great women of Australia — the pioneer women who have shown it possible to carry the ideal of home-life out into the untamed Bush … Mrs. Gordon lived an ordinary life and gave us a most extraordinarily good tea and breakfast. It was here we started to call the last meal of the day 'tea', after the custom of the Bush, and commenced to enjoy this typical Australian beverage whenever and wherever produced. After the hot, dry, dusty day, tea in a teacup with milk, or tea boiled in a billycan over an open fire, and drunk strong and hot, is equally delicious.

We busied ourselves drawing sketches of ourselves, the first tourists arriving at Pine Creek, in the guest-book, which contained about twenty names, and started with those of Lord and Lady Stradbroke, who had stayed a night there on their transcontinental trip by car in 1924, which was the first occasion on which any Governor had ever visited the Northern Territory. It was a gala night at the hotel, as, not only had two Englishwomen arrived from the blue, but there had been one of those rarities in the Territory, nearly as exciting as a local race meeting — a Police-Court Trial — and the plaintiff, defendant, counsel, constable and jury were all celebrating the dismissal of the case in amicable Bush fashion. This was the last night we used mosquito nets.

The following morning we went on by the same train to Emungalan, meaning a stony place, the end of the railway where a bridge is being constructed over the Katherine River which is nearing completion and will carry the railway on southwards. It is a tiny place with the usual store and hotel as its only public buildings. Here I might say a certain amount of heavy drinking goes on. The bush-man has to drink to break the monotony, and it is his only form of amusement, but on our arrival a fiat went forth by common consent that all drunkards were to 'knock off' for the week we were in the neighbourhood. The kind thought was rather pathetic, and we did not hear of it till weeks later. It shows how much women are wanted in the Northern Territory.

Here we said 'au revoir' to my husband, who had come with us thus far. We hoped to meet again at Wave Hill in the centre of the Northern Territory, but as time in the Bush does not count, and as all sorts of eventualities might turn up and there were no sure means of communication, we were a little uncertain. However, we had faith in the power of our respective leaders to get through all right and that things would pan out in the end, though possibly through unusual channels.

We stayed that night, and several more, at Manbulloo, a typical cattle-station in the Bush, built of corrugated iron, two stories high, of which the wide verandah above and the large store below formed important parts. They are built of corrugated iron (1) because it can be brought in sheets ready to be put up easily on the spot by unskilled labour; (2) because galvanised metal is the only form of construction which withstands the attacks of a small white pest called the 'white ant', which swarms everywhere in the Bush, devours woodwork of all kinds, and even eats its way through cement, and for which reason most of the chairs and table legs stand in empty jam tins, to the surprise of the 'newy'; (3) the rain water collected on the roof of such a building is invaluable in places like Manbulloo, where the available water is from the river, which, though perfectly wholesome, tastes unpleasantly of mineral deposits and is very hard for washing and cooking. The house was prettily placed, overlooking the Katherine River, at that time of year a sparkling, fast-flowing stream of sun-warmed water, in which it was delicious to bathe in the evening, a form of amusement it was only safe to enjoy in the shallower, swifter stretches, as a small type of crocodile often lurks in the deep holes, and has a playful habit of taking pieces indifferently out of legs, black or white, and this he does without any warning and with malicious intent ...

At Manbulloo we were the guests of Mr. Little, typical host of the Bush. He turned out of his own quarters for us and saw we had the best of everything at his disposal. He and the other men living there gave us a splendid welcome and taught us the rudiments of Bush life. A cattle station of this kind is as self-supporting as an old feudal castle. It has its own blacksmith, saddler, engineer, butcher, cook, storekeeper, stockmen, team-driver, etc. They made us real bushmen's leather belts, on which the bushman carries his valuables — his knife, matchbox, pipe, and occasionally a compass, watch, or a cure for snake-bite … In a few days they were teaching us the difficult art of stockwhip-cracking, which is a painful one to acquire as the Australian stockwhip is made of plaited kangaroo hide. The expert is as particular about its balance, finish, length of thong, silk 'flash' and raw-hide 'dropper' as a good golfer about his driver. Cattle in the Territory are controlled almost entirely by the cracking of whips from horseback, so that one of the first jobs of a 'jackeroo' (or new hand) is to learn the correct use of some fourteen feet of heavy thong under all conditions. It is a delight to watch an artist at work amongst cattle-flicking a cunning old cow here or a surly youngster there, or making a pistol-fire of cracks to turn a mob, or a quiet one to keep feeding cattle together in the open at night.

We had as 'ladies' maid' at Manbulloo a black Aboriginal woman called 'Maggie', who dressed in a long cotton garment and was employed with various friends and relations on the station … Lady Leighton and I used to rock with laughter when every morning a long, skinny black arm used to come round the corner of the screen on the verandah just before sunrise with a cup of strong tea, the owner of the arm being too shy to follow it, yet dying of curiosity to have another peep at the scarlet bound dressing-gown which she knew one of the 'white-fellah ladies' would be wearing to the shower-bath across the garden. The way the verandah was swept by Maggie leaving as much dust as she found, was also very comic; and as for dusting afterwards, neither Maggie nor her assistant had ever heard of it, which was not surprising perhaps, as Maggie herself slept on the ground in the open behind a shelter of leaves. My sleeping-bag was a great puzzle to her; she had been taught the intricacies of blankets and sheets, but she had never seen a 'flea-bag' before, and couldn't think how to combine it with sheets! Sometimes she put a sheet on the top of it, and sometimes underneath; if I tried to tell her, she only bolted or made funny noises at me like a dog ...

We left Manbulloo on July 22nd on the westward trail, and thenceforth were out of touch with letters, telegraphs, telephones, and the rest of the world, for several weeks. Our next nearest cattle station, eighty-two miles away. The 'road' was simply following where wheels had gone before. In the Territory every car carries food, petrol, water-bag and each passenger's 'swag' as one never quite knows where the next night will be spent. Mr. Moray drove us in his six-cylinder Buick car, commonly called 'Betty', which yearly covers thousands of miles of roadless country in the skilled hands of her driver, whose work as Pastoral Inspector for the huge stations belonging to his company, scattered through northern Australia, takes him these long trips at frequent intervals. A few years ago the only means of transport in the Northern Territory were horses, which can travel an average of twenty-five miles a day without losing condition; camels, which do sixteen, and donkey wagons, which do twelve, but now, if there is a supply of petrol along the route, cars save time and trouble. However, at present there are only some half-dozen cars in use in the Northern Territory, so one does not meet much traffic on the road, and must avoid a breakdown at all costs. The car needs to be kept in perfect mechanical order, as at the best it has to make super-efforts, and at, the worst has to do the sort of things that our own petted cars at home could hardly conceive in nightmares! The worst part to the passenger, whose own chassis suffers severely, appears to be the crossing of the dry river creeks, which have steep, rock-strewn banks, boggy bottoms in which one expects to stick, and patches of soft sand which holds the wheels, not counting such inconsiderable trifles as fallen trees, deep ruts, stones and long grass; but what bothers the driver more than anything else is the unseen danger of hitting an ant-hill or a tree-stump hidden by the long grass, which might irreparably damage the steering gear or the radiator ...

The only humans we passed in the day was one white man with a black boy attendant and a few loose horses with his packs. At the sight of the car the horses 'went Bush'. Again, at such a phenomenon, I shed a bit more of the veneer of modern civilisation. It seems as improbable that horses should bolt at the sight of a smooth-running Buick as that they should fly! Conversation under such circumstances is difficult, but we found that the stranger was a horse-breaker, paid so much a dozen to ride raw young horses for the first time.

In the Bush no one knows of the arrival of guests until they turn up. At Willeroo, Mr. and Mrs. Rooney did not know we were coming, but gave us the warmest of welcomes and an excellent supper of 'Bush mutton' — that is to say, goat — with 'corned' (i.e. lightly salted) beef, and fresh vegetables from their own garden, which included tomatoes larger, pinker and more luscious than any we had ever seen before. The garden at Willeroo proves what I have already said about watering dry soil in Australia: seeds had only to be planted, watered, and the difficulty was to prevent peas, beans and cabbages from growing too big.

Mr. and Mrs. Rooney's three children had been born and bred in the Bush, and were some of the finest and healthiest-looking children we saw in Australia, which bears out what a good many people say, that the Northern Territory is extremely healthy for young children. Of course, none of the trio had ever seen a railway, yet their chief delight was playing 'trains'. Bush children get their education from travelling teachers, who spend a few weeks at a time with them and set them work to do. The result seems to be highly satisfactory.

We left at 8.30 next morning for Victoria River Downs, a hundred miles farther on. The country quickly became totally different. Scattered everywhere were still the red-coloured ant-hills, but the country grew more open, till as far as the eye could reach stretched dry, dust coloured grass, with here and there a patch of stony country or a duster of large blue-grey gum trees. Every now and again we passed small mobs of cattle feeding in the open. They were generally Herefords or Shorthorns, as only horned cattle can protect their calves from the attacks of dingoes. The dingo is a fine looking creature, tawny-coloured, sometimes as big as a wolfhound, with a heavy jaw like a bull terrier, but untameable, wary, and plentiful, and one of the worst pests with which the cattle-men and sheep-breeders have to contend in Australia.

We passed mobs of cattle and horses feeding on the long dry grass which to our inexperienced eyes looked dead, but is really some of the finest fodder in the world. After the wet season, the grass grows green and luxuriantly, but is quickly dried by the sun in such a way that its juices are chemically preserved so that it becomes more nutritious than even our best 'old hunter hay' at home. In addition to drinking water this is all that is required for stock through eight months of drought. Under present circumstances, with no facilities for storing the immense rainfall, most cattle stations have to rely on water-holes which are the deep places of the rivers which seldom completely dry up, and, more recently, on artesian bores worked by a wind pump. The horses grazing in the Bush are terrified at the appearance of a car, and it is a fine sight to see mobs of from twenty to a hundred peacefully feeding animals suddenly throw up their heads, take one look at the surprising apparition, and depart at full tilt, mares and foals in a bunch, galloping without a falter over country that an Irish hunter would be appalled at if you asked him to walk over it — sand, rocks, thorns, loose shale, stones, creeks, cracks in the ground, 'washouts' and 'breakaways' as the run-offs made by the terrific rainfall in 'the wet' are called.

With few exceptions, cattle and horses looked in splendid condition. The previous season had been a very hard one for them, as the rain was extra late coming, and gaunt bones by the roadside, picked by the kites and dingoes, showed where wretched beasts, weakened by the long drought, had remained stuck in the soft mud which had once been water, too weak to go the necessary distance to find more. Owing to the lack of water conservation, dying of thirst is the commonest natural end in the Northern Territory. We passed one mob of 900 head of cattle on their way down to the coast. They were in charge of three white drovers and some half-dozen black boys and it was good to watch with what skill they kept the untamed cattle together without unduly frightening or hustling them. Australians have a distinctive seat on a horse, riding long in large, heavy saddles, which are extremely comfortable for the all-day riding which droving and cattle work necessitates; they always seem to go either at a walk or a gallop ...

Driving all that day we reached Victoria River station about sunset, and stayed two days on Victoria River Downs station, 13,000 square miles in extent, which is the biggest single estate in the world. Mr. and Mrs. Graham have made themselves a very comfortable homestead, and have a large family, from the eldest son studying for college to the youngest about nine, and they have been living in the Territory for many years. There is quite a little community at Victoria River, in the heart of the Bush, as besides the Graham family and the station staff, there is a married bookkeeper and his wife and two Mission nurses belonging to a beautiful little hospital, the result of the efforts of the Australian Inland Mission. Two trained nurses are maintained there, and the benefits thus conferred are far reaching. This hospital has only been established during the last two years, and when one considers that the nearest doctor is at least a week's journey away by car and may be said to be practically non-existent, owing to the lack of transport and communications, the advent of two nurses is an inestimable boon and an encouragement to white women to follow their husbands and fathers into the Bush. The great difficulty hitherto has been to get women to live in the inland of the Northern Territory, and one of the chief reasons up to now has been the entire lack of medical attention, so that the Australian Inland Mission is doing a great practical work for the development of the Northern Territory by making it possible for a married man to take his wife to live on these lonely stations. Moreover the social addition of two charming, unmarried white women fresh from town life is enormously appreciated by every man in the Territory, who sometimes never sees a white woman from one year's end to another. In the old days, before she had been able to make things comfortable, Mrs. Graham told me that she once was reduced to making herself hairpins out of fencing wire! We were not to see another white woman until we reached West Australia … We left the hospitable people of Victoria River on July 24th, for the last 125 miles of the trip to Wave Hill. We were held up for half an hour in a narrow way crossing the Wickham River by a sick bullock — to the inexperienced, looking just an ordinary bullock, but the bushmanship of Mr. Moray saved possible disaster to the car, as the suffering beasts sometimes go quite mad and will charge anything that comes near them. We passed through various kinds of grass lands … In some places the car was buried in long grass, and it was well over the height of a man standing upright … Some of the lower country that we passed through consisted of rich, dark loam, known as 'black soil' which, with irrigation, is likely one day to grow an adaptable upland cotton and Indian wheat. Owing to the fact that it bakes hard in the sun after being waterlogged and well poached by cattle moving over it, it is also called by the blacks 'Devil-Devil', and motoring over it is a severe form of penance. Now and again we had to go through creeks with water over the axles, so in the Territory the magneto and other vulnerable parts of a car are raised extra high to keep them from possible harm. Just before stopping for lunch, we had to pass over a long, dry river-bed, known as the 'Longreach Crossing'. It is an infamous place for cars, and one that, looking at the alternate patches of heavy sand and rocky boulders, you would not believe it possible for any car to cross alive. In the wet season, fourteen feet of water flow over the passage by which cattle, pack-horses, wagons and some half-dozen cars pass over the river-bed during the 'dry'. There are flood marks in the trees high over one's head and one can imagine how impossible travel in the wet season must be …

No car as yet designed seems perfect under the variety of conditions to be met in the Northern Territory, as the ordinary car is liable to stick in bog or sand, while the car with the usual type of caterpillar wheels, though excellent in sand, is likely to damage its tracks on rocks, is slow in the better places and consumes so much more petrol. The ideal compromise is awaited with eagerness by the men who tour the Bush.

That day, we lunched near a delightful water-hole like a large lake, which is a famous resort for water fowl of all kinds and small crocodiles, but the worst beast we happened upon was a large red and green ant, which took a great liking to the tinned raspberries and clotted Australian cream with which we were finishing our most excellent meal, and called up most of his relations. Mr. Moray had at first feared that we might not care for the usual Bush fare of tea, cold beef and bread, but the early starts, fresh air and invigorating dry climate and hot sun gave us appetites that it was unnecessary to tempt. At ten o'clock in the morning the sun was burning hot, but the air was so dry that the heat was not exhausting. High up on the inland plateau there were cool winds at night, and almost a touch of frost in the early morning. We wore drill coats and skirts and straw hats, and generally had veils to keep off the glare and the flies. I found red chiffon was most pleasing to the eyes and we occasionally wore yellow spectacles.

We lived for a fortnight on Wave Hill station while Mr. Moray carried on his work. Lady Leighton and I felt that we were enjoying the perfect rest-cure as advocated by fashionable nerve specialists — no worries, no letters (as the mail only comes once in six weeks and anyhow there was no one to write to us), or papers or bothers of any kind, plenty of good air, food, sleep and exercise. In the wet season there are mosquitoes, snakes, centipedes and scorpions, but in July and August we found no pests at all. Mr. Moray feared we might be dull, but we always found something interesting to see or do ...

Time passed very happily at Wave Hill. We used to get up about 6.30, with an early morning cup of tea. Water was brought to us in a large kerosene tin because there is always a shortage of buckets and pails on a station, but there was an adjacent wash-house with a shower bath. Breakfast at 7.15 consisted of porridge, beef, bread, butter and jam. This was followed by a light meal known as 'morning tea' at 10.30, beef tea, cake, honey, etc. An afternoon cup of tea at 3.30; and the final meal of the day, known as 'Tea', at 6.15, as the sun set, consisted of beef, vegetables, pudding and cups of tea. English people may marvel at the number of cups of tea, but in the hot, dry, dusty climate of Australia it is welcome at all times. In the evenings we used to play card games — Bridge, 'Slippery Ann', 'Thank you, Darling', and other old favourites. We introduced 'Thank you, Darling' to the Northern Territory, and it became a great favourite …

On August 10th a miracle occurred. We were all leaving next day, but as the time was near when it was possible that Terry's cars might be getting into the vicinity, Mr. Moray was taking us out to Barry's Knob, a distant hill whence one could see a three days journey in their direction. A puff of dust on the horizon might indicate their position and it would be worth while awaiting their arrival. We hardly expected to see anything of them, and it was more an expedition to amuse us, of which Mr. Moray was always thinking. Booted and breeched, I had just pulled on my old yellow silk high-necked jersey, and was idly waiting to start, when I saw a strange single figure on an indifferent horse coming along the trail up to the station. I did not much consider the fact, as all persons of the least consequence in the Northern Territory go about with a 'plant' of horses and attended by a boy or several boys. I casually noted that he rode with a cavalry-soldier's seat, and supposed he was a strange policeman calling in to have a chat with Mr. Marshall, the book-keeper, till suddenly something familiar caught my eye about the stranger, and at that moment an excited Chinese cook came running in shouting: 'The Lord has come! The Lord has come ... in blue trousers!' ...

Next morning early we all went off together — the largest fleet of cars that had ever been seen in the Northern Territory, consisting of Mr. Moray's 'Betty', which he drove with Lady Leighton and myself, a specially constructed Dodge car containing Mr. Easton [a government surveyor] and my husband; and Professor Ward, with his mechanic, in the Dodge lorry, by which he had come overland from the south. We started in such a way as to keep in touch with each other all along the route. Mr. Moray had had the track leading from Wave Hill to Soakage Creek 'fire-ploughed' most of the way, so that it was easy to follow and, in some places, excellent going. A fire-plough is drawn by some fifteen horses, and is a wide metal scoop on a timber frame, after the fashion of a snow-plough, which, used after the wet season before the ground is baked hard, cuts off the top vegetation and the surface irregularities, the primary object of course being to prevent bush fires ...

That night we slept out in the Bush, and the next day, proceeding on our way, we crossed into West Australia. There was nothing to mark the boundary except some initials cut by the first surveyor in a tree, but the difference was soon apparent as the country became flatter, more treeless, with fewer creeks and with patches of red sand-stone soil and lots more spinifex — the signs of less surface water. In some parts the country was so flat that we were able to career along at forty miles an hour and actually burst a tyre from speeding!!

We reached Soakage Creek (or Gordon Downs) Station on August 15th, the coldest day we experienced in the North, and unpleasantly dusty and windy. The station blacks gave a corroboree in honour of the first white women to stay at Gordon Downs, which was an eerie show to watch in the light of torches and a few stars, but rather shorn of its primeval character by the boots and trousers worn by the performers whose natural get-up would have been merely smears of red ochre and white cockatoo feathers stuck with gum on their naked bodies in fancy patterns. The 'dances' consisted of endless repetitions of certain movements to the rhythmic accompaniment of foot and voice and the deep tones of a 'didgeridoo', a saxophone-like instrument made out of a long hollow piece of tree.

Staying there a day, we then went seventy-six miles to Flora Valley across flat, plain-like country called 'downs' which in some places stretched like a yellow sea without anything on the surface to break the monotony for sixty miles on all sides to the horizon. Now and again, we saw a mirage of trees apparently standing on their heads in water in the haze of the great heat.

Flora Valley, about 1300 feet up in a fold of the Kimberley Ranges, once famous for the North Australian gold rush in 1885–88, produced some of the finest scenery we had yet seen, and we lived there a week, enjoying picnic trips, fishing, riding, bathing, camping, and the pick of the well-bred horses, under delightful conditions. This station was connected by private telephone to the telegraph office at Hall's Creek, so we were able to make final arrangements about the cars that were coming from Derby to meet us. There was an excellent Chinese cook, and we lived on the fat of the land — best beef, eggs, cream, fresh vegetables and milk.

The successful finish to a happy trip was marred by a nasty accident to Lady Leighton, who had a fall while riding out to see a muster of cattle, and the ground being hard as iron and covered with sharp stones, she unfortunately broke her ribs and her collar-bone. Once again the Australian Inland Mission proved its value, and before evening, thanks to the kindness of the manager of Moola Bulla Station seventy miles away and the owner of the only car in the district, the two nurses from the tiny Hall's Creek Hospital were able to come forty miles and to strap up her injury, making it possible for her to travel three days later. Hall's Creek in the Kimberley Ranges is quite the place of this part of West Australia, as it contains over a dozen white inhabitants.

Mr. Alec Scott of Fitzroy Crossing was waiting to take us down to Derby — 400 miles — in his car, in time to catch the Air Mail. Between Hall's Creek and Fitzroy Crossing the 'road' to civilisation was like an endless switchback, winding mile after mile over alternate rocks, stones, sand, creeks and hills severer on a car than any of our drove trails in the Territory. It had been picked out by the feet of prospectors and pack-horses, and followed by bullock-carts and donkey teams; it turned and twisted, never straight for more than 100 yards — a nightmare road — and the least suitable for motor touring imaginable. Small wonder that barely half a dozen times had the journey been done by car during a twelvemonth! It was a tiring two days for even the hale and hearty, and Lady Leighton had a wretched time, but we were anxious to reach comparative civilisation where she could be rested in comfort and her damages attended to as soon as possible. Only sheer pluck kept her going.

We stopped a night each at Margaret Station, Mr. Scott's hotel at Fitzroy Crossing, famous the length and breadth of the Nor'-West, and at the sheep Station of Nucumbar, where we said goodbye to our dear friend Mr. Moray, who had come with us thus far as one of the hired cars had broken down and his faithful and indomitable 'Betty 'was the most comfortable conveyance for Lady Leighton. Mr. Moray had been one of the kindest of hosts, best of companions and most interesting of guides. He is one of the little company of true lovers of north Australia, and in his position as Chief Pastoral Inspector of the cattle stations controlled by the Vestey companies is probably doing more for its actual development than any other man in the Territory ... Nothing is too hard or too difficult for this kind of Australian, who is made up of the old pioneering stuff, added to the modern scientific, calculating mind ... His is the sort of spirit that has held the Northern Territory together at a time when the price of meat does not pay for the labour of keeping the cattle, and so it was as interesting for us to see behind the scenes something of the driving ideas of the bushmen as it was to experience their lives on the stations ...

The final stage of our journey to Derby was made in a car sent out from Derby, as accidents occurred to both the others after leaving Fitzroy Crossing, one running into a sheep and the other damaging its steering.

The temperature here was hotter than anything we had yet come across — about 112 degrees in the shade — but it was so dry and exhilarating that it did not tire one at all, even in the middle of the day. Twilight was very brief, as we were still near the tropics and the nights were lovely for sleeping out, with no pests at this time of the year …

The last sixty miles of our journey were accomplished in the dark, owing to punctures due to the heat and rough going. We reached Derby about 10.30 on the night of Friday, August 21st and had to repack and be ready to catch the air mail at 3.00 the following afternoon … The local doctor, the first we had come across since leaving Darwin, put Lady Leighton's arm into plaster-of-Paris, to make it easier for the journey. He said he only had an accident of that kind once in a 'blue moon', and it is very evident everywhere in north Australia how well and healthy every individual is, and the older a man is, the better the climate seems to suit him and the more he is able to do. Personally, I never felt better in my life and thoroughly enjoyed what we were able to see and do in the Bush, and shall never forget the excellent time we had and the many good friends who were so kind to us.

The 2,000 mile air-trip southward to Perth along the Australian coast took four days of flying at a height of 4,000 feet with the wind behind at a speed of about 80 miles per hour …

I have endeavoured to put down a few of my impressions, but at the time I was too busy enjoying things to do more than keep odd notes and dates, which are no more than an amateur's conceptions of a fascinating and intricate country where twentieth century knowledge and thought meet the conditions of prehistoric man.

I can't say why Lady Leighton and I wanted to go. It may

have been some old Norse roving ancestry, or the workings of ancient Scottish Border raiding blood, or it may have been ordinary feminine obstinacy, but it was certainly with no useful purpose in mind that we went and so, unwittingly, became the first people who travelled for pleasure through this strip of northern Australia. Should I ever go back, as I hope to do some day, I know that the first man I meet in the Bush will know me or know those that I knew. The Brotherhood of the Bush is so strong that people who have lived in the Bush, even for a short time, know by sight or repute everyone there is to know. No one in the Bush ever forgets ...

From Lord and Lady Apsley, *The Amateur Settlers. Part II. An Interlude Through Northern Australia by Lady Apsley*, London, 1927. Courtesy Peter Bridge Collection.

1930

Angela Thirkell, writer and traveller, was the daughter of a Professor of Poetry at Oxford University. For a time she resided in Victoria and Tasmania before returning to England to pursue a literary career. She became a highly successful professional writer, selling her features to periodicals, newspapers and syndicates around the world. Her feature story of a typical voyage out to Australia, such as you might experience on a P&O or an Orient Line passenger ship at the height of the great days of sea travel, is both masterly and highly credible. By now travel almost everywhere was easy and comfortable for most, and was thought commonplace by a great many people. Regular passenger ship travel to and from Australia, as she described it, was to last until the 1960s.

JT IS AN ETERNAL MYSTERY that special boat trains for Tilbury Docks, which are away to the east, down the Thames, should start from St. Pancras [Railway Station] which one associates entirely with trains running north; unless it is part of the general scheme for making the last of England as dismal and depressing as possible. 'Let us', say the railway and shipping companies, 'let us lure our passengers to a station from which they might reasonably expect them to go to Edinburgh; let us then run a train over as many clanking points as possible; through as many goods yards; past as many gasometers, factories and homes for scrap iron; over as many sodden, dirty pieces of waste land. And let us see that no friends are allowed to accompany the departing pilgrims. Let us cast them out at Tilbury in bitter cold and driving rain in a little station beyond the world with a wet walk to a pier.' And so it is done.

St. Pancras on a Saturday morning falls into such a bellowing and hooting of engine whistles, such clankings of couplings and puffing of young engines fetching small loads along to sidings as never yet was heard. It is probably arranged with a view to drowning the lamentations and good-byes on the platform, on the principle of drums at an execution, but it makes one think of the old joke in an old

'Punch' whereby St. Pancras is hailed patron saint of railways.

While waiting on the platform one has leisure to admire the good fortune attending those whom Kipling calls the Sons of Mary [nuns], who, disregarding all notices about heavy luggage, take four cabin trunks and a gigantic wardrobe trunk to the special train with them, relying on their Lord to see it put aboard for them with no difficulty; which he accordingly does. Whereas we poor Sons of Martha send our trunks off on the Thursday morning at infinite personal inconvenience, being hypnotised so to do by a leaflet sent us by the shipping company (such is the power of print) and live miserably for two days in a suit case with a very insufficient wardrobe.

It was a cold, wet January morning when we left St. Pancras. 'We', in this case, consisted of myself and the Child, who is Australian born and has the independent outlook and unquenchable conceit of his birthplace. He helped us all and took the sting from parting by announcing his intention of being sick in the train. This is one of his talents and can also be carried out in a tram, carriage, or motor, with complete success, so his Loving Parent had hastily to devise distraction for him ... we arrive at Tilbury ...

The final touch of discomfort is given to the journey which takes one from the pier to the ship, lying out in the channel, looking very tall and grim and unhomelike. Little motor boats surged around us full of friends of the third-class passengers, all in excellent spirits; we had no friends to accompany us on the later stages of our journey. From the third-class promenade deck cheerful faces looked down and yelled witty remarks at the motor-boats; from our promenade deck a few cross, reserved faces looked coldly down as if to say, 'What is this dirt that is presuming to come aboard?' How pleasant is the survival of class distinctions, even in this levelling age …

It is not until Port Said is left behind that the sports committee get into their stride. People rush about the decks all morning with the aimless activity of ants; violent friendships are made over deck quoits, to be quickly disintegrated by the bridge tournament; no one knows anyone else's name, and the passenger list is at a premium. The barber's shop is besieged for tennis shoes; all the young creatures have their hair waved and wear a fresh frock every night. The young men, in a minority as usual, distribute their favours with nonchalance. The clergy come out in flannel trousers, alpaca coats and soft collars of a distinctly dissenting flavour. Business increases at the bar and all is joy. On the boat deck, quoits and deck tennis fill every open space, while in every corner young people sit on rugs in pleasant confusion and among them all are lines of deck chairs, where spectators stand an even chance of being killed by a quoit or tripping up a player.

And now we are well towards the tropics where the female hearts do so unaccountably melt towards unattractive males, and chairs gravitate in couples into corners, and every shepherd tells his tale under the porthole in the vale. And this is the moment for the fancy dress dance.

Passengers may flatter themselves that they got up a fancy dress ball which surpasses others for ingenuity and beauty; but the fact is, there is only one fancy dress ball, which surpasses other dances for ingenuity and beauty — an immutable type that scarcely varies from voyage to voyage from year to year. There is a great substratum of people that won't dress up at all, and just above them a layer of people (mostly men) who say that nothing will induce them to dress up, but when the night comes they are smitten with madness and, borrowing scarves and dressing-gowns from their female friends, arrive a half hour late for dinner as Arabs. Then there is a whole class which is doomed to dress up as unsuitably as possible. Men with very long, thin necks will go as Turks with low-necked Zouave jackets and a fez to add to their height; men with heavy moustaches powder their hair and appear as a kind of Charles Surface; tall, thin girls go as Pompadours; short fat girls are seized with frenzy, and come as Pierrettes, with short, stout, black, silk legs; females with flat figures and bony legs are inspired to be Hawaiians with insufficient clothing and no shoes and stockings. There are also the unimaginative who throw themselves on the barber's mercy. 'I have got a picture hat,' they say vaguely (or a fur boa, or a green shawl), 'what do you think would work in with it for fancy dress?' The barber treacherously feigns solicitude and makes a few impossible suggestions, but we all know what the end will be; the victim goes away with a cardboard box marked 'Jazz Pierrot', 'Lady Mephisto', or 'Gent's Comic'.

Then it always strikes two or three people as an entirely new and original idea to come dressed in their cabin curtain with cabin fittings hung about them. Almost inevitably, too, a female will drape herself in a Union Jack or an Australian flag; and there is the slightly pathetic lady who has a little circlet with a star on it and a spangled shawl, and goes as Queen of the Night. And there are others who just undress.

Dinner is earlier that night, and as each self-conscious

319

passenger enters the dining-saloon there is applause, perfunctory from some, champagne-inspired from others. The Grand Parade takes place; prizes are awarded by fearful judges; dancing begins. The Ship's Vamp makes a determined onslaught on the more personable of the men. Greasepaint runs and melts on many Sheikish countenances. South Sea Islanders find bare feet impossible for dancing, and put on golden shoes with jewelled heels. And all unperturbed among it, a few bridge players pursue their sacred calling. And so, in a blaze of glory, we come to Colombo.

Colombo affords great pleasure to travelled and untravelled alike. The untravelled enjoy rapturously their first sign of the East, its sights and smells. The travelled can enjoy themselves with less exertion by despising the raptures of the untravelled. If once you have seen the sights, the happiest way to spend the day is in a friendly bungalow in the Government quarters with a real rest on a real bed. One must have spent three weeks in a bunk and have nearly three more in prospect to appreciate its full worth on a bed on which one can sprawl and lie starfish-wise and turn without hitting a wall or a wooden side and sit up without crashing one's head into the springs of the upper berth. So I did not motor to Kandy (150 miles there and back at breakneck speed and half an hour to see the sights), nor did I lunch at the Galle Face Hotel (prices and food rather disproportionate, but they mix cocktails stronger than on the ship), nor did I drive to Nagombo (the mango tree miracle is worked for believers haggling as to terms), nor did I have tea at Mount Lavinia and bathe in the warm sea. I can only say that bougainvillea and hibiscus swearing at each other in gorgeous clashes of colour from every bungalow garden, and the great blue convolvulus added its contribution, and everything was looking green and leafy compared with the smug aridity of Australian towns.

We got back to the ship late at night and it was not too hot to sit on deck and watch the launches returning with the passengers who had been dining on shore. A powerful electric light was hung over the side of the ship above the ladder by which the shore-goers came up, and it illumined a half circle on the water very brilliantly. Suddenly out of the darkness beyond came gliding a fishing boat with seven sails spread dazzling and ghostly white and looking as fragile as a great moth. While one might count a hundred, it slid slowly past in absolute silence and vanished into the dark beyond. And then a motor launch gave its vulgar hoot, and voices yelled loud coo-ees from the lower deck and all was normal again. I was still enthralled by this vision when I was roused to consciousness by seeing what was apparently a small lighthouse moving past us on a piece of rock, under its own power. It was only a moment later that I realised with a slight shock that it was we who were moving and not the lighthouse; but we had started as silently and with as little effort as a cloud might move.

The older one gets, the more one finds out that literature is true. Every year's experience brings fresh insight into the wonder of poetry and lines which have seemed no more than lovely words stab one unexpectedly. Similarly, books of travel and adventure which have been agreeable make-believe, suddenly come alive. To-day I saw Coral Island and realised how perfectly right Ballantyne was.

Ship's rumour speaking the truth with her many tongues

for once had said that we were to pass near the Cocos Islands and on the following morning a line of palms appeared on the horizon, and as we drew nearer to them I saw exactly what Jack and Ralph and Peterkin saw. A chain of little islands lay encircling a lagoon. Each island had a dazzling white beach and was crowned with brilliant green palms. Between the islands the white line of surf roared ceaselessly, and within this rampart lay a calm sea of vivid blue — quite unbelievable till one had seen it. As we steamed slowly past the islands the same miracle of colour was repeated at every opening — green, white; sapphire; emerald, ivory — glittering in the sun. And always the sound of the surf.

From a landing place on one of the larger islands a motor boat came out across our course, followed by a little sailing boat. For some days past a notice had invited passengers to contribute books, newspapers, chocolate and tobacco for the few white inhabitants of the islands who manage the cable station, and these, together with some ship's stores, were packed into a barrel. As the motor boat came near we slowed down and almost stopped. A white man who was standing up in front of the boat shouted to us and evidently received instructions, for he ordered his native crew to change their course and they dashed off round the ship's stern to where the barrel was being lowered on the other side. It was quickly fastened behind the motor boat and the little craft circled us once more with shouts and hand-waving and plunged off towards the bank.

While we were waiting the sun had gone behind a cloud and a squall was coming up from the northwest, and in a few moments the crest of each wave was tipped with foam and the rain was hissing on the water. Before long the islands were blotted out by the driving rain and the little sailing boat disappeared in the mist.

It is all romantic enough to see, but what a life of monotony it must be, with no escape day or night from the sounding of the waters and no rest for the eye from the maddening brilliance of sea and sky and palm ... Next day the captain of our boat had a wireless from the island thanking him for the barrel and its contents, and asking for copies of the snapshots which passengers had taken of the boats and the island.

After nine days of tropics and sub-tropics we were due at Fremantle from Colombo. Quarantine and passport inspection were to take place at 7 a.m., and we all went to bed very early. But, bright and alert, the quarantine officers arrived well ahead of time and I woke with a jump at the sound of a steward's voice yelling abstractedly down the corridor, 'All passengers in the lounge' ... I hauled the angry Child out of bed while he said in an injured voice, 'I was sleeping very heavily,' and dressed him and myself and went up to the lounge. The doctor was already waiting and looked very unhappy, as if the sight of so many women with potential diseases was depressing him. Some heroic females had come with sleeveless frocks and others were rolling their sleeves back to the shoulder, saying bravely, 'He will want to see my vaccination'. But to no purpose were all these sacrifices, for all the doctor asked was that we pass before him, showing the backs and fronts of our hands ... all those who had hoped to have their blood pressure taken and the whites of their eyes examined were sent empty away.

This done, we went to the section to have the passports

stamped. The passport officers were kindness itself and got through the business expeditiously, not even alarming our dressing-gowned and bedslippered modesty by raising their eyes to our faces as they scanned the passport photographs. Nor were the customs officers at the gangway less apt in chivalry, and the glances they cast at the contents of my (perfectly innocent) handbag were as perfunctory as those St. Anthony cast on the devil. But a terrible fate overtook a large party of picnickers who went ashore with sandwiches and dried figs; for dried figs contain at least two million seeds, and is not the import of seeds forbidden except under the strictest quarantine rules? So I am sorry to say that the figs were all confiscated and sent back to the refrigerator, and the picnic party was deprived of the pleasure of these delightful fruits.

Perth looked very well as it always does to sea worn mariners, and a great many people bought more grapes than their husbands could possibly carry.

And here, at the Western Gateway of this Island Continent, a terrible thing occurs against which experienced travellers had been providing for some days beforehand: I allude to the raising of all drinks and smokes to the Australian prices. All, that is, except the Australian wines. The Commonwealth Government, by an ingenious exercise of its reasoning powers, has convinced itself that all ships travelling between one Australian port and the next are in its territorial waters, unless they call at a foreign port on the way. It would be so very difficult for a ship to call anywhere between Fremantle and Adelaide that the shipping companies have given up any thought of it. So the unfortunate consumer, be he Australian or British, has to pay duty on his drinks in port and out of port, whether he or she is in Fremantle, or miles out to sea, being very sick and urgently in need of brandy in the Bight — which all helps, doubtless, to bring down the prices in the Government Hotel at Canberra.

From Angela Thirkell, 'Unorthodox Impressions of an Itinerant Parent. Tilbury to Fremantle', *The Home*, October, 1930.

Amy Johnson
1930

While most travellers were now content to go out to Australia in comfort, a few were bent on exploring the newfangled idea of travel by air. Amy Johnson was the first woman to fly solo from the United Kingdom to Australia. She was aged twenty-seven. She flew a de Havilland Gipsy Moth named the Jason Wanderer G-AAAH, *which was refitted with a second-hand engine. It was perhaps the last great journey out to Australia undertaken by a woman. It took her twenty days to reach Darwin, and the whole world, it seemed at the time, breathed a sigh of relief when news came through that she had arrived safely. The King immediately made her a Companion of the Order of the British Empire, while letters, telegrams and cablegrams of congratulation from Empire prime ministers and others poured in by the thousands.*

MY FLIGHT WAS CARRIED OUT for two reasons: because I wished to carve for myself a career in aviation, and because of my innate love of adventure. My first object has not been realised exactly as I would have wished; the second object is still open to me. What I crave for more than anything else is adventure. I am, therefore, going to try to bring into my book [never completed], not only the construction and care of my engine, but little bits of the romance and adventure of my flight ...

My engine and machine were standard except for stub exhaust and fairing on the ailerons, rudder and elevator; and front cockpit covered in. This I had done to gain a little extra speed and probably gained a further 5 miles per hour; all of which was probably lost again by carrying my spare propeller strapped on to the side of the machine, but I dare not go without it, and events proved that my advisers were wise ...

I carried two extra petrol tanks, one in the front cockpit to hold 35 gallons, and one in the rear locker with a capacity of 26 gallons. The top gravity tank held 19 gallons, so I had a total petrol capacity of 80 gallons which should keep me in the air for 13 hours at a cruising speed of 90 miles per hour, and in temperate climate. Kingsford Smith had 100 gallons. You can, therefore, see that he was better off than I was, because in the hotter climates I used more petrol, and, therefore, I could not keep in the air for so long. He had a great advantage over me …

The first day I had slight head winds, and only reached Vienna after 10 hours flying, but after that, until I reached India, I had following winds, which was just as well, because my calculations had been based on a cruising speed of 90 miles per hour, and at this speed I was due to reach each stopping place before sunset. Doing such slow speed I could not carry them out quite as planned, but, fortunately I had these following winds and my calculations came out about right.

On the morning of May 5th at 4 a.m., I rose and breakfasted, and then went onto the aerodrome [Croydon, London], where two of my friends had been working all night, filling up, trying on the spare propeller, greasing, and oiling. As dawn broke the machine was run up, and I settled myself in the cockpit. Whilst fastening my belt and parachute straps I smelt petrol strongly, and tracing it I found one of the petrol pipe connections dripping badly. There was nothing to be done but stop the engine, and let my friends see the trouble. I soon saw it would be a fairly long job, so I went back to bed till the connection was repaired. It was 8 o'clock before I finally took off.

The journey to Vienna was uneventful except for my slow speed and pumping petrol. This was not at all funny. My pump was an ordinary hand air-pressure pump, and I had to pump 40 times (there and back counting as one) to pump one gallon into the gravity tank. There is no need to enlarge on the subject, but the only thing that kept me pumping was the ignominy of giving up my flight because pumping petrol made me sick. However, my muscles grew harder, and although I never grew to like it, yet later on I used to be glad of the job as a means of keeping me awake.

At Vienna the mechanics absolutely refused to let me do anything on my engine, and I danced hither and thither explaining what must be done, my head full of my last promise to my engineer tutor to do everything myself. The mechanics meanwhile endeavoured to amuse me by a story of their last lady pilot visitor who changed into overalls and mounted a ladder, insisting on looking over the engine herself. Now if there is one thing I cannot stand, it is the idea of being laughed at behind my back, so I left them to it, and went off to see about my passport, finding somewhere to sleep, as there was not time to go into Vienna. In the morning at 4 a.m. I rose, and went to my machine. I thought I was fortunate to find anyone up so early to open the hangar doors, but later I never wondered at this, because in other countries it seems the custom to start work early. We started up the engine, but she did not sound good ... The rear plug was badly 'oiled' up. After this experience I examined the plugs every day as I did not like early morning delays.

Vienna to Constantinople was fairly uneventful, except that the petrol pump developed another leak, and as I pumped, petrol spurted into my face, and made me feel so sick I had to do all my pumping with my face over the side of the ship.

I arrived at Constantinople with an hour's daylight to spare, but one and a half hours were wasted in the Customs, and by the time I was allowed to return to my machine it was pitch dark. A car was on the aerodrome, and I asked for its headlamps to be lit, and turned my way. By their light I cleaned and examined the engine (and generally carried out the usual daily overhaul), changed all the plugs, and drained the oil which was filthy. The Turks helped me fill up with petrol, and after about three hours' hard work the machine was ready. No one spoke English, and I made signs to ask if it could be put in a hangar for the night. I could see one at the other end of the aerodrome. Before I could protest several able-bodied Turks had lifted high Jason's tail, and over he went on his nose — heavily weighted as he was in front with petrol and tools, etc. Intuition (or strict training) had caused me, two minutes before, to straighten the propeller (put it horizontal) as I passed in front of the engine, so no harm was done. I was a bit worried, and insisted on testing it for truth … The Turks looked so shame-faced I was sorry I had been cross with them. Jason was then taken, oh so carefully, into a hangar, and off I went to find somewhere to sleep …

In the morning … no sooner was I installed in the cockpit than the ominous smell of petrol reminded me of the leak I had noticed the previous day. This had become worse, but as I wanted to reach Baghdad I would probably have pushed on with it. However, it was then long after dawn, and I knew I could not make Baghdad anyhow, so I went to rest whilst a French mechanic (conveniently working on a visiting French plane) mended the leak for me. Whenever there was a suitable man mechanic near I always left it to him.

When at last I was in the air I felt anxiously for vibration, because it seemed too good to be true that no harm had come from the upsetting incident of the previous night. However, all seemed O.K., and I went on. Over the Taurus Mountains, which are about 15,000 feet high in parts, I tried to climb, but as I had no altitude control and was heavily laden, I could not get higher than 10,000 feet, and even then my engine coughed and spluttered until I came down to 9,000 feet. I watched the oil pressure gauge with anxiety, but it stoutly remained at 40, and I blessed it.

At Aleppo I found the French Air Force most kindly and efficient. Filling up was quickly carried out from pumps, which I was rather surprised to find in the desert, and as I had landed fairly early I had plenty of daylight to finish the engine work by. With the aid of French mechanics I carried out an ordinary daily overhaul, including the plugs, changing the oil, and examining the plunger. Everything went well, and Aleppo was one of my happiest stops, as well as my first hint of romance. I shall never forget being at Aleppo, the very first time that I had been anywhere near a desert, and seeing the Sheiks there, or, as I learned to call them in Baghdad, the Shakes. I was off early in the morning, and everything went well until the dust storm. I forced-landed in the desert at about 110 miles per hour, and must have weakened the undercarriage left-hand radius rod, because when I later landed at Baghdad it broke clean in two, and my landing there, though heavy, did not warrant that …

The Royal Air Force mechanics at Hinaid, bless them, worked all night long making a new strut, and it was all ready fitted for me when I came the next morning. I was fortunate at Baghdad, because Imperial Airways mechanics did all my work for me, and I went for a drive through

Baghdad. I knew that proper men mechanics would do the job much better than I could, so I had no compunction in leaving it to them whenever I could.

Baghdad to Bundar Abbas was rather a nightmare. I was getting into terrific heat, and no matter how high I went (ceiling at 10,000 feet) my oil pressure would fall but it did not go below 35, so I just flew as high as I could, throttled down the engine, and hoped for the best. Besides this, my engine was missing, and I did not at all like the sound when I ran on to the right-hand magneto only. My revolutions dropped, but not very seriously, and I guessed one plug must be misbehaving. I hastily switched on to the other magneto so that I should not hear the unpleasant sound so plainly. There was nowhere to land, anyhow.

At Bundar Abbas I was not expected; the aerodrome was not marked in any way, nor was there any indication of the wind. Presuming there was a sea breeze I landed towards the Gulf in the only available large space, which proved to be the aerodrome. I landed fast, as usual, and rather heavily, also. as usual, in the terrific heat I was now flying in, and to my horror, the left wing drooped and trailed on the ground. This time it was the bolt securing the top of the new strut which had sheared, and I could not see any hope of help in such a Godforsaken place as Bundar Abbas. I was taken into the British Consulate situated almost on the aerodrome, where I succumbed to a blinding headache, and was utterly incapable of seeing to my machine. The Consul was very kind, and assured me he had an excellent man who looked after his car, and who would do everything he could for my plane. I was not so sure, but felt far too ill to take any active steps just at that moment. I was given tea, and made to lie down, the Consul's wife and daughter doing their utmost to cure my headache. By dinner time they were successful, and the headache marvellously vanished, but much precious time had been lost, and I had done nothing to my machine. Dinner was a long meal because the lights went out in the middle (the man in charge of the power house had run out of petrol, and so had taken a holiday, and gone out to see my machine). Dinner over, it was dark; but a beautiful moon was rising which after a time gave enough light to enable me to see to my engine, helped by a torch for inside jobs.

Feeling very anxious indeed, as it was getting so late (it was by then about 10.30), I insisted on going at once to the aerodrome. Here, to my intense surprise, I found my machine standing up properly, and on testing the strut and bolt I found a new bolt had been fitted, and the result all that could be desired. I could not imagine how anything so marvellous had been carried out in this place at Bundar Abbas. I was then introduced to the wonder worker, who went by the name of 'David', and he confided to me that when Royal Air Force planes had been using the aerodrome he had always hung around to help, and to learn all he could. He also said he had found the bolt amongst some spare parts which had been left behind. I was too thankful to be curious, and I blessed him for his interest in aero engines.

Two Englishmen had come on the scene from somewhere, but they evidently had not ever in their lives shown any interest in aero engines. Balanced precariously on petrol tins, as no steps were available, I tugged at the cowling, as I was anxious to discover the mystery of the 'missing' plug. It was not all missing, but the middle of it was. The electrode had blown clean out. Oh well, no harm was done fortunately, and from then on I vowed to add tightening of electrodes to the list of my daily tasks.

David worked hard under my instructions, and whilst he balanced on the petrol tins, I stood on the sand, and directed him whilst he took out the plugs. I impressed on him the importance of putting back the washer on each plug, and when the job was done I myself tightened the electrodes, and plugs. The rest of the work went on smoothly, if slowly, because of the lack of light, and the sand blowing over my tools, and large and small insects creeping in and out amongst them. I carried out the complete daily schedule, and by midnight had got as far as putting in the new oil, having drained out the old.

'Where's my XXL, David?' Consternation reigned. After a long search some Castrol R. was produced, and I was told that was all there was, and no one had any idea as to how many years it had lain there on the aerodrome. We opened it, but I did not like the feel of it. I had no experience of Castrol R., and had never seen any, as all my engine work had been done at the Club where XXL and Vacuum BB were the only oils used. There seemed no alternative but to risk this, so I decided to pour in two gallons, run up the engine, and note the oil pressure. However, when I saw what looked like weak tea running into my engine I had definite misgivings, and ordered a halt. After much questioning, and a journey back to the Consulate to get the Consul's views as to the whereabouts of my own supplies, it was decided to find out whether the oil was in the Customs shed. We got into the car and bumped across to the Customs Officer's bungalow where we hauled him out of bed (or rather the Consul did) and he gave us the key so that we could examine the place ourselves. This was about 1 a.m. I returned to *Jason* whilst two of the others went to look for oil. In about an hour's time they triumphantly returned with two gallons of XXL. I drained out the weak tea, and with great relief saw the thick green peasoup with which I was so familiar disappearing into the sump. By 2.30 a.m. I had finished all I intended to do (the air was wonderful, and I did not feel a bit tired), and went off to bed. I was up at 4, as I had left the petrol cap on the front tank to be fastened in the morning ...

Bundar Abbas to Karachi was a very worrying flight, partly because my engine was again missing on the right-hand magneto, and I could not imagine what was wrong, as I had been so extra careful the night before. On landing at Karachi the trouble was soon discovered. On the outside of the right-hand cowling I saw a round black bulge, and insider saw a black patch surrounded by a pretty rainbow halo. I did not stop to admire this, but turned my attention to the plug opposite. I found two washers on it, and again was thankful for my lucky escape, as the plug had been shorting across to the cowling during a journey of about 800 miles. Fortunately it was on the opposite side to the carburetor, or there might have been danger of fire; as I say, I was lucky ...

At Karachi I was taken over by Imperial Airways; told to be a wise girl, and rest a day whilst my engine was overhauled. I wanted to be wise, but had no intention of losing a day, and after a good deal of persuasion it was arranged that my machine should be done overnight. How mighty thankful and relieved I was. They examined my carburetor, and adjusted it for tropical flying as I explained the engine was running too rich … Early in the morning, whilst still dark, I ran up the engine in the hangar and was delighted to see the beautiful Bunsen blue flame which flashed out of each of the four stubs. The advantage of having stub exhaust is that you can see straight away if anything is wrong with the petrol mixture. They went through my tools, renewed those missing, cleaned all my plugs, and wrapped them in petrol rags. My next stop was to have been Allahabad, but I had head winds, and had not sufficient petrol, or daylight, to reach that aerodrome. I therefore forced-landed at Jhansi, on the [Indian Army] parade ground, as the aerodrome was not marked on my map, and I could not locate it. Anyway, the parade ground seemed to be the most suitable place that I could possibly land on. I landed with my wheels just touching the bushes on one side, and I ran across the parade ground. There was nothing at all to pull me up. There was no wind, and there was nothing to stop me, as I had no brakes. I therefore simply [had to] run across the parade ground. There happened to be a post on the opposite side, and I ran into the post, damaging my wing. There were a number of natives there who could have stopped the machine by holding on, but, naturally, they did not know anything about aeroplanes. My wing was slightly damaged. I was really heart-broken about it, because I could not see any hope of having it repaired there. Anyway, it was not quite so bad as it looked, and I found that I could mend it by strengthening the leading edge, and covering it with fabric, and doping it. I was told by the officers there that in the village there was a mystery man. I thought that this sounded very good, and I had in mind another miracle worker like David at Bundar Abbas. In the end, a bearded man came out, and I asked him who he was. He explained that he was known as the Village Mystery Man. He set to, and in a short space of time he had most marvellously mended this leading edge, and strengthened it, and it was stronger than it was before. I found out later that 'Mystery Man' is simply the village name for a carpenter. They also fetched out the village tailor to repair the wing, and to sew it up he used all my fabric, and all my dope [lubricant], and cotton. I had none left, and I very badly needed them on a future occasion.

The officers of the 3rd and 8th Punjab Regiment helped me to carry out my daily overhaul. Enough petrol was fetched in cars from the aerodrome ten miles away to enable me to reach Allahabad. Nothing very interesting happened over the engine; the heat was terrific, but I landed in the best place possible — the Colonel's front yard practically — and servants came constantly to and fro with long cool drinks. As time wore on my kind friends made me lie down on a camp bed near the machine, and direct operations. This was the nicest way that I had ever overhauled my engines: I liked it!! Eventually I was ordered off to bed with their promise to awaken me extra early in the morning to fill up with petrol. This was against my usual rule, but I was tired out, and gave in. Next morning I found they had finished everything for me, and most efficiently too.

From Jhansi I flew the odd 200 miles to Allahabad, where I re-fuelled. The engine had been spluttering slightly, and I knew the plugs must be all right, so I cleaned the magneto points (this sounds simple, but off the propeller had to come; the sun was blazing hot, and there was not a particle of shade), but it seemed to rectify the trouble.

Calcutta was reached with no incident, and my engine was there taken over by the Dum-Dum Flying Club, who did my work for me, whilst I spent my time trying to borrow clean clothes.

Rangoon was my destination next day, and a long tale of woe follows my forced landing at Insein. Everyone knows *Jason* ran into the ditch, and everyone wonders why I chose to land there instead of the racecourse. All I will say here is that I should not have been such a perfect idiot (or I hope not) as to have tried to come down on a football pitch if I had known that it was not the racecourse. It happened to be the compound and playing field of the Insein Engineering Institute, and I was at any rate relieved to know I was near an engineering school, and not a dancing academy. *Jason* ran smoothly and quietly past the goal posts head on for the ditch surrounding the compound, but there was not the slightest chance to take off again because of the high trees and buildings. I crashed into a wire fence, held up by posts which guarded a deep ditch. The wire pulled him up, and he went over into the ditch on his nose, one of the posts crashing through the left lower wing, ripping the left tyre open, shearing the bottom bolt on the undercarriage radius rod, and bending the oleo leg cowling into a very distorted shape. It would be too long a story to describe everything that was done to repair the damage, but I will briefly tell you the most interesting things.

The head of the Institute was exceedingly kind, and placed his works, staff, and pupils entirely at my disposal. It was examination time, so his kindness did all the more credit to him. None of them knew the first thing about aeroplanes! It poured with rain the whole time. The machine was in the ditch, and it had to be moved across the compound. The ditch had to be bridged to get the machine across, and then the machine had to be manoeuvred through trees right up to the Engineering Institute building. We took off the wing the next morning. Then came the task of repairing it. Two compression ribs were found to be broken, and several former ribs in the leading edge. They were all under the footboard, and there is a special stress on them there. We worked all the next day and night, and the following morning. I was very much helped by the Forestry Inspector there, who came along with some of his men, and took out the ribs, and pieced and glued them together. He chose timber from his warehouse which was as near as possible like my own ribs, and cut out new ones exactly to shape. These people did not know the first thing about aeroplanes, and yet they made all these important compression ribs, and the former ribs, which are not so important, to match exactly those which were broken. They worked all night fitting the wings.

The insects which I saw at Insein are the worst that I ever came across during the whole of my flight. They had to have several servants during the whole night through waving them off. The next morning they put on the wing, and they got several Burmese women from Rangoon, and the surrounding villages, to do the stitching. This was a long job. The stitching has to be done very carefully over and under, and it takes a long time to do it. I had no fabric. Several yards were needed, and somebody came forward with a brilliant suggestion that during the War a lot of aeroplane fabric had been dumped in Rangoon, and as there had been no other use for it it had been sold cheaply, and all the thrifty wives had bought it to make shirts for their husbands, as they had been told it would never wear out!! As many shirts as possible were collected and cut up into strips, and used for mending the wings. I had no dope left, and that is absolutely important for tightening up the fabric. A chemist was sent for from Rangoon, and he took my empty tin and made some more dope to match the smell. Over the dope there should have been a varnish of aluminum nitrate. There was none of this, and so we had to do without it. The dope had to be put on, according to the strict instructions of the makers, in a temperature of not more than 70° F., and a humidity of not more than 75 per cent was allowed. It did not seem much use worrying about things like that. The temperature, I expect, was well over 100° F. It poured in torrents the whole time, and I do not know what percentage of humidity that represents.

In between times I carried out my daily schedule on the engine, fitting on the spare propeller, which was very light, and not nearly as good as the one which was broken. I tested it for truth, because it was just possible that when the propeller shaft had been bent it might have thrown the whole engine out of alignment, which would have been perfectly hopeless. I tested the propeller, and I found that it satisfied all requirements.

The pupils made a new bolt, and straightened out the bent

cowling, whilst a Dunlop Rubber representative took away my outer cover to vulcanise it, as I only carried a spare inner tube, and an outer tube was not available. It speaks well for the care in carrying out this job that the same tyre still holds good, and also for my new strut made at Hinaidi, as it still held firm, in spite of being in the thick of the damaged part. I left in the oil so that we could run up the engine before taking the plane away, as the Engineering Institute was the best place for it as long as anything was wrong.

It was the following morning before we had the wing on and ready for test; the engine started easily, and I anxiously listened for any change in its note. I ran it up, and was relieved to find no vibration, and that everything seemed O.K. The oil pressure was only 30 lb. per sq. in., but I knew the old oil must be getting very thin after its long journey from Calcutta, so this did not worry me. The spare light propeller (a doped one) ran up to 1,900 revolutions per minute on the ground, and I was sorry my excellent heavy one was ruined.

I will not spend time on the difficulties of finding a vehicle to tow the plane to Rangoon, or getting out of the Institute grounds, and of its twelve mile journey at a speed of about three miles per hour; a native policeman going in front on a bicycle and importantly clearing all traffic off the road for *Jason*'s approach. Every fifteen minutes or so a halt was called for the tyres to cool down, because I was afraid of the long stress on the vulcanised cover, and if it had given way I was stranded until new tyres or wheels could be sent.

In due course our destination was reached, but it was sunset by then, and too dark to fill up that night. Early the next morning we filled up, I took the plane up with a light load for a test, and was all ready to take to my parachute if anything happened, but nothing did, and in due course I brought the machine down, packed in my kit, and after a long delay, due to wind squalls across the aerodrome, I took off in a blinding rain storm across the wind. The racecourse is only 100 yards wide, and about 750 yards long. Therefore one has to take off the long way of the aerodrome, no matter in which direction the wind is blowing. I do not know how I would have got away from Insein if it had not been for the excellent help given by the Institute and the forestry men; they were absolutely marvelous. In the air, at full throttle, my engine ran at 2,200 revolutions per minute, but my speed was greater. I throttled down to 1,900 revolutions per minute, and cruised at 90 miles per hour. This was a better performance than my old propeller gave, but I was grateful to my old friend because I knew it had saved my engine a lot on the journey so far. I was not happy with the light propeller, but it was much better than no propeller at all. The light propeller would not carry the weight so well, and my take-offs were much longer, often proving dangerous, because I needed so much more space. At the aerodrome in Atamboea I nearly crashed into a fence. I only just got over it in time before reaching the boundary of the aerodrome.

Nothing eventful happened to the engine between Rangoon and Bangkok ... At Bangkok I landed on Don Muang Aerodrome, over a mile square, and at the wrong end, so that I had to taxi at walking pace for nearly a mile behind a man with red and green flags. When the green flag was up I could continue to crawl, but at the red flag I must stop. My heart was aching for my poor engine working so hard in such terrific heat, but nothing could be done, and we must have been twenty minutes reaching the hangar. This was exceptionally bad for the engine. I soon developed a splitting headache again, so was persuaded to lie down a short time whilst the Siamese Air Force mechanic got on with some work on my machine. It was already dark, and there were no lighting arrangements in the hangar, the only torch was my own small one, and I was mighty thankful that this had not been souvenired. I had to give my instructions in English to the Shell representative, who repeated them in French to a Siamese, who translated them to the mechanics. As neither of the interpreters could translate technical words I was pretty helpless, and should have preferred to have cleared everyone out and got on with the job myself, but my head was too bad to enable me to cope with things at the moment, so I went to the barracks, having left instructions (or so I thought) to examine the plugs, clean all old ones, and drain the oil, by which time I expected to be back. When I did return I saw two new empty two gallon XXL tins on the ground, and at once I asked where my supplies of oil were. 'Inside the engine,' I was assured. 'But how much was inside?' I insisted. 'All that had been sent for me.' This was four gallons, and I knew the sump held only two gallons; I was very puzzled. I asked whether the old oil had been drained out. No, it had not. I asked if there was any more XXL? No. Any other similar oil? No. Only Castrol R., and I did not fancy that after my Bundar Abbas experience. There was nothing for it but to have all the four gallons, plus old oil, drained out, filtered, and two gallons poured back. I left them at this job whilst I went to have some dinner. On my return I found them struggling with the oil filter housing, in spite of my having shown them the drain plug. It was explained that they could not unscrew the drain plug, so had decided to take out the whole housing. This is not an easy job on a Gipsy engine, as anyone here who has done it will know. I cannot describe to you the muddle and mess; the awkwardness of working by the aid of one small torch, and the insects and my headache. There were about six mechanics helping me, and they worked hard, and joked and laughed the whole time. I have never seen such good humoured and happy people as the Siamese, but they are small, and do not seem to have much physical strength. They could not do any of the things which up to then I had called for a man to do for me because I could not do them myself. At long last, however, I went to bed …

At dawn the following morning I was off almost before it was light. I was always relieved and happy to get into the air, as my hardest work was certainly on the ground, and this morning, as usual, I headed towards the sunrise with pleasure. I had barely taken off, however, before the top cowling flew open so down I had to come with full load, the first time I had had to do such a thing, and I was a bit worried. I was devoutly thankful for the large aerodrome, but the landing, after all, proved quite easy. The cowling was well and securely fastened, and I took off once more. I had hoped to reach Singapore, but had already lost some time, and the bad weather I had to fly through that day made it necessary for me to make a halfway halt at Singora [Thailand]. I seemed to be expected, although I had certainly had no intention of stopping there if all had gone well. The aerodrome is not worthy of such a name, but it was great good fortune that I had landed near the sea, as the remainder was soft [beach] sand through [which] I could not taxi the machine. It took about 20 men eventually to carry it through the sand on to the road, where I decided it safest to take off next day ... I arrived at Singora fairly early in the afternoon, but I knew it was useless to try to reach Singapore before dark. For once, therefore, I was able to carry out my overhaul in daylight, but even then I had to wait till the sun had gone down a bit, because there was no shade on the aerodrome, and it was impossible to work in the mid-day heat. Fine sand was blowing all the time I was working, and the Siamese brought picnic parties out, and ice cream stalls, squatting themselves round the roped-in ring made by the efficient police. All these small people laughed at everything, and I even had to laugh myself at things which were not really amusing. I covered up the air vent hole in the petrol tank, the carburetor, and the air intake to prevent sand blowing in, and then set to work to fill up with petrol. There was one native who spoke English who had been sent down by the Siamese Government to help me, but there was no one who knew the first thing about an aero engine, and they had little strength. Quite a time was spent on undoing the front cowling which had been so securely fastened at Bangkok, unscrewing the plugs, oil drain plug, and relief valve. One man was fetched out of the crowd who was supposed to be extra strong, and every time I wanted anything doing I called out: 'Where is the strong man?' After a time the crowd recognised these words, and when they saw me looking round for some one to help they called out for me, 'Strong man', amid peals of laughter!!

It was a difficult matter filling up with petrol, because of the sand blowing about, and I insisted on tying my one chamois leather over both ends of the petrol filter, and the task of filling proved a very long one. The natives took off their shoes, and climbed on the wings and it took about four of them to hold up the heavy four gallon tin. One of them had a brain wave, and said there was a ladder which would make things easier, and went off to fetch it, and when I next looked round I saw them struggling to lean a huge ladder against the top wing, quite capable by its own weight of caving in the leading edge. The ladder had to be abandoned. The rest of the daily overhaul went off all right, but it was not pleasant working there in the hot sun with sand covering up the tools, and the sun scorching them as fast as I laid them out on the ground.

The next morning I had an exciting take-off along the road, which was lined on both sides with crowds of natives. My life and theirs depended on my keeping perfectly straight, and this was made much more difficult by the petrol which squirted in my eyes as the machine took up flying position. I must explain that at Karachi I was so tired of petrol-soaked kit that I had asked for a rubber tube to be attached to the air-vent pipe in the front petrol tank, and to have the petrol overflow led outside the cockpit. This was done, with the result that on the take-off I received a full burst of petrol in my eyes, because I take off looking over the left side. After that I used to take off looking to the right, but at Singora I had to look rapidly from one side to the other, and could not avoid the squirting petrol. I was devoutly thankful when I was safely in the air.

At Singapore the Royal Air Force took command of my machine, and as I was worried about the roughly repaired wing I asked if they would kindly look at it for me. Examination showed a large split in the rear spar. Fortunately they had a spare Moth wing handy. I left everything to them with a mind quite at ease, and was myself taken into Singapore for dinner. It was a great relief to know everything was being done for me very efficiently.

The next morning as I was strapping myself in the cockpit I noticed the air speed indicator looked peculiar. It was luminous, and graduated in 'Knots'. It was explained to me that my own indicator, graduated in 'miles per hour', had been tested, and found incorrect, and they had therefore lent me one of theirs. All their machines being sea planes, their reckoning was in knots. I did not much like this new idea because it looked too much like hard work translating knots into miles per hour, and vice versa. However, I remembered my shut indicator, which is a rough and ready but accurate speedometer so I did not worry much over the knots problem in the cockpit.

I left Singapore at dawn, and hoped to reach Sourabaya [Java] but had no luck. Rainstorms made going difficult immediately on leaving Singapore, and to make up for lost time I decided on what was to be a short cut across the Java Sea instead of following the coast line of the Islands of the Dutch East Indies. That short cut nearly proved my undoing. The terrific downpour of rain making visibility nil, forced me to seek the coast as quickly as possible, instead of keeping on my compass course across the open sea. There was neither sufficient petrol nor daylight to reach Semarang, never mind Sourabaya, and I forced-landed at Tjomal, a sugar factory, within five miles of an excellent emergency landing ground further inland, of whose existence I had not the slightest idea, as I had been unable to obtain a copy of the book in which a list of these landing grounds is given. The kindly Dutch people at the factory gave me some motor spirit which I carefully filtered through two layers of chamois (I was always extremely careful about filtering petrol as I had heard so many stories of forced landings due to a grain of dirt or drop of water choking up the jet; this was my downfall in Australia.

I refuelled at Semarang, and was there advised to follow the Dutch Air Mail to Sourabaya to show me the proper aerodrome as it was difficult to find, and there were two. I agreed, and about an hour later took off after the Air Mail, a three engined Fokker whose pilot had promised to go as slowly as possible. At full throttle I could barely keep him in sight, and I did not dare lose him as he was not following my compass course, and treacherous volcanoes were, I knew, buried in the clouds unpleasantly near. I had to fly full throttle, 2,200 revolutions per minute she gave, and a speed of 100 miles per hour the whole of the way, and on throttling down to land at Sourabaya the engine spluttered, and the propeller stopped dead immediately on landing. My propeller had been worrying me lately as it had had to bear the stress of the hundreds of miles of monsoon rains I had flown through, and it was looking much the worse for wear. At Semarang therefore, where I had been examining the propeller, someone volunteered to ring up a gentleman who owned a Moth, and ask him if he had a spare airscrew to lend me. He consented to take off his own propeller, and sent it to Sourabaya for me, and, as far as I can make out, he has never sent me the bill!! I should like to meet him, and thank him. I had great difficulty in explaining about this propeller to the mechanic who was given charge of my machine, as he only spoke Dutch, and my translators knew no technical words. With some misgivings I left the overhauling in his hands, but was assured he was very clever, and knew how to deal with a Gipsy Moth. This ultimately proved correct.

Later in the evening I came down to see how things were going on, and found practically nothing had been done. He said he would work all night, and I was taken away by my hostess and put to bed. Before dawn the next day I was at the aerodrome. On running up the engine I found the revolutions dropped considerably on the rear switch. The mechanic assured me he had cleaned the plugs and examined the magnetos, and he was sure it was all right. I was not, and when I ran it up again it spluttered badly on the right-hand magneto. The mechanic promised to look into the matter whilst I was taken into Sourabaya for some breakfast. I had already wasted too much time to reach Atamboea, and the midway halt was Binia, so there was not so much hurry. When I returned later on I found, to my dismay, the right-hand magneto lying on the bench in the hangar with bits of flexible coupling still sticking to the teeth of the driving gear wheel on the engine. The

Simms flexible coupling joining the magneto to the gears had evidently swollen, as it often does in the tropics, and it gets covered with oil and the teeth had sheared. I had no spare coupling with me, and no such thing was to be found in Sourabaya. We phoned the man with the Moth, but he had no spare, and could not take his own magneto to bits, which, of course, I could hardly expect. He had already been much too kind to me in the matter of the propeller. At length an ordinary motor coupling was obtained, and we made this do. I did not know whether the mechanic knew the timing of a Gipsy engine, and all my efforts to have this process explained to him through my interpreter proved futile, as he knew no Dutch technical words, and did not even understand what I said … I much wanted to stay and see it done, but was not allowed, and I realised it was hopeless to try to get off that day. I returned later when the work was finished to try out the engine, and found her quite O.K., the new propeller, I decided, being responsible for the slight drop in revolutions.

I was off at dawn the next morning heading for Atamboea. It is too long a story to tell of my forced landing, but sufficient to say I landed safely, if only just, and had to leave my machine where it was for that night.

The next morning preparations had to be made for me to get the machine to Atamboea. We got all the natives out of their huts, and bribed the headman to cut down the large heaps which were on the earth. I think that they were ant-hills. He got all the natives out with knives and swords, and they cut down these, and made me a run through. I had only a little petrol in the machine, and there was no petrol to be had anywhere. Where I had brought it down in a field was miles away from the road. As everybody knows, I had been cared for by the Pastor at this little village, and he happened to have one or two tins of motor spirit there. He sent these on donkeys and they were about three hours arriving at where I was. When they did arrive we spent about an hour trying to get the petrol through my two filters. It simply would not go through them, and at the end of about one hour I think that about an egg cup full of petrol had run through, so that I had to give that up.

I dared not waste petrol running up the engine. I tried to explain to the natives — as I had not much room for a take-off — that they must hold my machine back whilst I ran the engine up, and then when I gave the signal they must let go of the machine, and let me go straight off. There was a very amusing native there with large white eyeballs. He really was quite a comic character. He instructed the men to hold on to each wing, but every time that I opened the throttle out a little, in terrific fright they simply fled in both directions, and I had to jump out of the cockpit and bring them back again. Nobody understood a word of what I said, and I did not understand them. I had to make movements showing how, when I pushed the throttle open, it would make a noise, and the propeller would go round, but they must still stick to their posts. I tried about four times before they would do it, and even then, when I opened full throttle they ran, so I continued my take-off. I was just at about the last gasp of petrol, and I had to get to the aerodrome. It had had a bush fire on it, and I had not been able to locate it the day before. It was a mass of black, and the white cross on the centre of the aerodrome was covered over with black. I had been within seven or eight miles of the aerodrome, and not known it, because it looked like a black patch of hillside.

It was then too late to think of rushing through the work so as to leave that day for Port Darwin, so I decided to utilise the time overhauling my engine as thoroughly as I could, so that nothing should go wrong over the sea that could humanly be avoided. It worried me terrifically at Atamboea, because I had a long sea crossing, and the only petrol that there was at this aerodrome at Atamboea, which was nothing more than just a field, was in enormous casks. They had been there for so long that they were covered all over with red rust. As the petrol poured over the casks it naturally collected all the rust. This would have gone into my engine, so that I had to filter it out of the casks into smaller tins, and then out of tins through two chamois leathers into my engine. I was still very worried as to whether any pieces of rust had got through.

The thing that worried me most was that my oil supplies had not come through. I had a spare gallon with me, and there was less than half a gallon of dirty oil left in the sump after my long flight from Sourabaya (nearly 1,000 miles). There was nothing to do but add the fresh gallon to the dirty oil, and hope for the best. I anxiously watched my oil pressure gauge the whole way over the Timor Sea. I was worrying terrifically about whether I should have enough oil. Again, fortunately, I had.

I did every single thing I could think of on the engine. I put in a new set of plugs I had kept specially for this stage of the journey, tightened up every single nut and bolt on the engine and machine, carefully examined all petrol and oil pipes and connections for the slightest hint of leakage, and did all the other jobs which I have already detailed as coming under a daily overhaul. I worked long after dark by the light of a big fire built for me on the aerodrome. I even looked at my books to see that I had remembered everything. I was determined that I was not going to have any forced landing over the sea, owing to my having left out any small thing. Through the whole of the night they had to keep the natives out to watch for bush fires, which were all round, and which were steadily approaching the aerodrome. Fortunately they did not get as far as my machine.

The next morning I set off on the last stage to Port Darwin. My engine ran beautifully, but half way across it spluttered occasionally. It sounded like a slightly choked jet, and I wondered whether, in spite of all my precautions, some dirt or water had got into the petrol. Every time the engine spluttered I opened out quickly to full throttle to try to blow the foreign matter out, and then quickly throttled down again. Black smoke escaped from the stub exhaust, but the engine never stopped. This happened several times, and I was not sorry to, sight land.

AT PORT DARWIN THE CARE of my engine and, indeed, all other matters were taken out of my hands, and from then onwards throughout the whole of my journey through Australia I was not even allowed to think for myself.

Flight-Lieutenant Owen, who had been sent to Darwin by the Shell Company to meet me, saw to my engine, and after that it was seen to, or supposed to have been, by my escorting pilot. I believe that *Jason*'s daily overhaul (or my idea of a proper one) was carried out at Atamboea.

At Longreach, mechanics stayed up all night to give my plane a quick top overhaul … It is a well recognised fact that straightaway after a top overhaul an engine should not be run full out for any longer than necessary (that is, for the few minutes ground test), and that even if run full out in the air, the resulting speed is not so great as when the engine gets worn in.

The next day nothing particular happened, and then the day after that my engine still would not do any more than about 85 miles per hour. My escort, knowing that before I had been able to do about 100 miles an hour, evidently thought, for some reason, that he would like to get along quickly. My engine simply would not go beyond 85 miles per hour, and so my escort faded away in the distance. I simply could not catch him up, and in the end I completely lost sight of him. I had no idea where I was. I had tried to set my compass course on his machine, but the maps are not made the same way in Australia. The orientation keeps changing, and all the strip maps were just about as much use as a piece of blank paper, because there are no features on them. I continued on until I saw the railway. On my map Charleville was marked at the end of this railway. I came to this railway, and I naturally thought that I should have to follow it to the right. The railway was wrong on the map, and if I had gone to the left I was within about ten miles. I turned to the right and went about forty miles off my course. I landed where the railway petered out, filled up with motor spirit and had to come all the way back, landing after dark.

My crash at Brisbane was definitely proved to be due to carburetion trouble. On examination, the slow running jet was found to be choked … As I explained to reporters in Australia (who seemed to regard my version as the one least likely to be correct!!) I was forced high up on the approach to Brisbane by the tableland to the north and north-west of that city. I therefore throttled half down all the way to the aerodrome, still being about 1,500 feet up when I was almost on its borders. I had arranged with my escort that he was to go straight in and land, and I would do a circuit before landing. He came down in the middle of the aerodrome, and I kept to the outside. When over the crowds I was at 1,000 feet. I realised that I must throttle down then and make a circuit, and come in to land. I therefore throttled down. The engine went on to the slow running jet, which was choked, and the propeller stopped. I therefore had to lose height very quickly. I came down at as steep a side slip as I could. My wheels touched the ground a few feet off the boundary fence at the far side. The result was inevitable. It was hopeless to try to turn round at that speed, because I should have overturned, and there were other machines landing beside me. There was no alternative but to go on to the fence. The result was that I turned a somersault, and everything was over very quickly.

There ended *Jason*'s quest, so far as I was concerned. He was flown to Melbourne for me, and was there packed up and put on board the [P&O] *Naldera*. On examination in England on its return *Jason* was found to have a cracked sump, so he is now somewhere lying in the dust. I do not know where, but I am going in search of him soon, because he deserves a better fate. He has flown altogether a distance of, approximately, 50,000 miles, which is not bad for an engine.

I attribute my safe arrival in Australia to the excellence of the Gipsy engine, and to the careful training and wise advice of my engineer at Lane Aerodrome. Ladies and Gentlemen, that is the end of my address ... I thank you very much for your kind attention, and for the great compliment which you have paid me in asking me to come here, and to speak before you. I wish the Society of Engineers the very best of luck, and I thank you one and all. (Applause.)

From a speech delivered at a dinner given by the Council of the Society of Engineers to Miss Amy Johnson. CBE, BA, Hon. FSE, Commemorating her lone flight to Australia in May 1930. Held in The King's Hall at the Holborn Restaurant, London WC, on Trafalgar Day, Tuesday 21 October 1930.
The Engineer. 1930, London.

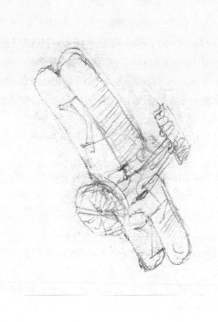

Bibliography

Australian Dictionary of Biography 1788–1939, University of Melbourne, Melbourne, 1966.

Australian Encyclopaedia, The Grolier Society, Sydney, 1963.

Dictionary of American Biography 1928–1955, Charles Scribner's Sons, New York, 1955.

Dictionary of Australian Biography, Australian National University, Canberra, 1963.

Dictionary of National Biography, 1901–1930, Oxford University Press, Oxford, 1939.

Encyclopaedia Britannica, 11th edition, Cambridge University Press, Cambridge, 1910.

The MacGraw-Hill Encyclopaedia of World Biography, New York, 1973.

The Shorter Oxford English Dictionary, third edition, Clarendon Press, 1970.

Tinling, Marion, *Women into the Unknown. A Sourcebook on Women Explorers and Travellers*, Greenwood Press, Westport, Connecticut, 1989.

Who Was Who, A. & C. Black, London, 1897–1960.

Webster's Biographical Dictionary, G & C Merriam Co., Springfield, Massachusetts, 1963.

Acknowledgements

I made use of many fine libraries around Australia and my grateful thanks for their help must go to the librarians, stack staff and their volunteers. I am particularly appreciative of the staff in the Petherick Reading Room at the National Library of Australia; the libraries of the Australian National University, the universities of Western Australia, South Australia, Curtin, Flinders, James Cook, La Trobe, and the Australian Defence Force Academy of the University of New South Wales; the State Libraries of New South Wales, South Australia, Victoria and Western Australia. At the State Library of Western Australia Sue McDonald and Ross Withnell of the Document Delivery Service helped enormously by finding several rare autobiographies for me, in some cases the only copies in Australia. Of public libraries, I must acknowledge the helpfulness of the City of Perth Library, the Nedlands Public Library and the Midland Public Library, whose Reference Section, comprehensive and splendid, is a great credit to its librarians, and should be the prototype for regional libraries.

Personal and professional thanks go to Peter Bridge of Hesperian Press for the use of his private collection; Louis Kirby, Editor of the *Daily Mail*, London; ArtsWA for the generous research grant; Ray Coffey and staff at Fremantle Arts Centre Press — promoting itself as one of Australia's finest small publishers is not an idle boast; David F Bird, the historian, who has shared with me much of his historical research and many splendid luncheon pies made by Beverley Bird; Scott Parsons, who continues to sort out all my frequent computer muddles; Gary Tonkin, for his lively interest in this anthology and for his expert drawings which form the illustrations to this book; Craig Burns, Warren Burns and Betty Burns, who made motoring to Perth less of a grind; and in Albany, Sue Lefroy Smith, Jennifer Reed and Paul Shaw gave courteous and patient assistance.

My warm thanks are also due to Philip Bennett, Andy Wilson, Sophia and Murray Gatti, Doris Freer Smith, David Harvey, Ron Bodycoat, Michael and Middy Dumper, Carl Smith, Kelly Hopkins and Nikki Jenkins whose kindness in taking an interest in my work is greatly appreciated.

Douglas Sellick

Douglas Sellick was born in Bridgetown, Western Australia in 1936. He studied at the Bishopsgate Institute and the Courtauld Institute of Art in London. He has worked variously in shipping and publishing, from Sydney to San Fransisco, and as a history consultant and researcher. He is currently a freelance history and literary researcher and anthologist.

First published 2003 by
FREMANTLE ARTS CENTRE PRESS
25 Quarry Street, Fremantle
(PO Box 158, North Fremantle 6159)
Western Australia.
www.facp.iinet.net.au

Consultant Editor Ray Coffey.
Production Coordinator Cate Sutherland.
Cover Designer Marion Duke.
Cover image courtesy Battye Library, 7265B/31.
Internal artwork Gary Tonkin.
Printed by Griffin Press.

National Library of Australia
Cataloguing-in-publication data

Venus in transit: Australia's women travellers 1788–1930.
Bibliography.

ISBN 1 86368 394 1.

1. Women travellers - Australia. 2. Women travellers - New Zealand.
3. Australia - Description and travel. 4. New Zealand - Description and
travel. I. Sellick, Douglas R. G.

919.304

The State of Western Australia has made an investment in this project through
ArtsWA in association with the Lotteries Commission.